ETNA THE VOLCANO

Love for this land is the common factor that binds all those who have contributed to the creation of this work.
The editor hopes to make the many beauties of Etna more widely known also through the editions in French, German and English.
Many thanks to Matteo Collura, Pino Correnti, Maria Teresa Di Blasi, Pippo Di Lorenzo, Antonino Di Maggio, Giuseppe Gangemi, Giuseppe Garozzo and Emilia Poli Marchese.
We took advice and suggestions from Sig.ra Palermo from Adrano municipal library, from Giovanni Giuffrida in Belpasso and Sig.ra Rapisarda from Sant'Agata Li Battiati library.
We would like to give special thanks to the photographers and the draughtsman who have illustrated this guide with images that do justice to the beauty of the places, and all the local councils who kindly sent us information and reference maps. Finally, thanks to all those who have helped to re-read, correct and improve this publication.

To Tiziana and Federica

AUTHORS: **Maria Rosaria Falcone and Romilda Nicotra**
Giuseppe Riggio and Giuseppe Vitali wrote the excursion itineraries

PHOTOGRAPHS AND ILLUSTRATIONS

G. Adamo: page 77, 78, 80.
Neil Bowman: page 61, 62.
Giovanni Callea: page 36.
Salvatore Centorrino: page 28, 40, 66, 67, 77, 86, 124.
Carlo Costa: page 18, 19.
Domenico D'Arrigo: page 105.
Antonino Di Maggio: page 61.
Alessandro Duca: page 97.
Biagio Fichera: page 10, 15, 34.
Alfio Garozzo: page 8, 9, 10, 11, 12, 13, 17, 19, 24, 25, 27, 28, 30, 31, 33, 34, 38, 40, 43, 45, 46, 49, 51, 52, 53, 55, 56, 63, 64, 65, 67, 72, 73, 76, 77, 81, 84, 89, 90, 92, 93, 96, 97, 98, 100, 101, 102, 106, 110, 111, 116, 117, 119, 120, 123, 126, 127, 134.
Gaetano Giudice: page 68, 69.
Giuseppe Iacono: page 14, 58, 67, 78, 79 .
Walter Leonardi: page 5, 11, 39, 40, 41, 42, 56, 58, 60, 117.
Riccardo Lombardo: page 37, 52, 53, 57, 88, 89, 102, 103, 134.
Marrara: page 79.
Nino Musumeci: page 1, 21, 26, 28, 35, 101, 135, 136, 137.
P. Pappalardo: page 11.
Alfredo Pisano: page 62, 84, 85.
Salvatore Russo: page 4, 21, 23, 25, 29, 33, 50, 69, 70, 71, 87, 132, 138.
Nino Statella: page 82, 83.
Foto Tomarchio: page 6, 7, 16, 17, 23, 32, 91, 107, 115, 117, 128.
Giuseppe Vitali: page 35, 47, 54, 59, 68, 74, 95, 99, 128, 129, 130, 131, 132, 139, 140.
Antonio Zimbone: page 5, 6, 8, 9, 26, 27, 28, 42, 44, 50, 80, 94, 104, 107, 108, 109, 112, 113, 114, 116, 118, 121, 125, 127, 129, 133, 135, 139.
Cover photographs: Front **Musumeci**, inside front **Tomarchio**, inside back **Tomarchio**, back **Musumeci**, **Russo**, **Tomarchio**, **Zimbone**, **Leonardi**, **Lombardo**, **Lombardo**.

GRAPHIC DESIGN: *Flavia Micari and Domenica Maimone* - MAPS AND STREET PLANS: *Francesco Galletta*
TRANSLATION FRENCH: *Bernard Michaud*, ENGLISH: *Nicholas Whithorn*, GERMAN: *Doreen Lamek*
Translations and editing with desktop publishing
EDITORIAL CONSULTANT: Margareth Donaldson
EDITORIAL CO-ORDINATION: Tiziana Leva
Copyright 2000 by Società Editrice Affinità Elettive - via Saponara res. 13 - 98168 Messina - Italy
tel. 090.353107 pbx - fax 090.359443 - www.affinitaelettive.it/ - e-mail: affinitaelettive@hotmail.com

Welcome

Tourists are kindly requested to fasten their walking boot straps, to carry a rucksack containing a camera, binoculars, video camera, compass and to follow the route we lay down for a wonderful journey of discovery around the most amazing active volcano on the continent and the towns that lie courageously and proudly at its feet.

You will find luxuriant landscapes, incredible scenarios, nights lit up by the fiery flashes from Etna, dawns with the blue sky streaked by smoke and ash from the volcano.

At the foot of this extraordinary mountain you will discover a beautiful collection of Arab fortresses, Norman castles, mediaeval streets and arches, baroque churches.

All of this is accompanied by folklore, religious feasts, cultural and sporting events, festivals, gastronomy, arts and crafts.

We can guarantee you a fantastic trip and we can predict, without any shadow of doubt, that you will want to come back here, to this magical land of Sicily.

Rosaria Falcone e Romilda Nicotra

Etna: the mountain that touches the stars

The whole province of Catania is dominated by Etna, the most majestic active volcano in Europe, the highest mountain in Sicily. Its presence is worrying, frightening, fascinating and seductive. It is typical of human nature to be able to dedicate to the same object both love and hatred at the same time.

Indeed, the people of Catania love and hate Etna, they submit to the charm of such a magnificent presence, they are proud of their regional park and of their mountain of fire, but they know that it could destroy them, that lava flows quickly. Yet, none of them would really like the activity of the volcano to end.

The lava of Etna is present just about everywhere, in the city and the towns, in the cliffs and the hills, in the church facades and lying alongside the road.

The colour of lava is dominant and even the local produce takes on this colour: cauliflowers and 'tarocchi' (a variety of orange).

Living with the volcano is now almost part of the genetic make-up of the people of Catania. Etna is not a mountain isolated by its height of over 3,300 metres (12,400 feet), it is not a volcano that makes its presence felt only when in full eruption.

Everybody here (from Giarre to Bronte, from Randazzo to Misterbianco) is accustomed to wiping the black sand of Etna from their cars, doing the washing again because the clothes hung out to dry have been stained with black ash, putting up with the earth tremors, sometimes slight at others more serious, that accompany the changing moods of the mountain, of not trusting the clouds in the sky, which might not be what they seem but smoke from Etna.

There is a certain amount of fatalism in all this, an ancient fatalism that has often gone hand in hand with faith, superstition, myth and legend.

What can be done against the unbridled forces of nature? Today scientists keep a watchful eye on Etna and are able to foresee activity, both great and small. Today technicians have the means at their disposal to try to divert the direction of lava flows.

Yet, now as in the past, people invoke patron Saints to protect the towns from the lava and the eruptions. While scientists busy themselves with lasers and highly sophisticated equipment, people continue to carry relics and simulacrums in procession to defeat the beloved-detested mountain of fire.

So every town has its heavenly champion in the fight against Etna. In Fornazzo the heavy responsibility lies with the Sacred Heart of Jesus, in Nicolosi with Saint Anthony, in Catania with the veil of Saint Agatha.

However, like all important natural phenomena, over the centuries Etna has not only aroused all kinds of emotion

tion, and liquefied rocks amass with roars/ boil up from below./ It is said that the body of Enceladus, half burnt by lightning,/ lies under this mass, and above giant Etna/ weighs down on him and puffs out the flames through cracks and chimneys./ And every time it moves its tired side, it shakes the whole/ of Trinacria and thunders, filling the sky with smoke".

Virgil refers to the myth of Enceladus, one of the giants that rebelled against Jupiter. The father of the gods punished him by striking him with lightning and throwing him against Etna, under which he remained imprisoned. The eruptions are the puffs of his body in flames.

There are two more mythological stories connected with the mountain. Another giant, Typheus, who had tried to climb up to heaven,

in the population, generating fear, veneration, amazement, legends. It has also aroused the interest of scientists and researchers, of travellers (especially in the Romantic period) fascinated by its beauty and its terrible majesty and has inspired poets and writers, such as Hesiod, Pindar, Virgil and Dante. It is perhaps Virgil, in the third book of the Aeneid, who left us the most lyrical and effective description of Etna.

"The port, sheltered from the winds, is large and tranquil;/ but up above Etna thunders with frightening shudders,/ and occasionally throws up, black, a cloud into the air/ dense vortices and smoking burning sparks,/ and sends up sheets of flame touching the stars./ Sometimes pieces of rock, from the bowels of the mountain,/ are thrown out by the erup-

was segregated by Jupiter in the mountain. The furious giant vomits flames and fire.

Finally, in the bowels of the mountain is Vulcan's black forge, in which the Cyclops worked making lightning.

The name of the volcano comes from the Phoenician 'attano' (furnace) or the Greek 'aitho' (burning) to which is also connected the Latin 'Aetna'

The Arabs called it 'Gibel Utlamat', in other words mountain of fire. Some sources, dating from around 1000 already use the name 'Mons Gibel', then changed into 'Mongibello' (Dante,

From the top: the snow covered slopes of Etna and the Gulf of Catania in the background, Etna in its winter colours, Lake Gurrida.
Facing page: Etna in a sea of clouds.

as regards the relationship between the volcano and man, the history of Etna is still fundamentally based on myths and the most important eruptions, even though the number of eruptions recorded is certainly much lower than the real number.

Several centuries before Christ there are already references to the activity of the volcano in historical sources. Two important eruptions were those of 475 BC and 396 BC.

From the end of the 1st century AD onwards more eruptions are documented, about 200 up to the present day. One of the most serious happened in 1669.

The volcanic activity was preceded and accompanied by strong earth tremors, new eruptive mouths opened up,

in the 1200s, also used this name in the 15th canto of Hell). Etna was formed about 500,000 years ago. The scientific explanation of its birth is directly connected to the phenomenon of continental drift and particularly to the colossal clash between the African and Eurasian shelves, the same clash that probably caused the creation of the Alps and the Himalayas.

The immense impact between the two shelves caused the compression of the magma that was deep below the sea and it came out violently, creating Etna.

Obviously, over thousands of years, the mountain has undergone considerable transformations and, although today its geological history can be partly reconstructed,

some of which created the Monti Rossi behind Nicolosi, and the lava almost completely devastated Catania and Nicolosi in just 18 days.

Another eruption with catastrophic effects was the one in 1811, which particularly affected the Bove Valley, where a new crater was formed.

The activity of 1843 was terrible. Running downhill, the lava crossed an area of marshland and, on contact with the damp ground, created tremendous explosions that killed several people.

On this page: images of recent eruptions.

There was a violent eruption in 1866, which created the crater of Monte Gemmellaro.

The eruption of 1892 was longer and more serious, forming the craters of the Monti Silvestri.

In the 20th century there have been numerous eruptions: in 1910, 1928, 1950 (the activity began in March and continued until the December of the following year, 372 days, during which the lava caused enormous damage overrunning vineyards, orchards, grazing land, broom thickets), 1952, 1971 (when the observatory and the cable car were destroyed), 1979 (when nine people were killed by the sudden expulsion of a lava plug from an eruptive mouth), 1983 (the lava damaged the Sapienza mountain hut and the lower cable car station) and in 1992 (the year that saw people all over Italy following with apprehension the news about the lava that was threatening the town of Zafferana).

The last two dates are worthy of particular attention because on both occasions

attempts were made to put an end to the atavistic fatalism of the local people faced by eruptions by trying to divert the lava flow with explosives, with partial success, in order to save the threatened towns.

The landscape of the Catania area is greatly influenced by the presence of Etna, which is visible even from a great distance.

It occupies a vast area of the province, indeed its circumference at the base is about 250 km.

Even though it is an old volcano, constantly active, numerous towns have grown up on its slopes, divided, in a certain sense, by the mass of the mountain, which is, as we have already said, over 3,300 metres high (even though its height, like its appearance, can change depending on the volcanic activity, which creates small cones, craters etc.).

It is true to say that life revolves around the foot of the mountain, so much so that the towns here are connected by the famous Circumetnea railway, opened at the end of the 19th century.

It could be said that each town has its 'own' volcano.

Top: a river of lava.
Left: a mountain of magma overwhelms farmhouses and crops.

Indeed, the appearance of the mountain changes according to the place from which it is viewed. So the Etna you see from Sant'Alfio is different from the one seen from Linguglossa, the one seen from Randazzo is different from the one you see from Adrano, and so on.

The continuous eruptions and lava flows over the centuries have not only created outright hills and mountains but also characteristic formations, closely linked to the process of magma consolidation. Some of these formations are called dykes, daggers (open spaces), the Crags of Acitrezza are nothing more than a rocky agglomerate that came from an eruption.

The lava of Etna is particularly fluid (the temperature of

the magma is about 1,000°C), which brings both advantages and disadvantages. The fluidity means that gases escape more easily, reducing the risk of explosions. However, fluidity also means speed; the lava flows quickly and can cover great distances in a short time.

It is the latter characteristic that makes Etna a seriously dangerous volcano because the rapidity of its lava flows make it more difficult to organise appropriate action to divert the flows and defend the towns.

Overall it can be said that Etna is rather moderate as regards explosions and expulsion of lava and lapilli. This is due to the fact that every day it gives off tons of gases

On this page: Etna in its autumn colours.

and sulphur dioxide into the air (looking like clouds from afar), maintaining an acceptable level of internal pressure. Obviously, however, pressure builds up to an explosion when lava plugs are created, blocking the eruptive mouths.

Etna has four summit eruptive craters (New Crater, Central Crater, South Eastern Crater and North Eastern Crater) and numerous lateral craters.

The Etna Regional Nature Park was set up in 1987, covers 60,000 hectares and includes 20 district councils of the province of Catania.

No form of life, vegetable or animal, is present in the areas affected by recent lava flows, while the areas of old lava flows are teeming with life.

The flora numbers over 1,500 species, including the soapwort, symbol of the Park, and the fauna counts numerous species of mammals and birds.

The natural landscape changes according to the altitude. At sea-level, along the coast, the vegetation is mostly halphilous. As you begin to climb up, you find land given over to growing apples, citrus fruits, pears, nuts, pistachios, almonds and, naturally, grapes.

These gradually give way to pinewoods, ilex groves, oak woods and chestnut woods.

From 1,500 to 2,000 metres the landscape is dominated by beech-trees, aetnesis birches and large fragrant gorse bushes.

Above 2,000 metres you only find extremely hardy plants, such as groundsel and mouse-ear chickweed.

The fauna is also very interesting.

On Etna you can find porcupines, foxes, wild rabbits, wild cats, hedgehogs, dormice and, pay attention, vipers.

The birds, above all, give particular joy to animal observers and especially to birdwatchers.

The Park is populated by both diurnal and nocturnal birds.

These include Golden Eagles, Peregrine Falcons, Kestrels, Rock Partridges, Scops Owls, Buzzards, Barn Owls, Cuckoos and Tawny Owls.

In the Gurrida lake you can also see ducks, herons and other aquatic species.

Although the Park can be visited freely and independently, we recommend visitors take the greatest care, especially when hiking.

You do not need special equipment, just hiking boots, a map, binoculars and, obviously, a camera. However, Etna is not a mountain like any other, it is and remains an active volcano.

Our advice is not to venture off on your own but to hire authorised guides when climbing up to the craters.

On this page: Etna welcoming spring.

Calender of feasts festivals and events in the Province of Catania

January
- **Patronal Feast of Saint Mauro: Aci Castello, Viagrande**. On the 15th.
- **Patronal Feast of Saint Anthony Abbot: Misterbianco, Aci Sant'Antonio, Camporotondo Etneo, Pedara**. On the 17th. In particular in Pedara ritual blessing of animals and vehicles, sale of natural products offered to the Saint.
- **Carnival: Acireale**. From the 20th. The most beautiful carnival in Sicily. Allegorical floats, cars decorated with flowers, folkloristic groups, musical bands, open-air shows, firework displays and local cuisine ('*maccarruni a setti purtusa*', artichokes, 'cannoli', 'castagnole', '*chiacchiri*').
- **Feast of Saint Sebastian: Acireale, Giarre, Maniace, Piedimonte Etneo**. On the 20th. In Acireale try the marzipan cakes traditionally prepared for the patronal feast.
- **Feast and Fair of Saint Sebastian: Santa Venerina**. On the last Sunday of the month.
- **New Year by the Sea: Riposto**. International swimming competition.
- **Livestock and Agricultural Implement Fair: Viagrande**.
- **Three days on Etna: Nicolosi**. Between January and March. International skiing competition.

February
- **Patronal Feast of Saint Agatha: Catania**. From the 3rd to the 5th. Grandiose celebrations in honour of the patron, spectacular Candlemas procession and procession of the precious litter with the remains of the Martyr.
- **Saint Agatha Trophy: Catania**. On the 3rd. International Athletics Event.
- **Feast of Saint Biagio: Bronte, Sant'Alfio**. On the 3rd. In particular in Sant'Alfio distribution of '*cuddureddi of San Brasi*', typical bread, blessed in the Calvary church.
- **Tour of Etna: Acicatena**. International cycling race.
- **Roast Suckling-pig Festival: Calatabiano**.
- **Nordic Ski Meeting: Sant'Alfio**. Excursions along the nature path of the Monti Sartorius.
- **Carnival: Acicatena, Belpasso, Biancavilla, Calatabiano, Castiglione di Sicilia, Fiumefreddo, Giarre, Mirabella Imbaccari, Misterbianco, Motta Sant'Anastasia, Palagonia, Paternò, Piedimonte Etneo, Tremestieri Etneo**.

March - April
- **Macaroni Festival: Calatabiano**. On the 4th. In Pasteria.
- **Feast of Saint Joseph: Adrano, Biancavilla, Fiumefreddo di Sicilia, Maletto, Mascalucia, Mazzarone, Mirabella Imbaccari, Nicolosi, Raddusa, Ramacca, Randazzo**. On 19th March. In Maletto traditional '*sfilateddi chi ciciri*' and rice 'crespelle' with honey. In Raddusa and Ramacca preparation of sumptuous feasts with all kinds of dishes and typical votive bread.
- **A' Truvatura: Caltagirone**. On 19th March, 16th April, 21st May, 18th June. In the town centre: antiques market, minstrels, exhibitions, concerts, puppet theatre, folk music.
- **Feast of Our Lady of the Annunciation: Bronte, Pedara**. On 25th March.
- **Display and Market of Pillow-Lace: Tremestieri Etneo**. In March.
- **Citrus Fruit Festival: Motta Sant'Anastasia**. Late March-early April.
- **Display of Easter Bread and Cakes: Giarre**. In Macchia. At the Museum of Customs and Traditions of the People of Etna.
- **Good Friday: Bronte, Giarre, Militello in Val di Catania, Randazzo, Sant'Alfio**. In Bronte and Randazzo processions. In Sant'Alfio procession of the simulacrum of the Dead Christ from the Cathedral to the Calvary Church.
- **La Diavolata: Adrano**. Easter Sunday. Performance of the religious drama dating back to 1752.
- **Easter Monday: Palagonia**. On Easter Monday procession of Saint Febronia and ritual "splitting of the pine-cone". On the Tuesday after Easter procession to the Hermitage of Saint Febronia.
- **Festival of Cheeses: Aci Bonaccorsi**. On the 3rd Sunday of April. Typical Sicilian products.
- **Festival of Peppered Pecorino Cheese: Castel di Judica**. On 25th April.
- **Autoslalom: Palagonia**. On 25th April.

From the top: Acireale Carnival, the Feast of Saint Agatha in Catania, Saint Sebastian in Acireale, the 'Diavolata' in Adrano.

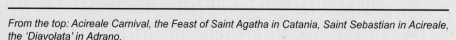

- **Festival of Ricotta and Cheese: Vizzini**. On 25th April.
- **Arts and Crafts Display: Linguaglossa**. From 29th April to 1st May.
- **April Festival: Nicolosi**. In April. Folklore and tasting of typical products.
- **Artichoke Festival: Ramacca**. In April.
- **Ricotta Festival: Mirabella Imbaccari**. Late April-early May.
- **International Exhibition of Terracotta Whistles: Caltagirone**. April-May. Popular display in the "town of ceramics".

May
- **Festival of Cheeses, Ricotta and typical Sicilian products: Aci Bonaccorsi**. On the 1st and 2nd.
- **Patronal Feast of Our Lady of the Chain: Castiglione di Sicilia**. On the 1st Sunday of the month.
- **Feast of Saints Alfio, Cirino e Filadelfo: Trecastagni**. From the 7th to the 12th. In Trecastagni procession of devotees called "nudes" and fair with stalls selling fresh garlic. Specialities made with lamb and mutton.
- **Festival of Sicilian Carts: Trecastagni**. On the 10th. In concomitance with the feast of the patron saints.
- **Regional Folklore Festival: Trecastagni**. On the 1st Sunday after the 10th.
- **Festival of Flowers and Arts and Crafts: Aci Bonaccorsi**. On the 2nd Sunday of the month. With kite festival.

- **Medlar Festival: Calatabiano**. On the 2nd Sunday of the month.
- **Feast of Mompilieri: Mascalucia**. On the 3rd Sunday of the month, also in August. In memory of the discovery of Our Lady of the Sciara or of Mompilieri.
- **Festival of the Mountain: Sant'Alfio**. In the second half of the month. Excursions to the most charming locations on Etna, exhibitions, mountain songs.
- **Feast of Sant'Alfio: Adrano**. On the last Sunday of the month. Sicilian carts pulled by sumptuously harnessed horses, players of typical ancient instruments.
- **Festival of Cherries and Roses: Giarre**. Last week of the month. In Macchia.
- **Spring Festival: Bronte**. At the end of the month. Arts and crafts and tasting of typical products.
- **Ecological May: Mascalucia**. All month.
- **Flower Decorated Stairway: Caltagirone**. From the 3rd Sunday of the month to the 1st Sunday of June. Feast in honour of Our Lady of Conadomini.
- **Olive Tree Trophy: Pedara**. Late May-early June. Archery competition at the municipal stadium.
- **International Hockey Tournament: Catania**. May-June.
- **Calatino Rally: Caltagirone - Scordia**.
- **Feast of Our Lady of La Strada: Giarre**. In Santa Maria La Strada. Popular sausage festival, 'crispelle' of various flavours, singers, band music, eat as many *calia* and nuts as you want.

- **Mascalese May: Mascali**. Traditional games.
- **Antich...età: Motta Sant'Anastasia**. Ancient arts and crafts display.
- **Our Lady of Valverde: Valverde**. With procession from the site of the apparition of Our Lady to the sanctuary.

June
- **Patronal Feast of Saint Anthony of Padova: Gravina di Catania, Nicolosi**. On the 13th.
- **Patronal Feast of Saint Vito: Mascalucia**. On the 15th and also on 15th August.
- **Strawberry Festival: Maletto**. 2nd half of the month. Display-market of strawberries and typical products, tastings, folklore, drama and music.
- **Feast of Saint John the Baptist: Aci Trezza**. On the 24th. Festival of '*u pisci a mari*' in the waters of the port.
- **Feast of Saint Peter: Riposto**. On the 29th. Procession of boats and entertainment.
- **Piedimontese Summer: Piedimonte Etneo**. From June to September. Drama, entertainment and gastronomy in the streets.
- **Night of Fire: Misterbianco**. Display of Italian wrought iron.
- **Corpus Domini: Mascalucia, Riposto, Valverde**. In Riposto procession through the town with stops in front of the votive shrines and the altars set up for the occasion.
- **Cherry Festival: Ragalna**.

July
- **Patronal Feast of Saint James: Caltagirone**. From the 1st to the 30th.

From the top: Feast of Saint Alfio in Trecastagni, the attractive stairway of Santa Maria del Monte in Caltagirone, Mediaeval Festival in Randazzo.

For the occasion the picturesque stairway of Santa Maria del Monte is illuminated by thousands of coloured lanterns.

- **Pepper and Aubergine Festival: Aciplatani**. On the 2nd Saturday of the month.
- **Mediaeval Festival: Randazzo**. Last week in July. In the centre of the town. Commemoration of the story of Bianca of Navarra. Concerts, round tables, mediaeval displays and banquets.
- **Patronal Feast of Our Lady of the Carmel: Catania, Santa Maria di Licodia**. On the 16th.
- **Etna Week: Linguaglossa**. From the 18th to the 25th. In the streets. Some of the most interesting events are the "Etna Pentathlon" and "boards and brushes".
- **Etna Jazz: Mascali**. On the 23rd. In Puntalazzo. Jazz music review.
- **Patronal Feast of Saint Venera: Acireale**. From the 24th to the 27th. Religious rites and folkloristic displays.
- **Etna Jazz: Bronte**. On the 25th. In the streets. Jazz music review.
- **Display and Market of Local Craft Products: Fiumefreddo**. In the middle of the month. In Piazza Botteghelle.
- **Sanconese Summer: San Cono**. From the 26th July to the 31st August. In the streets. Games, competitions and concerts.
- **Antiques Exhibition: San Giovanni La Punta**. On the 27th.
- **Summer Evening Music: Mascali**. From 28th July to 12th September. Open-air art exhibition and entertainment.
- **Tench Festival: Licodia Eubea**. On the last Sunday of the month.
- **Patronal Feast of Saint Andrew: Milo**. Last Sunday of the month. Religious traditions and folklore.
- **Arts and Crafts Display: Acireale**. July-August.
- **Adranita, Belpassese, Biancavillese, Malettese: Adrano, Belpasso, Biancavilla, Maletto Summer**. July-August. Review of music, drama, dance, cabaret.
- **Brontestate: Bronte**. July-August. Review of music, drama, cabaret, fashion in the streets.
- **Catania Summer of Music: Catania**. July-August. Review of chamber music in the ancient Roman Odeon.
- **Le Ciminiere and Stars: Catania**. July-August. At Le Ciminiere. Review of music, dance and drama.
- **Fiumefreddese Summer and Asclepio Prize: Fiumefreddo**. July - August. Music, cinema, drama, dance.
- **Etneadi: Nicolosi**. July-August. Review of music, dance and drama, cinema and cabaret.
- **Rocca Normanna: Paternò**. July-August. Music, drama, cinema and ballet in the streets.
- **Pedarestate: Pedara**. July-August. Drama, music and sport in the Belvedere park.
- **Summer Fair: Pedara**. July-August. In the municipal park and in Piazza Don Bosco.
- **Sounds of Verses: Catania. July-September**. Music, cinema, prose and literature.
- **Old Steam Train: Catania**. July-September. Visit to Militello, Vizzini, Grammichele, Caltagirone, Castiglione, Randazzo. Departure from the station.
- **Giarre Summer: Giarre**. July-September. Review of music and drama.
- **Palagonese Summer: Palagonia**. July-September. Music, drama, open-air cinema.
- **Mottese Summer: Motta Sant'Anastasia**. July-September. Review of music, dance and drama in the streets.
- **Etna on Stage: Zafferana Etnea**. July-September. Review of cinema, music, drama and dance in the streets.
- **The Frying-pan: Aci Trezza**. Fish festival.
- **Bunches of Lemons Festival: Giarre**. In Carruba. Beautiful and heavy bunches of lemons.
- **Autoslalom: Giarre-Milo**.
- **Etna Jazz: Trecastagni**. Review of jazz music.

August
- **Octopus Festival: Aci Castello**. On the 1st Saturday and 1st Sunday of the month. Scardamiano sea-front.
- **Patronal Feast Our Lady of Providence: Zafferana Etnea**. On the 1st Sunday of the month.
- **Poseidon Prize: Fiumefreddo**. 1st week of the month. Prize awarded to a figure who has been foremost in the spread of environmental awareness.
- **National Firework Festival and Patronal Feast of Saint Stephen: Aci Bonaccorsi**. On the 2nd.
- **The Flight of the Angel and Feast of Saint Nicolò Politi: Adrano**. On the 3rd and the 4th.
- **Peach and Pear Festival: Maniace**. From the 6th to the 8th. With tastings in the streets.
- **Cinema Festival: San Gregorio**. From the 8th to the 18th. At the Piano Immacolata sports ground.
- **Night of Saint Lawrence: Nicolosi**. On the 10th. At the Sapienza mountain hut. Music and picnic.

Top: vines on Etna. Right: specimen of octopus.

- **Patronal Feast of Saint Lawrence: Sant'Agata Li Battiati**. On the 10th.
- **Mediaeval Festivals: Motta Sant'Anastasia**. From the 10th to the 22nd. Folklore and historical parades.
- **Puntese Summer: San Giovanni La Punta**. From the 10th to 4th September.
- **August Holiday on the Praca: Aci Castello**. On the 15th. Characteristic festival on the beach.
- **Patronal Feast of Saint Anthony of Padova: Nicolosi**. On the 15th. In concomitance with the display and market of arts and crafts and folklore.
- **'A Vara: Randazzo**. On the 15th. Solemn procession of the triumphal carriage of Our Lady of the Assumption with living characters.
- **Summer Feast of Saint Agatha: Catania**. On the 17th. Commemoration of the removal of the remains of Saint Agatha from Constantinople to Catania.
- **Rock Evolution: Bronte**. From the 18th to the 20th. Review of rock music in Piazza Cimbali.
- **Home-made Bread Festival: Piedimonte Etneo**. On the 20th. In Vena.
- **Show beneath the stars: Viagrande**. On the 20th. In Piazza S. Mauro.
- **Band Meeting: Santa Maria di Licodia**. On the 21st and 22nd. In the streets.
- **Patronal Feast of Saint Anastasia: Motta Sant'Anastasia**. From the 22nd to the 25th. With flag-waving festival.
- **Patronale Feast of Santa Venera: Santa Venerina**. On the 26th.
- **Patronal Feast of Saint Joseph: Santa Maria di Licodia**. From the 28th to the 30th.
- **Feast of Saint Gerardo: Piedimonte Etneo**. On the 29th.
- **Bread Festival: Ramacca**. Last week of the month. In via Risorgimento.
- **In...song on the Riviera: Catania**. On the last Saturday of the month. Review of Italian songs. At the port.
- **Table Grape Festival: Caltagirone**. On the last Sunday of the month. Tasting, music.
- **Arts and Crafts and Gastronomy: San Gregorio**. From 31st August to 5th September. Tasting of sausages, polenta and wine in Piazza della Repubblica.
- **Holidaymakers' Festival: Mascali**. Late August-early September.
- **Baroque Week: Militello in Val di Catania**. In August and September. Historical parade, drama, music, living chess match and jousting.
- **International Etna Motor Meeting: Belpasso**.
- **Calatabianese August: Calatabiano**. Sporting and cultural events on the San Marco coast.
- **Etnalquantara: Castiglione di Sicilia**. Review of music, drama and dance in the streets.
- **International Women's Tennis Tournament: Catania, Mascali, Tremestieri, Nicolosi**.
- **Fish Festival: Mascali**. On the beach at Fondachello.
- **Milo's Venus: Milo**. Beauty contest. In Piazza Madonna delle Grazie.
- **National Basketball Meeting: Nicolosi**.
- **Arts and Crafts Fair: Nicolosi**.
- **Riposto Summer Project: Riposto**. Music, drama, dance, sport.
- **Randazzese August Holiday: Randazzo**. Various kinds of events throughout the month.
- **Battiati Effect: Sant'Agata Li Battiati**. Review of music, drama and cabaret in the streets.
- **Arts and Crafts Fair: Trecastagni**. Display of local craft products.
- **Anchovy Festival: Valverde**. Part of the celebrations in honour of the patron Saint. Tasting of sandwiches with anchovies and as much wine as you can drink.

September
- **Etna Nut and Apple Festival: Mascali**. From the 1st to the 10th. In Puntalazzo.
- **Semeraro-Pellegrino Band Competition: Catania**. From the 3rd to the 5th. At Le Ciminiere.
- **Milo Wines: Milo**. On the 4th, 5th, 11th and 12th in via Etnea. Display and sales of wines from Milo and Etna.
- **Arts and Crafts Fair: Santa Maria di Licodia**. From the 4th to the 12th. Display, sales and entertainment.
- **Sausage Festival: Grammichele**. On the 6th and 7th. Tasting and folklore in the streets.
- **Arts and Crafts Fair: Grammichele**. From the 6th to the 10th.
- **Flower Festival: Giarre**. 1st week of the month. In Trepunti.
- **Grape Festival: Licodia Eubea**. On the 1st Sunday of the month. Grapes, wine, must-cake and desserts made with cooked wine.
- **Wheat Festival: Raddusa**. On the 1st Sunday of the month. Historical reconstruction of *pisatura*; *cuccìa*, seasoned bread, pasta; music, show-jumping, mythological parade.
- **Flower Festival: San Gregorio**. On the 1st Sunday of the month. Displays and entertainment.
- **Feast of Our Lady Child and Fish Festival: Catania**. On the 8th. With procession of boats at Ognina.
- **Grape Festival: Mazzarone**. On the 2nd Sunday of the month. In Piazza Concordia.

- **Inside the Volcanoes**: **Catania**. From 11th September to 3rd November. Exhibition of archaeological finds in the caves on Etna. At Le Ciminiere.
- **September Fair**: **Paternò**. From the 13th to the 23rd. Crafts and gastronomy. In the municipal park.
- **Enoetna**: **Santa Venerina**. On the 17th, 18th, 19th 24th and 25th. Displays and sales of Sicilian and Etna wines. In Piazza Roma.
- **Etna-Wines**: **Sant'Alfio**. In the first half of the month. Wines from Etna and local produce.
- **'Ampanata' Festival**: **Misterbianco**. On the 3rd Saturday of the month.
- **Grape-Harvest Festival**: **Piedimonte Etneo**, **Viagrande**. In Piedimonte from the 24th to the 26th. Music, folklore, costume parades, pressing of grapes in traditional ways, gastronomy and crafts. In Viagrande on the 24th.
- **Festivities of the Virgins**: **Palagonia**. Last Tuesday of the month. At Annunziata. In honour of S. Febronia, votive bread, *cicili* (local biscuits), music, fireworks.
- **Exhibition of Brickwork, Lava Stone and Wood**: **Gravina di Catania**. From 30th September to 4th October. In the Borsellino park.
- **Mushroom Market**: **Nicolosi**. September-October-November.
- **Palio of Our Lady of Graces**: **Belpasso**. In the main street.
- **Kalat Expo**: **Caltagirone**. Local produce. Tasting and stands.
- **International Rugby Matches**: **Catania**.
- **Gravinese September**: **Gravina di Catania**. Popular theatre in the Borsellino park.
- **Tribute to Luigi Capuana**: **Mineo**. Theatre review.
- **Etna Race**: **Nicolosi**. Uphill race.
- **Brancati Literary Prize**: **Zafferana Etnea**.

October
- **Sea, Mountains and Art in Sicily**: **Catania**. On the 2nd. At Le Ciminiere. Vintage cars.
- **Grape and Wine Festival**: **Sant'Agata Li Battiati**. On the 3rd and 4th.
- **Grape and Sausage Festival**: **Trecastagni**. On the 2nd Sunday of the month. Tasting, display, folklore.
- **Pistachio Festival**: **Bronte**. 2nd week of the month. Exhibition and tasting of local dishes made with pistachio.
- **Prickly-pear Festival**: **San Cono**. 2nd weekend of the month.
- **Golden Bellini Prize**: **Catania**. On the 14th. Awarded to great interpreters of Bellini's works. At the Massimo Theatre.
- **Verghiano Festival**: **Catania**. On the 14th and 15th. At Le Ciminere.
- **Must-cake Festival**: **Castel di Judica**. On the 17th. Folklore, gastronomy.

- **Monte Judica Autoslalom**: **Castel di Judica**. On the 17th.
- **Prickly-pear Festival**: **Vizzini**. From the 11th to the 20th.
- **Honey and Cake Festival**: **Trecastagni**. 3rd Sunday of the month. Tasting and folklore.
- **Must-cake and Prickly-pear Festival**: **Militello in Val di Catania**. 3rd week of the month. In the castle hall.
- **Chestnut and Wine Festival**: **Trecastagni**. 4th Sunday of the month.
- **Meletna**: **Pedara**. From the 23rd to the 31st. Promotion of tasty local apples.
- **Mycological Exhibition**: **Catania**. From 27th October to 2nd November. At Le Ciminiere.
- **Olive Festival**: **Biancavilla**. At the end of the month.
- **Mycological Exhibition**: **Riposto**. Late October-Early November. Fresh and dried mushrooms, wild herbs, mycological information.
- **Festival of Seasoned Bread and Roast Chestnuts**: **Aci Sant'Antonio**. At Lavinaio. In Piazza Maggiore.
- **Lava Stone Exhibition**: **Belpasso**. In the streets.
- **Craft and Agriculture Exhibition**: **Belpasso**. In the Martoglio Garden.
- **Ottobrata**: **Calatabiano**. Gastronomic displays, sales and events.
- **Women's International Open Golf Tournament**: **Castiglione di Sicilia**.
- **Arts and Crafts Fair**: **Gravina di Catania**.
- **Grape Festival**: **Maletto**.
- **Mascalese Autumn**: **Mascali**. Drama, music and sports events.
- **Must-cake Festival**: **Mascali**. In the streets.
- **Mycological Exhibition and Mushroom Festival**: **Nicolosi**. In Piazza della Cisterna.
- **Mushroom Festival**: **Pedara**. In the municipal park and Piazza Don Bosco.
- **Apple Festival**: **Ragalna**. Every Saturday and Sunday. Market of Etna produce.
- **Grape Harvest Festival**: **Randazzo**. Entertainment and tastings.

Top: pistachio flowers. Facing page top: October Festival in Zafferana. Bottom: crib in Acireale.

November
- **Chestnut Festival**: **Trecastagni**. Tasting of mushrooms, home-made bread, ricotta, honey, must-cake.
- **Ottobrata Zafferanese**: **Zafferana Etnea**. Every Sunday of the month. Festival of grapes, must-cake, mushrooms, honey, wine and chestnuts.
- **All Souls Toy Fair**: **Trecastagni**.
- **Sausage, Goblet and Wine Festival**: **Ragalna**. 1st week of the month.
- **Feast of Saint Martin**: **Linguaglossa**, **Milo (contr. Fornazzo)**, **Raddusa**, **Ramacca**. On the 11th. Gastronomy, tasting of Wine and local Etna produce, folklore, shows. In Raddusa wine competition and sausage festival.
- **Festival of Saint Martin**: **Giarre**. From the 11th to the 14th. In Macchia. Tasting of sausages, must-cake, hot ricotta, mushrooms, chestnuts, honey, citrus fruits.
- **Festival of Roasted Chestnuts**: **Piedimonte Etneo**. On the 13th.
- **Chestnut and Wine Festival**: **Zafferana Etnea**. Mid-month.
- **Ornithological Exhibition**: **Catania**. From the 17th to the 21st. At Le Ciminiere.
- **Feast of Saint Catherine**: **Pedara**, **San Pietro Clarenza**. On the 25th.
- **Olive Oil Festival**: **Mineo**. Late November-early December. Local produce and crafts, folklore.
- **Mannino Trophy**: **Catania**. Fencing competition. In the sports centre.
- **Golden Trinacria Trophy**: **Catania**. Rhythmic gymnastics competition.
- **Exhibition of Local Wines**: **Linguaglossa**.
- **Secular Livestock Fair**: **Mascali**. Displays, antiques and folklore.
- **Good Taste Festival**: **Misterbianco**. Typical Sicilian produce. In Piazza Mazzini.
- **Olive Oil Festival**: **Motta Sant'Anastasia**, **Santa Maria di Licodìa**.
- **Indian Summer**: **Nicolosi**. Preparation and tasting of ricotta, display and sales of local agricultural produce and folkloristic shows.
- **Wine Festival**: **Raddusa**.
- **Oil and Wine Festival**: **San Michele di Ganzarìa**.
- **Feast and Fair of Our Lady of the Lamp**: **Santa Venerina**.

December
- **Feast of Saint Barbara**: **Paternò**. On the 4th.
- **Patronal Feast of Saint Nicholas of Bari**: **Trecastagni**. On the 6th.
- **Patacò Festival**: **Licodia Eubea**. 1st or 2nd Sunday of the month. Tasting of *patacò*, a local pulse, with broccoli and sausages.
- **Olive Oil and Local Produce Festival**: **Ragalna**. 2nd week of the month.
- **Patronal Feast of Saint Lucy**: **Belpasso**. From the 12th to the 14th. Parade of allegorical floats and singing competition.
- **Feast of Saint Lucy**: **Acicatena**, **Licodia Eubea**. On the 13th.
- **'Cuccia' Festival**: **Mirabella Imbaccari**, **San Michele di Ganzarìa**. On the 13th.
- **Chess Tournament**: **Catania**. From the 17th to the 19th. At Le Ciminiere.
- **Sounds and Lights of Christmas**: **Sant'Alfio**. From 20th December to 10th January. Exhibition of cribs and musical events.
- **Large 18th Century Crib**: **Acireale**. From 22nd December to 20th January. Church of Santa Maria della Neve.
- **Christmas in Catania**: **Catania**. Concerts, traditional events, cribs and craft market. Crib in the Ulysses cave at Ognina.
- **Christmas 'A Cona**: **Catania**. Performance of the popular *cona* inspired by the liturgy of the Novena. In the churches.
- **Christmas around Yule Log**: **Pedara and other towns on Etna**.
- **Christmas in the Streets**: **Randazzo**. Living crib, novenas in dialect. On the night of Christmas Eve lighting of *zucchi*, bonfires of wood.
- **Patronal Feast of Saint John the Evangelist**: **San Giovanni La Punta**. On the 27th.
- **New Year's Eve by the Sea**: **Catania**. On the 31st. Swimming competition in the Gulf of Ognina.
- **Terracotta Crib Exhibition**: **Caltagirone**. December-January.
- **Crib and Cribs**: **Catania**. Exhibition of artistic cribs. At Le Ciminiere.
- **Arts and Crafts at Le Ciminiere**: **Catania**. At Le Ciminiere.
- **Town of Cribs**: **Caltagirone**. Classical music, parades, decorations in the streets.
- **Christmas in Nicolosi**: **Nicolosi**. Concerts and cribs.
- **Park Festival**: **Randazzo**. Excursions on horseback and mountain-bike. Entertainment in the town centre.

ETNA IN ANCIENT TIMES

The oldest human settlements on Etna can be traced back to the Neolithic period (6th-3rd millennium BC), when man developed his knowledge of the production of tools for deforesting, tilling and farming the fertile lands on the slopes of the highest volcano in Europe.

Certainly, apart from building villages of huts, they also took advantage of the numerous caves created by lava flows, which offered safe, warm and comfortable shelter. There is very little archaeological material available to allow the formulation of hypotheses about these early phases of life on Etna, also because of the continuous disastrous events that have frequently changed the landscape.

At the end of the Copper Age and the beginning of the Bronze Age (from 2200 to 1500 BC) the inhabitants of Etna learned to use caves as large tombs, for both single and mass burials. As was usual in other parts of Sicily, everyday objects, such as water vessels and drinking cups, were offered to the deceased.

Among the most interesting sites, from an archaeological point of view, we should mention the Petralia Cave in the Barriera del Bosco district of Catania, which has yielded decorated terracotta vessels and bowls.

In the district of Adrano (S. Marco hill) a tomb from the late Bronze Age has been brought to light. It was built with large blocks of lava stone and inside various objects were found: four terracotta vessels, an amphora, two bowls and a vessel with filter, all objects that would also have been used in everyday life.

In this area there are numerous phenomena of secondary volcanism, known by the name of 'Salinelle of Paternò': tiny volcanoes that give off gases and boiling water rich in minerals. The native and Greek settlements on the slopes of Etna can be dated to much more recent times, between the 9th and 6th centuries BC. Near Paternò, in the district of Pietralunga on a bend of the River Simeto, a village of oval huts was built and the objects found date back to the 9th century BC.

The native settlement of Mendolito, named after the present day district near Adrano, was much more important and has yielded an enormous quantity of bronzes, dating from the 7th century BC.

Adrano is also the site of one of the most important Greek settlements of the whole Etna area, and that is Adranon, dedicated to the god of the volcano that cast its huge shadow across the town and surrounding area. Inside the museum, situated in the castle, thousands of objects found in digs or from private collections can be seen: decorated Greek amphorae, oil-lamps, terracotta statuettes depicting young girls, coins, grinders in lava stone, frame settings, amphorae for wine and oil, jewellery, arms and numerous other objects used by the inhabitants of this splendid city.

The arrival of the Greeks on the slopes of Etna modified the landscape profoundly, the trees of the forest were used to build houses and ships, the sides of the mountain were dug to create terraces for planting vines, large blocks of lava were hewn and cut in order to construct formidable walls to defend the city, the river beds were used to transport stones, trees and agricultural produce.

The volcano naturally induced a feeling of inferiority and this was accompanied by an attitude of civilised and respectful cohabitation, leaving deep traces in mythological and literary tradition.

For the ancient Greeks the eruptions of Etna were attributed to the monster Tifeo or the giant Encelado, imprisoned by Zeus under the volcano. In some texts Etna is described as the workshop of Efesto-Vulcan; Pindar recorded some eruptions.

The devastating fury of Etna is also referred to in the classical legend of the Pii Brothers, who saved their elderly parents from the advancing lava.

Another well-known legend of Etna is the one about the Agrigento philosopher Empedocles, who lived in the 5th century BC and is said to have died throwing himself into the crater of the volcano.

This episode inspired the Romantic German writer Hoelderlin, and is connected to the presence of a brick and terracotta construction, situated at above three thousand metres of height, known by the name of Philosopher's Tower; now believed to be from the Imperial Roman age, this monument has been attributed with various functions: the ancient temple of the god Vulcan, the dwelling of the philosopher Empedocles (hence the name), Empedocles' tomb, a house built to host the Emperor Hadrian, who during his reign 117 - 138 AD went up Etna twice to admire the incredible view and the majesty of nature.

Maria Teresa Di Blasi

CHRONOLOGY OF ETNA

500.000 years ago circa: birth of Etna linked to the phenomenon of continental drift and, in particular, to the clash of colossal proportions between the African and Eurasian shelves. The huge impact between the two shelves caused the compression of the magma, which was situated deep below the sea, which then violently rose up creating Etna.

200.000 years ago circa: beginning of the activity of the so called Ancient Eruptive Centres. Change from volcanic activity of a fissure type to that of a central type.

80.000 years ago circa: origin of the Trifolium, a collection of volcanic structures whose activity partly covered the material produced by the Ancient Eruptive Centres.

30.000 years ago circa: end of the activity of the Trifolium and shift of the main eruptive axis towards the north-west, where the summit craters are to be found today. Origin of the Mongibello, whose activity is distinguished in two phases called Ancient Mongibello and Recent Mongibello.

475 BC and 396 BC: eruptions of considerable entity reported by historical sources.

End of 1st century AD: from this century onwards historical sources begin to report a greater number of eruptions (about 200 to the present day) but certainly considerably fewer than those that really happened.

1669: one of the worst eruptions in the history of Etna. The volcanic activity was preceded and accompanied by strong earth tremors. In just 18 days the lava almost completely destroyed Catania and Nicolosi.

1811: eruption with catastrophic effects which interested above all the Bove Valley, where a new crater was formed.

1843: the lava, while flowing down the mountain, crossed marshland and the contact with the damp ground caused tremendous explosions that killed several people.

1866: violent eruption that created the crater of Monte Gemmellaro.

1892: during this long eruption the craters of the Monti Silvestri were formed.

1910: eruption on the southern side lasting twenty-six days.

1923: eruption on the north-eastern side with mouths at an altitude of 1,800/2,500 metres above sea level and a lava flow eleven kilometres long.

1928: eruption on the eastern side with a lava flow eight kilometres long and 18 days of eruption.

1950: the activity began in March and continued until December of the following year, 372 days during which the lava caused enormous damage overrunning vineyards, orchards and grazing land.

1971: the observatory and the cable car were destroyed.

1975: an eruption lasting 406 days.

1979: this eruption caused the death of nine people, killed by the sudden expulsion of a lava plug from an eruptive mouth.

1983: the magma destroyed the Sapienza mountain hut and a cable car station lower down.

1992: this year saw all Italians, through numerous television reports, following with great apprehension the news about activity on Etna, with lava flows threatening the town of Zafferana Etnea. These last two dates are worthy of particular attention because on both occasions attempts were made to overcome the ancestral fear of the local people faced with the eruptions by trying to divert, with partial success, the direction of the lava flow with explosives in order to save the threatened towns. 473 days of eruption with a lava flow almost nine kilometres long.

1999/2000: the volcano puts on a display with explosions and hurling out incandescent material. For months and months Catania and all the towns round Etna are showered with ash.

THE CIRCUMETNEA RAILWAY

Generally, when you find an obstacle in front of you, you have only two alternatives, jump over it or go around it.

The latter is the solution adopted by the people of Catania with regard to Etna, the majestic and terrifying volcano around which numerous towns are situated. The people of Catania are quick-witted and are accustomed to living with the explosive nature of the fiery mountain and in 1895 they inaugurated the first stretch of the Circumetnea railway with the audacious aim, which was completely fulfilled, of linking all the towns round the volcano. If you take the Circumetnea railway from Catania today, you will also travel along the new stretch of the city's underground, now being extended, which goes from

Piazza Galatea to Piazza Lincoln (they are thinking of turning the old line above ground into a cycle lane). Your journey begins just outside the city and the railway line begins to climb up, passing through countryside which, at first, is hilly and rapidly becomes mountainous until you come to the Ionian coast, where you find an indolent seascape. It is a charming journey, unique, one that famous visitors have also undertaken and recounted. This is the case with De Amicis, who wrote: O Dear reader, if you go to Catania one day, remember to make a trip on the Circumetnea railway, and you will say that it is the most charming round trip you can make on the face of the earth in seven hours.

This railway goes around the great volcano, with a length of more than a hundred kilometres, linking all the largest towns on its slopes. It seemed a utopian task from the outset and faced a thousand difficulties, not being completed until 1895. Now, it is hard to understand why it was not built twenty years earlier, so great are the advantages it has brought to the thirty-eight towns, large and small, scattered around Etna. The population density here is higher than that of the most densely populated areas of Germany. It is a railway that passes through a paradise on earth, interrupted here and there by pieces of hell. It starts out from Catania and, until it reaches the coast, where it joins the main line back to Catania, it is a series of marvellous views of Etna and of the sea, of gardens and of lava, of small extinct volcanoes and lush green valleys, of pretty villages and parts of ancient forests of oaks, beeches and pines, which supplied material for the building of the fleets of Syracuse and which have largely been devastated by lava from above and farming from below. The line goes up to altitudes of more than one thousand metres, goes down, climbs up again and passes through vineyards, olive groves, vast plantations of almond trees and chestnut woods; it runs through wide areas covered with the debris of eruptions, between lava walls as high as houses, between piles of volcanic material, arabesqued, streaked and moulded into a thousand strange shapes of snakes and monstrous human bodies, where you cannot see a single blade of grass; it passes other

Top: rail-car near Biancavilla.
Left: a prototype carriage of the new Catania underground.

areas where nature is beginning to reclaim the land from the ashes and scoriae, already broken up and disintegrated by the new vegetation; it passes over flowering hills from which you can look down onto green valleys with charming white villas, churches, roads winding around dark patches of orange, mandarin and lemon trees, alongside silver streams that look like streaks of snow, sparkling in the sunlight. Throughout the journey Etna is always visible, but from a hundred different viewpoints, changing according to the view of the cone it lets us see. The regularity of its conical shape, as seen from Catania, is no longer apparent. Going round it, you see enormous sheer sides, immense stairways, pyramids within pyramids, which follow one another like instantaneous transformations; in some places it seems to have lost its upper cone, at various points it seems broken in two, at times completely covered with snow, at others white only on top, at others still it seems so different from the fixed image you have in your mind that it makes you suspect it is another mountain hiding Etna from your view! The summit offers a host of different images, sometimes coloured pink by the sun, at others clouded by smoke. Rising up like a giant plume, either the smoke stretches out one way like an oversize waving banner, or it goes down and stretches out

on the sides of the cone in light white veils, as delicate as lace! Towards the end of this spellbound journey the sea opens up before your eyes and you can still see the outline, against the white snows of Etna, of what remains of the huge chestnut forest of Cento Cavalli, while in the other direction you see the great beauty of Taormina, almost hanging in the blue sky. Then, finally, you come to the most wonderful coastline of the island, the site of its first settlers; marvellous because of its lovely vegetation and the poetry of its legends: here is the charming beach where Ulysses' ship was hurled, where Aeneas landed and where Polyphemus grazed his goats; and at the end of the archipelago of the Cyclops, the seven strange rocky islets, a fantastic line of conical black heads, decreasing in height, which stand out of the sea, like the heads of a family of underwater giants, who lift up their foreheads to bid farewell to the 'Island of sun'.

O divine Sicily! How many Italians, who have run around the world for pleasure, died or will die without having seen you!

Edmondo De Amicis

Extract from "Memories of a journey to Sicily" - Editore Cav. NICCOLÒ GIANNOTTA 1908.

Top: the Circumetnea railway passes through pistachio orchards near Bronte.
Left: "Boveri" type locomotive near Adrano.

ITINERARIES ON ETNA: USEFUL INFORMATION

alf you want to fully enjoy the places these itineraries will take you to, it is necessary to have adequate equipment and to know what facilities exist to help hikers, particularly signposts and mountain huts.

It is essential to carry only what is absolutely necessary with you on your walk, remembering, however, on the basis of the time of year and the route you take, that you are dealing with a mountain of over 3,000 metres (11,000 feet) in height in the middle of the Mediterranean, where sudden changes in the weather are always possible. This means, even on short easy walks, choosing strong boots, because of the rough surface of the lava; then consider clothing, adequate to protect you against the cold and the wind, with changes. It is a good idea to carry sufficient water since there are almost no natural sources and it is very difficult, especially in summer, to find water in the mountain huts with water tanks.

Signposts are still few and far between. You will only find those put up by the Park Authority along the 'nature footpaths' (M.Nero degli Zappini, M. Sartorius), while on the north-western slopes you will find those put up by the Forestry Service. These are made from pyrographed wood and are placed at the base of 'cones' or at the most important junctions, along the network of tracks that lead up from the towns and villages into the woods.

On the lava flows it is possible to find small piles of stones marking the way, left there once upon a time mostly by shepherds.

The mountain huts demonstrate the peculiarity of this territory, not only because of the volcanic and tectonic events, but also because of the inability of the men that live here to manage it. Many of them were built when man's relationship with the mountain was different and are no longer usable, either because they have been destroyed by earthquakes or eruptions (Puchoz, Conti, Piccolo Rifugio, Osservatorio and in part Torre del Filosofo), by man's neglect (Casermetta, M. Spagnolo) or by a combination of the two (Menza). Others, while being in perfect condition, cannot be used because they are forestry service huts reserved for personnel (M. Grosso, M. Gemmellaro, M.

Denza, Case Pappalardo, M. Ruvolo, Case Zampini, Case Pirao, M. Crisimo, Due Monti, Case Paternò). There are, however, a series of forestry huts, unmanned, equipped with fireplace and wood and almost all with water tanks, mostly situated along the so called high mountain route

and subject to regular maintenance (Galvarina, Poggio La Caccia, M. Scavo, M. Maletto, M. La Nave, Saletti, M. S. Maria).

There are then unmanned huts belonging to the Province, normally closed, equipped with fireplace, water and beds, run by the Italian Alpine Club (CAI), which allows its members to use them. These can be found on the north-eastern slopes (M. Corvo, M. Nero and M. Nero delle Concazze). Finally, there are manned huts, open all year round, which can generally be found in the fianl stretches of the two traditional access routes to the higher parts of the volcano. Two of these belong to the CAI (Sapienza, on the southern side, and Citelli on the north-eastern side), others are outright hotels (Corsaro, on the southern side; Nord-est, Le Betulle, Brunek, Ragabo, Clan dei Ragazzi, on the northern side).

Everyone who ventures out onto the mountain will realise that in this delicate game of adaptation to external factors and internal ones (not least the awareness of your own limits) it is important to be temperate, as a sign of common sense, in order to establish a trouble-free relationship with the volcano.

Top: a walker on the summit of the central crater.
Right: signposts placed by the Etna Park near the Citelli mountain hut.

Giuseppe Riggio and Giuseppe Vitali

grande traversata etnea

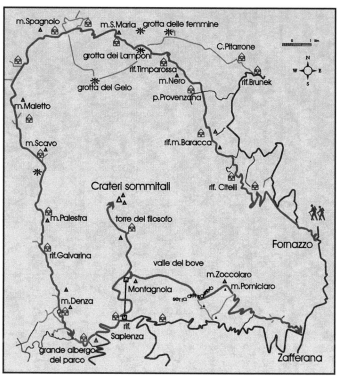

HIKING AROUND THE VOLCANO

The GTE (Cross-Etna Walk) is a hike of five days all around the volcano, allowing you to appreciate all its various features, the peculiar environments created by fire, as well as secular woods.

The GTE has already been tried out with satisfaction by hundreds of enthusiasts, largely from other parts of Italy, and can be fully considered one of the 'classic' hikes in Europe, thanks to the beauty of the mountainside landscape through which it passes.

In this publication the GTE is presented in great detail for the first time, so that even those excursionists who are not familiar with the area can organise their five day trip across the volcano (needing only the help of a topographic map).

This is necessary while waiting for the authorities responsible for tourism on Etna to set up the necessary facilities (above all the walking routes and a minimum number of signposts).

In the meantime the hiking route suggested here can be enjoyed anyway, adding to the description supplied just a little touch of spirit of improvisation and adventure, which are still necessary for those intending to appreciate the charming beauties of the mountains in the south of Italy.

1ST STAGE
FORNAZZO - DISTRICT OF MILO - (824 M.)
PIETRACANNONE HOUSE (1,130 M.), PIANO PROVENZANA (1,800 M.).
DIFFERENCE IN HEIGHT: climb of 976 metres

POINTS OF INTEREST

The first day of the GTE is dedicated to a gradual climb across the south-eastern face of the volcano.

You start from the highest village on this side of Etna, first passing through a cultivated area (vineyards, orchards) and then following an old mule track that was once the main access to the woods and crossing various stretches of vegetation until you arrive in one of the two ski stations on Etna.

The points of interest are mainly of botanical and anthropological nature (signs of human presence, the old 'snow grottoes', the paths used by shepherds and charcoal burners.

DESCRIPTION OF THE ITINERARY

An ancient nettle tree (loved by generations of Sicilian children who have played with its fruit) welcomes excursionists to the square of Fornazzo at the start of the GTE. Before leaving, however, you should pay a visit to the small church, just a few yards away, inside which you can see a large naive style painting of one of the more recent eruptions (1979), which threatened the houses of this quiet mountain hamlet.

From the square of Fornazzo (which can be reached by the regular AST bus service from Catania railway station) you set off along a narrow road that passes the last few houses of the hamlet ('Ideal Italian Village' according to the magazine 'Airone') and this soon becomes a simple track. You continue to climb for about 400 metres, until you come to the Mareneve road to Piano Provenzana.

You follow this road for about 1 kilometre, until you reach a characteristic votive altar, built on the edge of the 1971 lava flow.

This is one of the many put up over the years as a sign of thanksgiving and devotion, but this one has become extremely famous because the next lava flow, in 1979, went around it without destroying it, leading to claims of a miracle.

About 100 metres after the altar, on the left, you will see the start of an old cart-track, which was tarmacked, as an emergency measure, after the 1971 eruption. The route of the GTE in this stretch is of great interest, despite the tarmac, since you can still get an idea of the ancient origins of the track, which winds among shady chestnuts, locked between two high walls.

This takes you as far as Pietracannone, where the Etna

track, which now becomes narrower, and you climb up steeply among the broom.

After about ten minutes you will see the edge of the 1971 lava flow in the distance. You will have to deviate a little to the left to avoid the ilex grove (follow the signs), until you come out onto a forest path a little further on, in front of the Paternò Houses (lovely country houses, once part of the Paternò Estate, provided with a large water tank and sheep pen).

After reaching the group of houses, it is better to follow a pathway that starts just to the left of the buildings (seen from below).

After ten minutes more walking you find yourself on a wide forest path again. You walk through the pleasant woodland until reaching a barrier just before the first part of the 1971 lava flow.

You can follow the flow down to the right, as far as the Fanciullo House (not open to excursionists) or continue along the route turning immediately left when you reach the lava and entering the wood again (beeches, birches, pine-trees and poplars). You go right through the wood, until you come out onto a tarmacked road, after about an hour of

Park Authority has bought and restored an old farm-house with the idea of turning it into a 'base camp for excursions', in other words a visitors' centre for tourists arriving in the protected area.

The locality is named after a curious very smooth cylindrical shaped duct, situated below the house (in Sicilian 'a petra cannuni', in other words the cannon shaped stone). The origin of this strange duct can probably be explained by the sudden burying of a large tree by a lava flow.

The trunk gradually dried up inside the flow without burning, leaving a sort of mould impressed into the lava stone once the wooden fibres had decomposed over the years.

From Pietracannone you take a mule track that still seems to echo with the sound of the 'burdunari' (the mule drivers) who passed this way with their animals loaded down with charcoal and broom.

Up to this point the type of track was also suitable for carts to use.

You continue (following signpost n. 16.3) between two high drystone walls, until you reach a small wood of poplars alongside the cart-track. Here you can find one of the last remaining artificial 'snow grottoes' still in existence on Etna.

It is no more than a wide trench dug into the ground, seven metres deep, protected by thick lava stone walls and provided with a wide access chute: in this 'reservoir' snow was collected and stored in winter and sold when the hotter weather arrived.

Beyond the 'snow grotto' you continue to follow the mule

walking. From here in just ten minutes you can reach the Citelli Mountain Hut (owned by the Italian Alpine Club and situated in a beautiful position at 1,740 metres) to stay overnight, or you can walk on for about an hour and a half

On this page from the top: eruption of 1973; car park at the Citelli mountain hut; Piano Provenzana.

in order to reach the accommodation at Piano Provenzana.

If you do this, you go down the tarmacked road for about 100 metres, until you see an obvious pathway (initially, follow the signs for the M. Sartorius nature path), which disappears into a wood of aetnensis birches, a very rare botanical species.

Once you are among the white trunks of the birches, make sure you stay on the main path without following the signs for the nature path of the park, which lead to the crest of Sartorius Mounts (dating from 1865).

After going round these last craters on the western side, you move on past a hut (partially open), then past a diversion to the right (not to be taken) and, finally, a steep descent at Mount Baracca.

At this point the birches give way to secular Corsican pines. Careful observation will show you that at the base of the higher pines there are incisions in the bark, dating back to the time (up to the end of the Second World War) when resin extraction was a lucrative business in the forest.

The itinerary continues along a relatively flat path, partially disused, situated at 1,750 metres, until you come to a wider path, also used in winter as a Nordic ski piste, which brings you to Piano Provenzana.

In this important tourist locality you get a magnificent view

towards the north-eastern summit crater and the gorges of the Pizzi Deneri and there are two places to stay.

PRACTICAL INFORMATION 1ST STAGE

Fornazzo (800 m.) can be reached by bus from Catania (bus terminus near the railway station, AST service to Sant'Alfio, tel. 095 7230536).

Overnight accommodation can be found at the Citelli Mountain Hut (bookings on 095 930000), or at Piano Provenzana in the North-East Mountain Hut (tel. 095 647922) or at the hotel Le Betulle (tel. 095 643430).

At Piano Provenzana there is an emergency medical service.

WALKING TIMES 1ST STAGE

Departure Fornazzo
Piertacannone House 1hr
Cubania Houses 2hr 20m
Road for Citelli Hut 3hr 20m
Piano Provenzana 4hr 35m

> ## 2ND STAGE
> PIANO PROVENZANA (1,800M), MONTE NERO (1,920M)
> RUINS OF BARRACKS MONTE SPAGNOLO (1,440M)
> BIVOUAC MONTE SCAVO (1,700M) OR BIVOUAC MONTE MALETTO
> DIFFERENCE IN HEIGHT: CLIMB OF 385M
> DIFFERENCE IN HEIGHT: DESCENT OF 460M

POINTS OF INTEREST

This is a long walk on three sides of the volcano, among the lava and secular woods, in an incomparable natural setting that never ceases to amaze you. The first part of the itinerary lets you discover one of the most beautiful and breathtaking stretches of the whole five-day walk: the slopes of Monte Nero, which you cross thanks to a narrow path created by shepherds.

This is one of those Etna landscapes in which the ancient lava flows almost seem to liquefy in a rediscovered harmony of multi-coloured pioneering plants, solitary vigorous Corsican pines sticking up, impressive volcanic bombs spread around the ground by the terrifying forces that the volcano has let loose in this area.

The excursionist enters this very interesting environment thanks to a narrow trace of a pathway, which is hardly noticeable among the volcanic sands, and yet this trace shows that it is possible today, as in the past, for man and nature to live together, above all when this happens in an area that has been designated a nature park.

However, this day's walk on the GTE does not consist only of the landscape on the slopes of Monte Nero, but continues further on with one of the best known caves on Etna (the Cave of Raspberries) and then with the unspoilt beau-

Top: view of Etna. Left: the eastern slopes at Fornazzo.

ty of the northern slopes, where the secular beech-wood of Monte Spagnolo leads us to the final climb towards Monte Maletto and Monte Scavo.

DESCRIPTION OF THE ITINERARY

From one of the stage posts you have to go down the tarmacked road for about one hundred metres, as far as the entrance to Piano Provenzana (naturally, if you spent the night at the Citelli Hut, you will have to finish the first stage), just below the Nordic Ski School, where a cart-track heads off northwards into the pine-forest.

The track climbs gradually with various sharp bends and, in a short time (15 minutes), leads to a wide clearing on the edge of which is the Monte Nero Mountain Hut (usually closed, but available to members of the Italian Alpine Club by contacting the Linguaglossa section).

You continue across the wide clearing and enter a thick beech-wood inside which the track is still very clear. Suddenly, you will find yourself facing the imposing mass of Monte Nero (2,042 metres). You climb up again through wide stretches of volcanic sand until you reach an obvious pile of stones - placed on the edge of a lava flow - which indicates the start of a path that takes you first to a fissure, dating from 1923, and then to the slopes of Monte Nero. The alignment, called button-style, of the explosive mouths that have formed on the fissure is characteristic: it is like an open wound in the surface of the earth from which - during the eruption - pyroclastic material came out and fell into the surrounding area. In the meantime - as is easily seen if you descend into the 'chimneys' (the hornitos) that were formed - the liquid lava, with little gas, flowed quickly downhill, bringing destruction to the countryside around Castiglione di Sicilia.

A few metres further on you come to the highest point of the second stage, passing through a landscape of incomparable beauty. When you arrive at a junction right under Monte Nero, you turn right and go down without delay - across lava flows with sparse vegetation - to the Timpa Rossa Mountain Hut (open but unmanned, consisting of two small rooms and an outside water tank). From this point you follow a forest path which, after a couple of kilometres, joins the high mountain ring (a circular route around the volcano from the pinewood of Linguaglossa to the southern side in the Piano Vettore area). At the same point where the two paths meet there is a sign-posted track that leads you in a few minutes to the entrance of the Cave of Raspberries (1,750m), a long lava tunnel (the main part measures 300 metres in length) that was created inside the lava flow of 1614/24. It is worthwhile going into the tunnel as far as a point where the ceiling has caved in. You can leave through the gap created in the ceiling and return to the junction of the high mountain path. The itinerary continues, with no particular problems, westwards over a rough surface. You gradually go down as

On this page from the top: Raspberry Cave; hornitos formed during the eruption of 1999; the small sanctuary of Piano Vetore.

far as the Monte S. Maria Mountain Hut at a height of 1,450 metres. This junction can be recognised because it is at a place where the main path takes a sharp turn to the right. It is advisable here to turn left and follow an old rough track that ends at the huge lava flow of 1981.

From here you can continue by taking a narrow but clear path that passes right through the explosive-effusive mate-

rial of that eruption, impressive piles of volcanic sand, lapilli, scraps of lava and volcanic bombs, until it brings you to the beech-wood that surrounds Monte Spagnolo. Just a few hundred metres further on you come back onto the main route of the high mountain path near a small barracks (1,440 m), now in ruins, and a small building of the Forestry Service used as an emergency shelter. A few hundred metres from the ruins of the barracks you come to a turning to the right that allows you to go down quite quickly to Randazzo, passing the western slopes of Monte Spagnolo (see the section on town connections).

From the turn off to Randazzo you begin to climb again gradually, staying on the high mountain route.

To the north you can see the Nebrodi mountain chain and will recognise Monte Soro, the highest peak in the chain (1,840m), from the radio-television transmitter.

Below, through gaps in the vegetation, you will see the Randazzo plateau, which divides the Alcantara Valley, to the

Top: hornitos and sulphurous concretions. Right: a fox at sunset.

east, and the Simeto Valley, to the west. After about an hour's walking from the Monte Spagnolo barracks, you come to the sign-posted turn (1,470m) for the Monte La Nave Mountain Hut (open) from where you can descend to Maletto.

The final stretch of the second stage is a gradual climb up to the slopes of Monte Maletto, where you find a first sign-posted turn-off allowing you, in 15 minutes, to reach the mountain hut of the same name (two rooms with fireplace and water tank, in a building in the pine-forest, unmanned) and a second turn-off downhill, which lets you get to the Pappalardo Houses and then the village of Maletto (see town connections).

For your second overnight stay you can use the above-mentioned Monte Maletto Hut (cosy and secluded) or - if you want to stay on the high mountain route - the other Mountain Hut of Monte Scavo (one large room with fireplace and outside water tank, also unmanned).

WALKING TIMES 2ND STAGE

Departure Piano Provenzana
Timpa Rossa Mountain Hut 1^{hr}
Cave of Raspberries 2^{hr} 20^{m}
1981 lava flow 3^{hr} 30^{m}
Monte Spagnolo 3^{hr} 45^{m}
Turn-off for Monte Maletto Hut 5^{hr} 20^{m}
Monte Scavo Mountain Hut 6^{hr}

PRACTICAL INFORMATION 2ND STAGE

There are no manned huts for the entire stage, so you must be completely self-sufficient as regards food and water for about 30 hours. In case of emergency you can drink the water from the water tanks of the mountain huts, there is, however, no guarantee that it is fit for drinking.

POINTS OF INTEREST

This is a day of wide open spaces and lava fields, only partly colonised by pioneering plants. This is because of the prevailing winds that usually blow eastwards and prevent sand and ashes given out by the summit craters from falling on this side.

Very little of the tons of material constantly sent into the atmosphere by Etna ends up covering the lava flows in this area, so, barren and exposed as they are, they seem to be flows of a few months ago and not centuries old.

For a good part of the stage you walk in the shadow of the steep overhanging western face of the volcano, the one that clearly demonstrates the presence of a large eruptive complex in existence before the present day 'Mongibello'. Looking up towards the smoking summit, you notice a distinct gap at the point where the ravines finish and before the beginning of the present summit cone. This is where the 'elliptic' crater, as volcanologists call it, existed.

The ravines that characterise the morphology of this side of the volcano are the ones that inspired the admiration of Goethe, who observed them when travelling down from Enna and described them in his "Journey to Italy" thus: "It was streaked with white and grey and seemed to be something bodily, but how could something bodily hang in the sky? The coachman explained to us that our admiration was caused by a side of Etna that appeared through a gap in the clouds…"

This then is the Etna of wide open spaces, which the Sicilian Regional Forestry Service began to administer as early as the 1950s. It should be visited slowly, passing from one mountain hut to another, with an eye on the scenery below, where you will see the towns and villages that circle the volcano pass by, like in a panning shot in a film.

On this page: details of the volcanic eruption in 1999.

DESCRIPTION OF THE ITINERARY

If you stayed overnight at the M. Maletto bivouac, it is best to continue uphill for about 20 minutes, until the track ends at a lava flow from 1975, and then cross this petrified river of fire along a narrow path that allows you to reach another track on the other side.

This will take you quickly downhill and onto the high moun-

27

tain route in a short time, less than a hundred metres south of the M. Scavo bivouac (1,700m).

If you chose the latter as your stop off point, then you need only continue southwards along the high mountain route.

At the top of the first climb after leaving the hut, you find the Cave of M. Nunziata, a few metres to the right of the track, a cave created by lava flows and very difficult to gain access to.

You walk on through a landscape of wide lava flows, touched here and there by a few pieces of woodland.

To one side you will see the Simeto Valley (with its numerous towns), while on the other side your view is blocked by steep ravines that come down from the summit of the volcano.

In the autumn of 1999 a lava flow from one of the summit craters ran down one of these ravines and, due to the steep gradient, reached the track we are using in just a few hours.

After an hour you reach another bivouac built by the Forestry Service (the M. Palestra Hut, also called Poggio la Caccia) and just after this, on a rise, you pass the highest point of this stage (at a height of almost 2,000 metres).

After passing the Galvarina mountain hut (1,850m), the track gradually becomes more shaded, thanks to the presence of a large pine-wood near Monte Denza.

At the point where the track becomes a tarmacked road (reserved only for Forestry Service vehicles) you can climb

up to the left towards the large mountain hut of Monte Denza (1,812 m, closed), which has a large picnic area, or continue downhill, rapidly reaching the small altar dedicated to Saint John Gualberto (patron Saint of Forestry workers).

A few hundred metres further down the road you can choose to follow the nature path set up by the Etna Park Authority

(take the path to the left), walking alongside the fence of the Nuova Gussonea mountain garden (only open to visitors by prior arrangement) and then heading towards an obvious lava stone building, flanked by a sheep-pen, after which the path climbs steeply and rejoins the nature path in the stretch near Piano Vetore (1,750m).

In this way you will visit a typical high altitude Etna environment, on the border between the tree line and the pioneering plants, remembering, however, that you will have to climb up about 100 metres and then go back down again towards Piano Vetore.

On the other hand you can continue - after reaching the Nuova Gussonea botanical garden - along the tarmacked

road, straight to Piano Vetore (avoiding all the detours).
It is useful to note that, on the edge of the plateau (which can also be reached along the provincial road n° 92 from

On this page from the top: eruption from the south-eastern crater; Monti Silvestri; Piano Vetore; grazing flocks in the high mountain meadows.

Nicolosi), there is a 'base camp' run by the Etna Park Authority, located in the Etna Grand Hotel (currently undergoing refurbishment), where you can watch videos about the natural beauties of the volcano and use the small snack bar.

Finally, to reach the stage point, you have to follow a tarmacked road for about 4km from Piano Vetore to the tourist zone of Etna South, where you can stay overnight, either at the Sapienza mountain hut (1,910m) run by the Italian Alpine Club, or at the restaurant-hotel Corsaro.

WALKING TIMES 3RD STAGE

Departure Monte Scavo
Galvarina Mountain Hut 2hr
Start of detour along nature path 3hr 30m
Etna Grand Hotel 4hr
(if you take the nature path calculate about 45m more)
Etna South tourist zone 5hr

PRACTICAL INFORMATION 3RD STAGE

Hotel-restaurant Corsaro, tel. 095 914122
Sapienza Mountain Hut, tel. 095 911062
Nicolosi Tourism Office, tel. 095 911505
Etna Park Authority, tel. 095 914588
SITAS Etna Cableway, tel. 095 911158

4TH STAGE
ETNA SOUTH TOURIST ZONE (1,900M)
TORRE DEL FILOSOFO MOUNTAIN HUT (2,920M)

POINTS OF INTEREST

After three days of walking around the volcano this is the big day of the climb to the top of the living mountain, the Sicilians' 'muntagna'. That peak, which has been smoking for thousands of years, provokes fear and curiosity at the same time.

Since the time of the philosopher Empedocles, the mystery of that inextinguishable fire that brings both destruction and fertility has continuously fascinated men's hearts and minds, whether they be educated travellers or simple spectators of its activity. Why so much fascination? In order to explain this phenomenon we need only consider that still now, in the 21st century, volcanism remains one of the great natural phenomena that man cannot control.

When faced with an erupting volcano, it is of little use to remember the experiments carried out on Etna in the last 15 years to 'divert' lava flows. Some regard these interventions as miraculous, but their effectiveness is limited to a specific type of flow.

Despite the enormous publicity the media gave those experiments, the bulldozers used against the rivers of lava and the explosives detonated along the edges of the flows

gave the impression of a little mouse pinpricking a giant. When everything goes right, the giant may, at most, redirect his anger somewhere else, but nothing more can be done today, and even this operation involves numerous risks. You need only think what it means to divert a lava flow in a highly populated area or in areas of outstanding natural beauty.

This happened in the Bove Valley, where numerous secular beech-trees, growing on the edge of the valley, were sacrificed in the name of civil defence.

Anyway, the stages of the GTE that you have already finished will have helped to create the right atmosphere for the day when you meet the living volcano. Above all because having waited for this day walking long distances around the huge mass of the volcano, having seen the far-off smoking summit dozens of times, you will not experience the climb to the top in the same state of mind as the large masses of tourists in jeeps who quickly arrive a few hundred metres from the summit and then move on, ready to take in another tourist trap.

In your heart you should try to be like the 18th and 19th century travellers for whom the climb to the top was an experience worthy of a scholarly account, a long letter to a distant friend, worthy of expressions full of adjectives.

Those were the times when you left from Nicolosi by mule. The first stop-off was inside the Cave of Goats; late at night the travellers and their guides were already at the base of the central crater and took shelter, before the final stretch,

On this page: images of the central crater.

in a hut that the Gemmellaro brothers had built, thanks to funds collected from the British officers stationed in Messina during the Napoleonic Wars.

It is a good idea, therefore, to read some of the accounts written by the 18th century travellers before leaving the Sapienza mountain hut to begin the 4th stage of the GTE. It helps you to face the climb in the right spirit, with due respect for a mountain that still remains in many ways inscrutable and unpredictable.

Certainly, the cable car will save you some exertion, the mini-buses loaded with tourists will sweep past you on their way to the Philosopher's Tower hut, that is the demarcation line traced around the top of the volcano for safety reasons.

That is also the point at which the fourth stage of the GTE ends because it is impossible to trace a permanent pathway beyond here, in an area that is the absolute domain of the volcano (with its four mouths in full activity). A 'planet' on which ashes, lapilli, and bombs given off during explosions, without mentioning the lava flows that occasionally come out of the craters, continually change the landscape and constitute a real threat to those who wish to go and take a peep into the mouth of the volcano.

Those who wish to beyond the Philosopher's Tower hut should, therefore, take all necessary precautions to avoid turning their visit to this area into an unpleasant experience, first of all by contacting the mountain guides (if necessary, engaging their services beforehand) and the appropriate tourist information offices (see box) to ask for up-to-date information on the warnings issued periodically by the Civil Defence Authorities regarding access to the summit craters.

However, in the unfortunate event that the volcano should surprise you near one of the craters with one of its not infrequent explosions, remember the advice often repeated by volcanologists: as far as possible stay calm and watch where the material thrown into the air is falling and avoid at all costs running away blindly, a course of action that greatly increases the risk of being struck.

DESCRIPTION OF THE ITINERARY

From the tourist zone of Etna South a rough track goes up towards the summit and is usually used by the off-road vehicles carrying tourists. Unfortunately, there is at present no real alternative route for walkers. To shorten the walk you can use the faint pathway that follows the ski slopes, remembering, however, that this involves a considerable increase in gradient.

The first stretch of the climb can also be covered by cable car, which takes you up to a height of 2,500 metres, in the Montagnola zone, in about 15 minutes. From here, if visibility is good, it is better just to start off along the rough track towards the Philosopher's Tower and then leave the track after about 15 minutes of walking, in order to continue straight on (eastwards) towards the precipices on the edge of the Bove Valley.

This allows you to avoid the continual coming and going of the smoky off-road vehicles and above all to get a glimpse of the gorges that drop down into the Bove Valley, almost 1,000 metres below. At a height of around 2,800 metres you come to the lava flow that developed in the last few months of 1998 after very long explosive activity from the south-eastern sub-terminal mouth.

If you want to continue towards the Philosopher's Tower, you need good visibility since the pathway ends near the recent lava flow and from here onwards you have to cross the lava by sight towards the north-west (also using occasional faint pathways) and then zigzag up the steep pile of ashes below the mountain hut. If there is fog or low clouds it is much better to stay on the track used by the off-road vehicles right from the Montagnola.

The route of this stage ends at the Philosopher's Tower (a large two-storey building, in a highly panoramic position) since - as we have already said in the presentation of this stage - beyond this point you enter the domain of the volcano.

In the same way as ancient geographers traced a line in the African continent accompanied by the words "hic sunt leones", the same thing could be done in this area of Etna, with reference to the savage tendencies of certain volcanic activity. If you wish to go on, at your own risk, towards the craters, you will have to come down the track from the mountain hut for about fifty metres and then take a pathway to the

Departure from Etna South tourist area
Top cable-car station 1hr 30m
Philosopher's Tower 3hr

PRACTICAL INFORMATION 4TH STAGE

For overnight stays you can contact SITAS (tel. 095 911158) if you want to stay in the Philosopher's Tower mountain hut.
If it is not available you will have to go back down (2hr 30m) after visiting the craters and stay a second night at Etna South.

right which heads westwards and goes around the summit cones.

At present there is violent activity in the terminal craters with lava flows that have considerably altered the morphology of the zone.

Usually, however, there is a faint pathway on the ground going up to the summit from the west (mostly used by guides and researchers) and this can be used, with all the dangers we have already mentioned, to continue the tradition of the 18th century travellers, going to take a glimpse into the mouth of hell.

It is impossible to describe the summit area, beyond the vague indications we have given, because of the constant changes it undergoes, caused by the incessant activity. A crater that is clearly defined and has a regular shape today could be torn apart tomorrow by a new lava flow and completely change appearance.

To stay overnight you can apply to SITAS to use the Philosopher's Tower mountain hut (owned by the Province of Catania, but not yet regularly open to the public). The advantage of putting up with a Spartan bivouac at an altitude of 2,900 metres (with no water or toilets) is that you can wake up in the morning and enjoy one of the most extraordinary views in Italy, the one celebrated by poets and travellers of every age: the sun rising slowly from the sea, the shadow of the cone of the volcano stretching across half of Sicily, the sky alight with red and orange until the spectators are bathed in the first rays of the sun, while the far-off cities still sleep in the half-light.

Dawn from the crater, according to AUGUSTO DI SAYVE (quoted in *the Illustrated Mediterranean, its islands and its beaches*; Florence, 1841, reprinted Palermo 1988, pag. 243).

"Of all the optical effects it is possible to see, the most singular for sure, but which only lasts a moment, is that of the pyramidal shadow of Etna, projected on the horizon westwards, at the moment the sun rises (…) I have travelled a lot, I've described the Alps and the Pyrenees, but nowhere have I found a view equal to this. It seems that the sea and the horizon make up he frame of this immense picture, offered for man to admire, and being here he feels he is the only living thing in the universe. The whole world and its monuments seem to disappear before his very eyes. Nothing that lies below him attracts his attention, since the forest area hides part of the town that forms the base of Etna; and only when daylight comes, striking each of the confused objects in that immensity, it seems, so to say, that they come out of the chaos one by one and come to life under the gaze of the man contemplating them."

Facing page: the central crater.
On this page from the top: details of the southern slopes.

DETOUR FIFTH STAGE

If you go back to the tourist zone of Etna South at the end of the fourth day of hiking, it is convenient to start the fifth stage going down the provincial road towards Zafferana for about 1.5 km, as far as the first turn-off, opposite which you will clearly see a forest track that goes back uphill and takes you to the edge of the Bove Valley at a height of 2,000 metres, near the so called 'Malerba memorial stone'.

Just below the stone (which is placed right on the edge of the Valley) you see the traces of a pathway, once also used by shepherds, which goes down into the deep depression along the steep Serra Perciata gorge.

At the bottom of the descent you rejoin the GTE at the 'Carmelo and Riccardo' path, which crosses the difficult lava flows of 1991/93.

This alternative way down into the Bove Valley should be used if you are in a large group, even if you stayed overnight at the Philosopher's Tower.

Instead of using the Montagnola gorge (see the description of the stage), you cut across the slope of the Montagnola and continue walking along the edge of the Valley, following the highly scenic Donkey's Back ridge, which brings you quite quickly to the 'Malerba memorial stone' (see above) at an altitude of 2,000 metres and from here you can go straight down into the Bove Valley .

5TH STAGE
PHILOSOPHER'S TOWER (2,920M), BOVE VALLEY,
SALFIZIO CREST, MONTE ZOCCOLARO, CASSONE,
PIANO DELL'ACQUA, ZAFFERANA ETNEA (620M)

POINTS OF INTEREST

The time has come to go back down the mountain: just as the shepherds used to do at the end of the summer. After five days walking around the living mountain, admiring its various natural beauties, you return to civilisation. Before doing so, however, it is indispensable to experience the terrifying beauty of the Bove Valley: a strange place, fascinating for some, repulsive for others.

It is the symbol of Etna's mutability, made famous in the 1930s as the place chosen for the skiing challenges of the time, then becoming farming and grazing land for the people of Zafferana and finally the domain of the volcano, which from 1991 to 1993 poured tens of millions of cubic metres of lava into the valley.

Those who saw it before those events (which can only partly be described as natural, since they were heavily influenced by the attempts made by the Civil Defence Authorities to divert the lava flows) are dismayed by the scene of devastation before their eyes, once they reach the edge of the enormous valley.

Where once there were meadows of pioneering plants and shepherds' huts, now lava flows dominate, where large secular beech-trees once grew, tongues of lava were diverted by the bulldozers of the Civil Defence Authorities. If, however, you manage to ignore the complex problems regarding the attempts to divert lava flows, made on Etna since 1983, and the resulting environmental damage, the transformation of the Bove Valley into an immense lava field can simply be considered a great natural event, part of the wide range of activity that the volcano offers. Those who enter the Valley for the first time will fortunately not be able to make comparisons.

They will see before them a huge basin, with sides more than a thousand metres high at some points, and the

bottom covered by a surprising variety of lava flows. This is the fascination of the Bove Valley - formed between 80 and 100 thousand years ago - , which has never been the Valley of Eden and which today comes close to the image of the infernal valley par excellence, but which is still a physical place - but also spiritual - which it is absolutely necessary to visit before leaving the land of the god Vulcan.

DESCRIPTION OF THE ITINERARY

If you were able to see the sunrise from the Philosopher's Tower the day will already have begun in the best possible way. So, tie up your boots and launch yourself down the first descent of the day, the scree below the Philosopher's Tower, along clear traces of path towards the Montagnola, staying on the wide stretches of ashes of Pian del Lago, which have now been greatly pushed westwards by the 1971 lava flow, the same one that destroyed the 19th century volcanological observatory and the original Etna cable car. For this stretch we offer the same advice given for the climb: in case of thick fog it is advisable to follow the main track.

Coming down from the scree and following the traces of

Attention: if you are in a large group, it is better to go down into the Bove Valley using the alternative route described in the box, since with a large number of people even a small stone falling can prove dangerous. Moreover, it is difficult even to hear falling stones because they usually bounce off the soft volcanic sand.

After arriving on the 1991/93 lava flow the nature of the itinerary changes completely.

After descending among dykes and breathtaking views, you find yourself in the chaotic reality of a lava flow.

Rocks, depressions, conglomerates of jumbled stones, seams of fluid lava, disturbing shapes, sudden hollows; this is the scene you will walk in for a couple of hours, enjoying the experience (indispensable for understanding Etna)

pathway, it is possible to reach the slopes of the Montagnola (a crater dating back to the 1763 eruption) and look over the steep western walls of the Bove Valley. From here you can drop down into the Valley jumping on the impalpable ash of the Montagnola gorge, which you enter by turning into the first gorge you meet coming down from Pian del Lago (on the eastern slopes of the Montagnola) and in which you can usually clearly see the traces left by other excursionists.

The steep slope of this stretch makes you take great care at first, until your legs get used to the sand and the descent gradually becomes easier and more pleasant. You immediately find colourful tuffs (left by impetuous explosive activity), enriching the scenery of one of the most extraordinary places existing in Italy.

The geological marvels of the area gradually become more evident as you descend among dykes (the old endogenous feeding channels of lava flows) and millenary stratifications.

The faint path takes you progressively to the right and you change gorge twice (at clear viewpoints) until you enter the Montagnola gorge itself, characterised by finer ashes and a steeper slope, thanks to which you soon arrive at the bottom of the descent (about 40 minutes after entering the first gorge), where you immediately come to the 1991/93 flow.

of crossing a lava flow not yet worn down by time. A short distance from the exit to the Montagnola gorge you will notice a hole in the roof of a lava cave (the Cutrona cave, one of the many that formed inside the flow), which is very difficult to enter.

The next reference point is a short channel covered by beech-trees, about 3km further on, which will allow you to leave the valley and take you to the edge of the great depression. To reach this point you have to follow the occasional signs that distinguish the faint path winding along the edge of the flow, a short distance from the walls of

*From the top: the Bove Valley, Etna in eruption, the eastern slopes.
Facing page: attempt to divert the lava flow in 1983.*

the Valley. It is important to pay the greatest attention here, since leaving the path would greatly increase the time you take.

From the Cutrona cave you head southeast until you come to a sudden change in gradient. Here you go down, staying on the edge of the recent lava flow and the older lands covered with pioneering plants. You continue along side the lava flow until you come (after having crossed a sort of narrow canyon created by the lava) to the Serra Perciata gorge (the one followed in the alternative itinerary described in the box) and a large bend of the Valley which, however, you do not follow. Instead, you follow the faint path straight on (as far as this is possible with this fascinating chaotic jumble of lava formations) towards some large piles of rocks that mark the edge of the Valley. The route then continues on seams of fluid lava (which form the characteristic structures called 'ropes') with a hard consistent surface, interspersed by occasional areas of chaotic stony ground.

As the softer substrata become prevalent, the pathway becomes clearer and easier to follow, making the going more pleasant.

After another steep climb, which you complete easily on the now distinct pathway, you finally arrive on a vast plateau in which the morphology of the lava flow changes again, becoming an expanse of compact material and of large slabs of rock.

The traces (piles of stones and paint marks) guide you across, with some zigzags to avoid the worst piles of rocks and hollows, as far as the beginning of the beech-tree gorge, marked by a pale wooden post placed on the lava. A short distance away a small wooden plaque fixed to the rocks informs walkers that the path they have just used is dedicated to two young men from Catania, Carmelo Di Stefano and Riccardo Pistone, who died while climbing on Easter Day 1997.

You quickly go back up along a path that winds in the shade of the wood and, in about 15 minutes, arrive at the Salfizio Crest, which marks one of the edges of the Bove Valley.

From this panoramic hill it is possible to go down quickly, if necessary, to Acqua Rocca and Piano del Vescovo (on the provincial road between Zafferana and the Sapienza

mountain hut), otherwise you continue along the ridge. In this area you must look out for dangerous precipices that appear suddenly on the side of the Bove Valley, especially if visibility is poor.

Otherwise this part of the route, while tiring because of the continual climbs and descents and the thick vegetation, offers unforgettable views over the geological conformations of the Valley and the coastline between Catania and Taormina.

After an hour and a half of walking along the ridge you arrive at the summit of Monte Zoccolaro, marked by a distinct metal cross. From this point one of the nature paths of the Etna Park will take you down to a lay-by on a branch of the Zafferana-Sapienza provincial road in about 30 minutes.

Our itinerary does not end here, however; from the point where you meet the tarmacked road you have to go under the railings and start to follow a pathway, which gradually becomes clearer, in the narrow space between the wall and the precipice that drops down into the Calanna Valley. This is an old route that once connected the town of Zafferana with this area full of fruit orchards. The path continues along the edge of the escarpment, bordering private property.

In some places the vegetation has overgrown the path, making occasional detours necessary. The path meets the tarmacked road twice but it is necessary to stay on the path at these points. When you come to the road for the third time, near a large house on the left with a red roof and surrounded by a wooden veranda, you walk down the road for about fifty metres, as far as a lane that goes straight down the hillside.

This is the access to the 'scalazza', the mule-track that winds through the chestnut wood and leads - with various sharp bends - to Pian dell'Acqua. The surface of the track has been partially repaired and it is particularly charming in the final stretch (when going down), where it is paved with lava stone.

When you come to the end of the 'scalazza', you follow another path for about 300 metres, as far as the tarmacked road (after 50 metres on the left there is a fountain and lay-by where the 1991-93 lava flow stopped). From

Top: typical Mediterranean scrub.
Bottom: Calanna Valley during the eruption of 1992.

here there are only three kilometres of tarmacked road to the town of Zafferana and the end of our grand tour round the volcano.

WALKING TIMES 5TH STAGE

Departure Philosopher's Tower
Montagnola 20 minutes
Bottom of Montagnola gorge 1^{hr}
Bottom of beech-tree gorge (end of Bove Valley) 2^{hr} 30^{m}
Salfizio Crest 2^{hr} 45^{m}
Monte Zoccolaro 4^{hr} 15^{m}
Lay-by on tarmacked road 4^{hr} 40^{m}
Piano dell'Acqua 6^{hr} 30^{m}
Zafferana 7^{hr} 15^{m}

PRACTICAL INFORMATION 5TH STAGE

Accommodation in Zafferana Etnea:
Hotel Airone, tel. 095 7081819
Hotel Emmaus, tel. 095 7081888
Hotel Primavera dell'Etna, tel. 095 7082348
Hotel-Guest House Villa Pina, tel. 095 7081024

TOWN CONNECTIONS

The GTE has been described here as a sequence of stages we believe to be suitable both in terms of climbs and descents and because it allows you to experience the different natural environments at different altitudes. If, however, for unexpected reasons you need to get down the mountain quickly, this is possible using the itineraries we briefly describe below.
It is also possible to start the GTE in other towns, if you need to shorten the walk.
From Randazzo you can reach Monte Spagnolo via Rocca Mandorla, leaving from Piazza S. Giovanni Bosco, which is situated on the western outskirts of the town.
You climb up along a tarmacked road that winds through a sparse ilex grove for a couple of kilometres, you cross a wide road that leads to Linguaglossa and you climb up again along a farm track.
You have to pay attention to the carriage roads that lead up the mountainside: the third one is the one that will take you to Monta Spagnolo, passing very near Monte Piluso. From the point of departure you should calculate 2^{hr} 30^{m} to reach Monte Spagnolo, 15 minutes less if descending.
From Maletto you can use the itinerary described before for the Pappalardo Houses, considering that to walk from the town to the high mountain track (where the route of the second stage of the GTE passes) you take about 4 hours, a little less when descending.
It is also possible to begin or end the GTE at Etna South

- Sapienza mountain hut, thanks to the daily bus service linking the high altitude tourist location with Nicolosi and Catania (bus terminal near the railway station).

MAPS

We advise using the map edited by the Italian Touring Club (scale 1/50,000), which can also be obtained from the Catania Provincial Tourist Board (tel. 095 7306222 / 095 7306233) or from the Etna Park Authority (tel. 095 914588).
For the more demanding parts of the itinerary you can use the IGM maps (scale 1/25,000), for example Etna South for the 5th stage (although not updated since the last eruption).

Giuseppe Riggio

Top: Monte Spagnolo.
Right: night-time view of Etna.

MISTERBIANCO: THE BELL THAT ESCAPED THE LAVA

Less than 8km from Catania stands **Misterbianco**, one of the most heavily populated districts in the province, which owes its economic prosperity to the numerous shopping centres, industries and craft workshops that prosper here. Yet the more distant history of Misterbianco would not lead you to think that it could become a rich town.

The name of the town derives from that of a Benedictine monastery on the slopes of Etna, 'Monasterium Album', in other words White Monastery. In 1640 Misterbianco was no more than a hamlet and to make some money out of it the Royal authorities could find nothing better than to sell it to Gianandrea Massa, who then resold it to Baron Vespasiano Trigona.

The Baron was, however, unable to enjoy his purchase for long. A few years later the hamlet was swept away by a volcanic eruption in March 1669. The inhabitants could only run away, quickly but 'sensibly'.

Despite the lava being right behind them, they managed to carry off with them most of the livestock, farm implements and, curiously, the bell of the church, which weighed no less than 1.8 tons.

They did not get very far, however, perhaps because of the weight of their burden, and they stopped about 5km from the original site on land belonging to the monks of the monastery of Saint Julian.

The refugees asked the monks for a piece of land on which to rebuild the hamlet. The monks were happy enough to grant their wish in return for the payment of a handsome sum, which they piously allowed them to repay in four annual instalments.

So, Misterbianco was founded anew and, although it had to face the destructive forces of nature again in 1693, it grew slowly, tenaciously and courageously until it became the present day rich town of entrepreneurs and tradesmen.

In Misterbianco it is worth visiting the **Church of Saint Nicholas**, in which you can admire 17th century paintings, and the **Cathedral**, which stands on a wide square that makes its clear facade stand out.

This facade is characterised by a central portal framed by a rounded arch, supported by two thin columns; to the sides are the two secondary portals, smaller than but identical to the central one, to which they are architecturally connected by delicate bow lace.

In the middle part of the central body there is a large niche with a statue of Our Lady with Child. Inside it is worth seeing the statue of Our Lady of Graces, exquisitely fashioned, commonly attributed to Antonello Gagini.

If you are interested in buying terracotta objects, we suggest you take a look round the numerous shops selling such articles.

A good place to go is **Artigianato del Sole** in via Santa Margherita. Here it is possible to find everyday objects or furnishings, bricks or floor and wall tiles of great beauty and with artistic decorations. **Franco Chisari** in via Vespri also has beautiful pottery and objects in enamelled lava.

For the greedier among you we list the three best **confectioners'** in Misterbianco: **Belfiore** in via G. Bruno, **Cacciola** in via G. Matteotti and **Costa** in via G. Matteotti.

If you love burying your head in books, then head for the **bookshop Lux Libri** in via G. Matteotti.

Finally, a list of events, beginning with the picturesque **Misterbianco Carnival**; the **Arts and Crafts Fair** in May; the competitions at the sports ground and in the streets for **Sports Summer**, from 19th June to 5th July; the **Regional Amateur Dramatics Festival**, from 26th June to 17th July; film shows and dance and drama performances as part of the **Summer Magic** event in August; the music review **Sonica**, from 2nd to 5th September in Piazza Pertini; the **Misterbianco International Road Race** on 18th September.

RESTAURANTS

- CATANIA GOLF CLUB: SS 417 Catania-Gela km 68 (tel. 095 572147). Restaurant-pizzeria. Sicilian cuisine.
- DEGLI AMICI: contrada Vazzano, 19 (tel. 095 303730). Local cuisine mostly based on fish. We recommend the pennette with pistachio, linguine baked in paper. Good selection of regional wines.
- TRATTORIA DA PIPPO: Corso C. Marx, 53 (tel. 095 476668). Characteristic trattoria. Exquisite grilled fish.

PIZZERIAS

- CRISPELLERIA PRESTIGE: via Di Vittorio , 40 (tel. 095 481746).
- IL COVO: via G. Garibaldi, 658 (tel. 095 461689).
- PIZZERIA CRUISE: via G. Bruno, 129 (tel. 095 463368).
- VANNI: via G. Garibaldi, 256 (tel. 095 463232).
- VOGLIA DI PIZZA: via G. Garibaldi, 646 (tel. 095 301235).

Left: detail of the facade of the Cathedral.

HOTELS

- IL GELSO BIANCO ♥ ♥ ♥: A19 km 3 at Gelso Bianco (tel. 095 7181159 fax 095 7181270). With restaurant and bar.

FARM HOLIDAYS AND RESIDENCE

- AZIENDA AGRICOLA ALCALÀ: SS 192 km 78 (tel./fax 095 7130029). Rural building on a hillside. Sales of fresh citrus fruits and bottled products.

MOTTA SANT'ANASTASIA: FROM UP ON HIGH

Following the SS 121 road from Misterbianco you arrive at the turn off for **Motta Sant'Anastasia** after just a few kilometres. The town is situated in the Simeto valley, on the southern slopes of Etna, in the lee of a rocky cliff of ancient volcanic origins. A lava flow of huge proportions rapidly solidified and gave rise to a formation of which there are very few examples in the world (called necks), characterised by vertical columns of basalt making up the interior of the struc-

protection of the area from Saracen raiding parties arriving by sea. In Norman times, under Roger, a tower was built here and formed a vitally important defensive system with the ones in Paternò and Adrano.

From the 1500s onwards the town became a feud of the Moncada family. The urban development of the town largely took place in the 18th century. It became a municipality in 1820.

TOWER AND SURROUNDINGS

The oldest part of the town, which still has an evident mediaeval appearance, is the area around the Norman castle. This is where the most interesting buildings are to be found.

The Norman Tower, in Piazza Castello, was built in the 11th century, probably on top of a previous Arab fortification. The massive quadrangular structure on three levels still maintains intact its battlements and has all the characteristics of a late mediaeval defensive tower.

Some of the openings are the original ones, the round-headed arches on the first floor, while others date from the renovations carried out in the 15th century. On the ground floor, which housed the garrison, there are some loopholes obviously used for defence against enemy attacks. The upper floor served as accommodation for soldiers of higher ranks. For centuries, right up until the 1900s, the building was used as a prison.

ture and which have been uncovered by weather erosion over the centuries.

The meaning of the name of the town, according to many researchers, is linked to the two expressions 'motta' and 'anastasia', which, despite having different origins, have the same meaning of 'high place', in obvious reference to the location of the town.

The two words were put together in late Mediaeval times, when the word 'anastasia' was also used to refer to the patron Saint. Archaeological digs around Motta have shown the ancient origins of the town. It is certain that a town was situated here in the Greek period (burial places in the surrounding areas) and that the Romans also lived here (remains of mosaic floors belonging to a Roman villa). The town's strategic position meant that it played an important role in the

A short distance away, in the small square of the Immacolata, stands the **Church of the Most Holy Sacrament** or Our Lady of the Immaculate Conception, rebuilt in the 1600s, which houses works of art of great value, including a statue of Our Lady of the Immaculate Conception from the 17th century and a half-bust of Saint Agatha on a high pedestal enclosed in a pretty frescoed niche with painted wooden doors.

Top: the Castle and town centre of Motta Sant'Anastasia.

In nearby Piazza Matrice stands the Cathedral, preceded by a short stairway in lava stone. It is dedicated to Our Lady of the Rosary and was originally constructed in the 13th century, but was rebuilt and enlarged in the 16th century. Inside the layout is that of a basilica of three naves and you can see a 16th century crucifix and works from the school of Antonello da Messina.

FLAGS UNFURLED

Motta Sant'Anastasia is a town that has kept up with the times, while maintaining its historical roots. The locals are jealous of their traditions and still today conserve the ancient **quarters**, each with its own characteristics, with which the members of the various professions and social classes once identified themselves.

Even today any occasion is an excuse for unfurling the flag to show which quarter you belong to. Joking aside, each quarter of the town has its own group of **flag-wavers**. The various events in town, both religious and civil, are always an opportunity for local rivalry between the quarters and for seeing these skilful flag-wavers, who are greatly admired at home and abroad.

Another source of pride in the town are the juicy citrus fruits, especially the tasty blood oranges, and the excellent olives, from which delicious oil is obtained. The best way of discovering the spirit of Motta is to participate in one of the many enjoyable events held throughout the year.

In mid-March you can attend one of the interesting performances organised as part of the **Cultural Week**. In late March and early April the colourful **Citrus Fruit Festival** is held. In May there is **Antich…età**, an exhibition of crafts and antiques. During the **Mottese Summer**, between July and September, there is a review of music, dance and drama in the streets of the town. August sees the **Mediaeval Festivals** from the 10th to the 22nd, with folklore and historical parades. For several days the streets are full of characters in mediaeval costume, recreating scenes from everyday life of those times. Motta is enlivened by dancing and music and the lucky visitors can taste traditional foods. As part of these celebrations the **Palio dei Martino** is held, naturally inspired

by the Middle Ages, in which modern 'knights' contest the horse-race. Also in August, from the 1st to the 10th, the **Festival of the Five Continents** is an international meeting of young people with the participation of folkloristic groups from all over the world, parades and flag-wavers; the patronal **Feast of Saint Anastasia** takes place from the 22nd to the 25th, with the **Festival of Flag-Wavers** and historical parades. Finally, in November there is the **Olive Oil Festival**.

RESTAURANTS-PIZZERIAS

- BAHAMAS: via Napoli, 8 (095 308620). Restaurant-pizzeria.
- TRATTORIA DEL BUONGUSTAIO: via V. Emanuele, 192 (tel. 095 308066). Also a bar. Traditional cuisine. We recommend the classic onion soup, the tasty stuffed mushrooms and the fillet with mushrooms. Excellent home-made cakes.
- PARADISE: corso Sicilia, 4 (tel. 095 308225). Restaurant-pizzeria. Specialities: spaghetti 'alla Paradise' and chef's fillet.
- SIGONELLA INN: SS 192 - contrada Fontanazza (tel. 095 7130002). Hotel restaurant-pizzeria. Italian and Mexican cuisine.
- VALENTINO: corso Sicilia, 12 (tel. 095 307348). Restaurant-pizzeria. Sicilian cuisine.

HOTELS

- SIGONELLA INN ♥ ♥ ♥: SS 192 - contrada Fontanazza (tel. 095 7130002 fax 095 7130040). With restaurant, swimming-pool, meeting and reception rooms, pizzeria and bar.

RESIDENCE

- RESIDENCE GARDEN ♥ ♥: SP 13 - complesso Ninfo, 2 - contrada Tiritì (tel. 095 7131956 fax 095 7131358).

APARTMENTS FOR RENT

- DAYS INN T.L.A. ♥: contrada Perticone Palazzello, 23 (tel. 095 7130222 fax 095 7130150).
- HAPPY PLACE ♥: via Stazione Motta, 54 (tel. 095 308899).
- HOLIDAY T.L.A. ♥: via Adua, 28 (tel. 095 307275).
- KITCHENETTE APARTMENTS: SP 13 (tel. 095 7131426).
- LIVINGSTON ♥: via P. Mascagni (tel./fax 095 309223).
- MARCHESE GREGORIO: via Vittorio Emanuele, 311 (tel. 095 308687).
- NEW PLACE ♥: via Enrico Toti, 9 (tel. 095 308639).
- PALACE IN ♥: via XX Settembre, 207 (tel. 095 7554101).
- STARS & STRIPES ♥: corso Sicilia, 10 (tel. 095 307778 fax 095 308565).

Left: town centre dominated by the mass of the Castle.

PATERNÒ: THE CASTLE ABOVE ALL

You can easily reach **Paternò** from Motta Sant'Anastasia along the SS 121 road.

Some researchers claim that Paternò corresponds to the ancient city of Hybla Maior, referred to by Livy and Thucydides. We are not really qualified to give an opinion on the matter but there is no doubt that this site has been inhabited since ancient times, as is shown by the numerous archaeological artefacts.

The first nucleus of present day Paternò was very probably founded under the Arabs, and this continued to expand in Norman times around the fortress-castle. Endowed with numerous important holy buildings, the hamlet of Paternò was made a county. On the arrival of the Swabians in Sicily, Paternò was ceded to the De Luca family and then passed on to the Lancia family.

They were fierce enemies of the Angevins and, when they fell into disgrace, power passed into the hands of the Bonifacio family. From this moment on the history of Paternò is a continual succession of powerful families who held the reins of economic and social life in the town: the Alagona, Speciale, Moncada and Hernandez families.

Paternò is peacefully situated on the southern slopes of Etna, at the foot of an imposing basalt **cliff**. On top of the cliff stands the **Norman Castle** built on the orders of Roger in 1072. It is probable, however, that during the Arab domination of

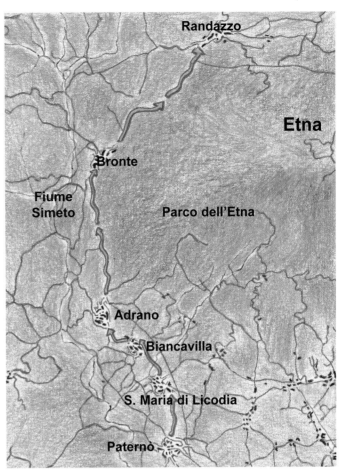

Sicily a fortress already existed on the site of the Castle and this was renovated, with all necessary modifications, by Roger the Norman when he occupied the Island and threw out the infidels.

The massive structure of the Castle, with a quadrangular layout, was made lighter by the opening of elegant two-mullioned windows to illuminate some of the rooms during renovations carried out in the 13th and 14th centuries. The fortress is an excellent state of repair both outside and inside. On the ground floor you can see the central well, designed to collect rainwater, a small chapel with traces of frescoes on the walls and rooms used for keeping provisions and as accommodation for the guards; on the upper floors there are rooms of various sizes, the large armoury being worthy of particular note, illuminated by the two-mullioned windows. From the bastions you can enjoy a beautiful wide view over Etna and the plain of Catania.

More evidence of the ancient fortified nature of Paternò is easily seen in the **Church of Santa Maria dell'Itria**. This was built in the early 17th century, incorporating an old mediaeval tower called the **Falconers' Tower**. You can still see the upper part with battlements, now used as a bell-tower, characterised by the contrast between the black lava stone and white limestone around the windows and in the corners. Access to the Tower is from inside the Church.

Left: Paternò Castle.

Very little is left of the original mediaeval structure of the **Church of Santa Maria della Valle del Giosafat**, built in 1072, although it does have a lovely 14th century portal.

The **Cathedral** also Norman origins, although it was rebuilt in 1342.

It has a characteristic tiled floor in the interior with three naves; you can see a Black Madonna, of uncertain date but probably from between the 12th and 15th centuries, and a 17th century wooden crucifix.

On the subject of 14th century churches we should mention the **Church of Saint Francis**, built at roughly the same time as the Cathedral in 1346.

Jumping forward in time we find the **Church of Christ on**

the Mount, constructed in the 1500s, with a baroque style interior.

The **Church of Saint Catherine** and the **New Cathedral**, also called Our Most Holy Lady of the Annunciation or Abbey, can be dated to the late 1600s.

The latter has a valuable 'Christ at the Column', a 17th century wooden statue.

Finally, the **Church of Saint Barbara**, patron of Paternò, is clearly 18th century and can be recognised by its characteristic cupola.

From the top: Cathedral, Sanctuary of Our Lady of Consolation, Church of the Benedictine Monastery and Piazza Indipendenza.

MISCELLANEOUS INFORMATION

If you visit Paternò you really must try the **citrus fruit**, the **tomatoes** and the **olives**, all of renowned high quality. The town is one of the most important agricultural centres in the province.

These and other farm produce can be bought from all the town's greengrocers'; moreover, if you are travelling with your own transport, you can stock up on genuine fragrant **extra virgin olive oil**.

You should also taste the local cakes and pastries.

Excellent cakes can be found at the **confectioner's Parisi** in via G.B. Nicolosi and at the **bar-confectioner's Cristallo** in via Vittorio Emanuele.

For a good night out we recommend the **pubs Capricci di Gola** in via Circumvallazione (it is also a pizzeria), **Top Gun** in Corso Sicilia (also a pizzeria and take-away) and **Fast Food** in via Bellia.

If you want to take home a souvenir of Paternò, you need do no more than pay a visit to the local artisans' shops. In particular, we recommend **Le Nid** in via Fonte Maimonde, a workshop situated on the slopes of Etna selling objects made from lava stone and pottery.

For those who love reading we recommend the **bookshop Ronsisvalle** in via Vittorio Emanuele and the **stationer's-bookshop Gulisano** in via G.B. Nicolosi.

One of the major attractions of the area the **Sicilian Zoo-**

logical Gardens in contrada Valcorrente. It is a lovely parkland area inhabited by exotic animals and large…statues of dinosaurs.

We recommend visiting the Zoo if you are travelling with children (it is well organised and you are guaranteed a pleasant visit).

For accommodation you can head for the **Hotel Sicilia** in via Vittorio Emanuele, with restaurant, bar and car park.

Now let's change the subject and move on to the most interesting religious and secular events in Paternò. It is almost obligatory to begin this section with the most important non-religious festival in the town, **Carnival**, which can be compared to the one in Acireale for splendour and entertainment.

The celebrations involve six days of fun, folklore and parades of allegorical floats (we can certainly say that when the locals joke, they take it seriously). July and August see the **Rocca Normanna** review, with music, drama, cinema and dancing in the streets.

For 13th to 23rd September the **September Fair** is held, with arts and crafts and gastronomy displays in the Municipal Park.

RESTAURANTS-PIZZERIAS

- AI PORTICI: Viale dei Platani, 92 (tel. 095 852885). Restaurant-pizzeria.
  We recommend the caserecce with scampi and prawns with sesame.
- AL BONTANDE: via Nicolosi, 237 (tel. 095 857173). Restaurant-pizzeria.
  Excellent pasta 'alla carbonara' and meat roulades.
- CRISTALLO: via Stazione, 2 (tel. 095 859768). Restaurant-pizzeria. We recommend the farfalle 'Cristallo' and the cutlets with mushrooms.

- LA RUOTA: SS 575 road to Schettino, 70 (tel. 095 623953). Home cooking. Very good mixed grills.
- LA TORRETTA: contrada Santa Maria.
- RIMINI via Nicolosi, 361/b (tel. 095 857698). Pizzeria-restaurant. Delicious pizza 'a Modo Mio' (ingredients include ostrich ham).
- SCUTO: via Maurici, 11/15 (tel. 095 621443). Elegant restaurant, very refined cuisine. Try the *'funci i ferla'* and the seafood dishes. Interesting wine list.
- SICILIA: via Vittorio Emanuele, 391 (tel. 095 845193). Hotel restaurant. Mediterranean cuisine. Excellent pasta 'alla Norma' and side dishes.
- TRATTORIA MONDELLO: Piazza M. Grippa, 3 - Sferro (tel. 095 623677). Exquisite penne with pistachio.

HOTELS

- SICILIA ♥ ♥: via Vittorio Emanuele, 391 (tel. 095 853604 fax 095 854742). With restaurant, bar, car park.

Right: Catania Plain near Paternò.

BELPASSO: THE PHOENIX AT THE FOOT OF ETNA

The distance from Paternò to **Belpasso**, situated at an altitude of 553 metres on the southern slopes of Etna, is just a little more than 10km.

The history of this town, which once had a less auspicious name, has also been marked by the looming presence of the volcano.

The terrible eruption of 1669 razed the town, then called Malpasso, to the ground, forcing the inhabitants to move elsewhere.

Two theories exist regarding the origin of the name. Some say that it derives from the Latin 'mali passus', or apple tree pass, while others say it comes from 'malus passus', or dangerous pass, referring to the threatening presence of brigands who infested the area in those days.

The new town grew up at the locality of Valcorrente with the name of Fenicia Moncada (Fenicia in reference to the ability of the phoenix to rise from the ashes and Moncada from the name of the noble family), but suffered an equally disastrous fate when it was destroyed by the earthquake of 1693. Once more the inhabitants moved and rebuilt the town again. In this way the present day Belpasso was born.

In the 18th century reconstruction of the town the town plan was drawn up by the architect Giovanni Bellia and provided for an orthogonal street layout, which can still be seen today in the older part of the town.

In Piazza Duomo, at the top of a stairway, stands the **Cathedral**, dedicated to Our Lady of the Immaculate Conception, the first building erected after the 1693 earthquake and designed by Bellia.

The beautiful linear facade is characterised by the large central portal and the bell-tower. The top of the crowning tympanum is decorated with statues.

The interior is decorated with frescoes and contains a precious wooden crucifix, some interesting canvases and the remains of Saint Lucy. The Cathedral has the largest bell in Italy, brought here from the destroyed Cathedral of Fenicia Moncada.

In Piazza Dante you can admire the **Church of Christ the**

King, built in the 1600s. Very nearby you can see the interesting 18th century **Palazzo Lombardo-Spina**.

Also from the early 18th century is the **Church of Saint Anthony**, in the square of the same name.

In Piazza Municipio stand the **Church of Saint Anthony of Padua**, with a beautiful baroque portal in lava stone, and the **Town Hall**. The latter is housed in the premises of the ex-Franciscan Convent and contains a collection of contemporary art.

Belpasso is the birthplace of **Nino Martoglio**, the famous author of important plays, one of the most important being, without doubt, 'L'Aria del Continente'.

The **Municipal Theatre**, built at the end of the last century in liberty style, and the **Municipal Park** are both named after the comedy writer.

There are other buildings that are worthy of attention because of their artistic and architectural characteristics, including the 18th century **Palazzo dei Baroni Bufali**, in via Roma, with a facade decorated with lava stone; **Palazzo Butera**; 18th century **Palazzo Scrofani**, with a beautiful lava stone portal; **Palazzo Spampinato**, in liberty style.

On the outskirts of the town, near Piazza Aragona, you can see the so called **Queen's Water Tank**, named after Queen

Top: Church of Our Lady of the Guardia. Left: Palazzo Scrofani.

Eleanor of Anjou, who lived alone near here after the death of her husband Frederick II of Aragon. It seems that this tank was used to keep fish destined for the Queen's table.

SUGGESTED EXCURSIONS

In the valley, at San Biagio, there are phenomena of secondary volcanism, similar to those of the Aragona Mud Volcanoes (Agrigento), called **salse**, which occupy a wide area completely covered with yellowish mud.

In the Gianpasquale-Pietra Forcella district you can visit the **Cave of Doves**, one of the many lava flow caves in the area. Around here there are numerous **rural buildings**, in a good state of repair, and some mills, evidence of another age and of old agricultural activity.

At Valcorrente (SS 121) is **La Pergola Zoological Garden**, one of the biggest in Sicily. Here you can see hundreds of animals from all over the world, while walking through a pleasant natural garden.

Two other zones are dedicated to life-size models of prehistoric animals and to animals housed in open areas. The latter can be seen from the cable car that goes around the park.

A RIVER OF NOUGAT

In the Belpasso district, at lower altitudes, **almonds**, **prickly-pears**, **olives** and especially **table** and **wine grapes** are all grown. The particularly sweet prickly-pears are used to make **must-cake**, a traditional speciality made with cooked prickly-pears flavoured with cinnamon.

Even those who have never heard of Belpasso before will certainly recognise the name of the most famous nougat in Italy and possibly in the world, the delicious soft **Condorelli nougat**, which became well-known in every household recently thanks to a television advert with a popular Sicilian actor. These popular sweets can be bought by weight or in various characteristic colourful gift packets. They exalt the flavour of the excellent almonds, which are their main ingredient, covered with delicious sweet frosting of various flavours, chocolate, vanilla, citrus fruit. The nougat and other speciality sweets can be admired, tasted and, obviously, purchased at the **confectioner's Condorelli** in via Vittorio Emanuele III, founded in 1920.

You can also buy excellent cakes from the **confectioner's Seminara** at crossroads XX.

If you want to try the local cuisine, which makes good use of mushrooms and game, we recommend the **restaurants Feudo Delizia**, at Segreta, serving pasta in extravagant shapes and excellent mushroom based dishes; **La Cantina**, on the Provincial road to Nicolosi, offering mountain specialities; **La Nuova Quercia**, at Piano Bottara, serving game and mushroom based dishes.

If you want to spend a good night out, halfway between a pub and a restaurant, you should head for **The Eight Horses**, in via III Retta Levante. It is housed in the former Carabinieri barracks and serves local cuisine with a touch of imagination and has a good wine list.

Now some advice for your souvenir hunting.

In Belpasso artisans are very active, especially those producing **pottery**, **sculptures** in **clay** and **lava stone** and, a pleasant rarity (unfortunately) **carts**. The carts of this area are different from those of Palermo, which are usually considered to be the Sicilian carts par excellence, especially because of their decorations. The carts of this area are char-

Top: Cathedral. Left: the famous Condorelli nougat.

acterised by sculpted figures. Finally, a mention for the specialist artisans who make **guitars** and **mandolins**.

FROM THE THEATRE TO THE STREETS

We begin our look at events in Belpasso with the **Theatre Season** at the Nino Martiglio Municipal Theatre, organised by the Brigata d'Arte company.
This company is closely connected to the name and memory of the famous comedy writer and promotes the best of Sicilian theatre, 'exporting' it to the rest of Italy.
Now we can take a look at the rest of the main events.
During the Easter period there is the procession of the Dead Christ and traditional songs on **Good Friday**.
In July and August the **Belpassese Summer** sees a review of music, drama, dance and cabaret.
In August there is the **International Motorcycle Meeting**, a meeting of motorcyclists from all over Europe.
In September the **Palio of Our Lady of Graces** is held, in the main street, a horse race in which the various districts of the town compete against one another. The course is a straight run of about 800 metres along which a crowd of enthusiastic locals gathers. It is followed by a parade in mediaeval costumes. Also in September, on the third Sunday of the month, the **Feast of Our Lady of the Guardia** is held in Piazza Stella Aragona. October sees the Lava Stone Exhibition, in the streets, and the **Exhibition-Market of Crafts and Agriculture** in the Martoglio Park. On 12th-13th-14th December the patronal **Feast of Saint Lucy** includes a parade of allegorical floats and a singing competition among the various districts of the town. The floats are real works of art, complete with various devices and mechanisms. On the 13th the simulacrum is placed on an 18th century silver litter, finely chiselled and sculpted in relief, and carried in procession. The celebrations end with fireworks.

RESTAURANTS

- FEUDO DELIZIA: contrada Segreta (tel. 095 918950). In an old mill on the slopes of the volcano. Sicilian cuisine. Exquisite first courses with pasta in extravagant shapes, game, dishes with mushrooms, desserts. .
- LA CANTINA: SP to Nicolosi. Traditional cuisine. Try the mushrooms, the country starters and the mixed grill.
- LA NUOVA QUERCIA: contrada Piano Bottara (tel. 095 911277). We recommend the home-made maccheroni, the game, the mushrooms (maybe while the friendly owner tells you about the eruption of 1983, which destroyed the original restaurant).
- MIRANEVE: Monte San Leo (tel. 095 7911966). Starters and first courses with mushrooms. We recommend the stuffed leg of lamb and rabbit.
- MARASCA: via Silva, 9 (tel. 095 913939). Restaurant-pizzeria. Dishes made from genuine local ingredients, excellent grilled mushrooms and caserecci with Marasca cherries. Also a discotheque.
- SALA INCONTRO: 19 Traversa, 62 (tel. 095 918646). Restaurant-wine cellar. We recommend the characteristic sweet and sour horse meatballs.
- UNDERGROUND "MARIGIÓ" PUB: via Provinciale, 5 (tel. 095 912992). Restaurant-pizzeria-bar. Try the "Marigiò" pizza.
- VILLA ANGELO MUSCO: contrada Monte Sona S.P. 92 Nicolosi - Etna (tel. 347 6663972). Restaurant-pizzeria. We recommend the casarecci 'alla montanara' with with fresh mushrooms and the game.

PIZZERIE

- LA BOHEME: via Monfalcone, 2.
- ZAMPANÓ: via Vittorio Emanuele II, 5 (tel. 095 918168).

HOTELS

- LA NUOVA QUERCIA ♥♥♥: contrada Piano Bottara (tel./fax 095 911277). With restaurant and car park.
- ETNA HOTEL ♥♥: via III Retta Ponente, 21 (tel. 095 7912640). With restaurant and bar.

FARM HOLIDAYS

- BRUCA: contrada Finocchiara (tel. 095 7130015). Restaurant service on booking (lunch for groups of at least 15 people), fishing, horse-riding, archery. Accommodation available.

Top: Palazzo Bufali.

RAGALNA: RELAXATION AND NATURE

There are just over ten kilometres between Belpasso and **Ragalna**, a small town at an altitude of over 700 metres on the southern slopes of Etna. The healthy air, the favourable climatic conditions and the splendid panoramic position (which has earned the town the name of 'terrace of Etna') make it an ideal place to spend a healthy relaxing holiday.

The name Ragalna is of clear Arabic origin and leads us to presume that the town already existed at the time of the Arab domination.

The first documented historical references, however, date back to the Norman domination of Sicily. In these the town is referred to with the name of Rachalena.

Over the following centuries the fate of the small town was linked to events in Paternò and in the 15th century Ragalna became a feud of the Moncada family.

The nearness of Paternò, which administrated Ragalna until 1985, meant that the two towns not only shared their administrative and economic destiny (even though Ragalna depended on Paternò) but also the dangerous moods of the mountain with the fiery spirit.

During the eruption of 1780, accompanied by violent earth tremors, Ragalna and Paternò used the force of faith against the lava flows and invoked Saint Barbara as their common protector.

The remains of the Saint were carried in a solemn procession in order to ward off the destruction of the towns. And, indeed, the eruption ceased.

The town does not have any buildings of architectural interest from before the 19th century.

However, some of the churches are worth visiting and this is an excuse for taking a stroll along the streets of the town.

These include the **Church of Our Most Holy Lady of the Carmel**, dedicated to the patron, built in the 1800s in a mixed style and preceded by a stairway in lava stone; the **Church of Saint Barbara** is named after the Saint dear to the historical memory of Ragalna.

Outside the town, in the district of Rocca, you can see the **Church of Saint John Bosco**, deep in the countryside.

If you want to venture to higher altitudes, you can head for the locality of Serra La Nave (1,700 metres), where you will find the **Church of Our Lady of the Snows**.

At the same locality you will see the **Astrophysical Observatory**.

Moreover, there is a pleasant nature walk that starts from the nearby Etna Grand Hotel, a starting point for numerous

Bottom: panorama of Ragalna.

the **Scalia oil-mill** in via Mongibello. For the greedier of our readers we now provide a list of confectioners' where you can satisfy your desires.

K2 in via Rocca (almond and mandarin nougat, ricotta roll), **Aetneus** in via Paternò (Sicilian 'cannoli' and almond nougat), **Parisi** in via Paternò, **Santa Barbara** in Piazza Chiesa Nuova.

For lunch and dinner you can head for the **restaurants-pizzerias Al Lume** and **Nuovo K2**, both in via Rocca.

If you prefer to dine out and spend the evening in a **pub**, you should try **La Vecchia Botte** in the village of San Francesco.

A quick mention also for traditional crafts, which offer numerous possible objects to buy as gifts and characteristic **souvenirs**.

At **D'Elia** you can buy objects in **lava stone terracotta** and **pottery**.

The calendar of events in the town offer further evidence of the gourmet disposition of the local people.

In June there is the **Cherry Festival**; every Saturday and Sunday in October the **Apple Festival** takes place with a market of Etna produce; the first week of November sees the **Sausage, Goblet and Wine Festival**; in the second week of December there is the **Festival of Olive Oil and Local Produce**.

Finally, an event that does not involve eating, the setting up of **living cribs** in the streets during the Christmas period.

excursions, and leads to the **Nuova Gussonea Botanical Garden**.

Other attractions in the vicinity, of particular interest to lovers of country walks, are the numerous **caves** and the chestnut wood at the locality of **Milia**.

The numerous **rural buildings** and **old mills** scattered around the area are of considerable interest, both from an architectural and from an ethno-anthropological point of view.

In Ragalna you can visit the **Ethnographic Museum**.

DELICACIES

Agriculture is the most important economic activity in Ragalna.

The principal crops are fruit, olives, from which fragrant **oil** is still made using traditional methods, and sweet grapes, which are expertly transformed into glittering full-bodied **wine** that you can buy from the wine-growers' co-operatives or private producers. Olive oil is also easily purchased but we particularly recommend

RESTAURANTS

- AL LUME: via Rocca, 31 (tel. 095 849105). Restaurant-pizzeria. In the centre of Ragalna. Mountain specialities, exquisite dishes based on mushrooms often accompanied by fresh vegetables.
- NUOVO K2: via Rocca, 131 (tel. 095 620066). Restaurant-pizzeria. Try the manicaretti with sausage and mushrooms.

From the top: Cathedral, ruins of an old mill, shrine of Santa Barbara.

MONTE NERO DEGLI ZAPPINI
NATURE PATH

RAGALNA: 1ˢᵗ ITINERARY ROUTE
Duration : 2 hours
Total distance: 4,5 km
Difference in height: 200 metres

This is perhaps the best known and most popular path among those laid down by the Etna Park Authority, an itinerary of great educational value which has the only defect of including a long stretch on a tarmacked road (although this road is closed to traffic), which in some way spoils the beauty and harmony of the first half of the walk. It is, however, still a walk worth taking because in just a few kilometres it has several points of interest. You start by crossing the plateau of Piano Vettore (colonised by pioneering plants and lined along its edges by poplars), you then climb up among beautiful lava flows until you reach a cone where you can observe the typical structure of fused scoriae ripped open at the side by a lava flow channel.

At this point you can shorten your walk by going down a short cut as far as a sheep pen, or you can continue to climb in order to visit an area characterised by sparse vegetation (old pines and a few beech trees). Further on you cross the bed of a seasonal torrent, where the force of the water has smoothed the lava, and then you enter the thick woodland of Monte Denza. Here you can see the difference between the grazing land and the area where the natural renewal of the woodland is protected.

A cart track then takes you comfortably downhill, running alongside the Nuova Gussonea botanical garden (if you want to visit it, contact the Botany Department of the University of Catania beforehand). Once you come out onto the tarmacked path you turn left and walk for two hundred metres until you come to a turn off sign-posted for the forest nursery, along which you can reach the carriage-road that comes up from the Adrano-Monte San Leo provincial road. You continue straight on, however, along the main route, leaving the wood behind you.

The final part of the itinerary, in order to get back to Piano Vettore, is very open and exposed to the sun and should therefore be covered in the cooler parts of the day if possible. To get back to the departure point of the nature path, marked by a large lava stone tablet, just follow the signs for the towns of Nicolosi, Pedara and Ragalna.

THE 'NUOVA GUSSONEA' BOTANICAL GARDEN ON ETNA

On the southern slopes of Etna, at an altitude of 1,700 metres, is situated the Nuova Gussonea botanical garden, set up over 20 years ago.
It is located in the territory of Ragalna, very near the Etna Grand Hotel, in the state owned Giovanni Saletti forest and covers an area of more than 10 hectares.
It was set up under a convention signed by the Sicilian Regional Forestry Service and the University of Catania; it is still being completed thanks to active collaboration between the University (Institute of Biology and Plant Ecology) and the Forestry Inspectorate of Catania.

The garden has been structured on the basis of synecological principles: it is home to plant species that are representative of the landscape of Etna at various altitudes.
The intention is for it to contain as many different species as possible from those that grow on the volcano, in order to protect the genetic variety that they represent.
The garden is the site of continual experimentation, not merely for scientific aims, but also as part of the important environmental education role played by the garden within the Etna Nature Park.

ASPECTS OF PLANT LIFE ON ETNA

Plant life on Etna is made up of a collection of elements which are diversified according to the varying factors of volcanic soil, climate and human presence.

In the area of an active volcano the layers of volcanic soil undergo continual changes because of volcanic activity, which changes the shapes of hills, creates new barren surfaces and profoundly alters every aspect of the landscape. Although the climate is a Mediterranean one, it varies according to the altitude, conditioning the type of plant life. Over thousands of years man has profoundly transformed vast areas, particularly on the lower slopes of the volcano, where there are widespread urbanised areas and farmland.

The landscape that results from all these factors is therefore singular. There are often a series of elements that contrast with one another: next to the forests and the more recent natural vegetation, next to the farmland that characterises the lower slopes of Etna there are the black lava fields, where plant life is forced to start over again its slow but tenacious colonisation, only to be destroyed yet again and once more colonise in a never ending process.

The changes in plant life according to the altitude are determined, above all, by varying climatic factors and allow us to recognise levels of vegetation on the slopes of the volcano, each characterised by precise aspects of the plant landscape.

These aspects correspond to the maximum expression currently possible in each of the distinct altitudinal levels. Therefore, they are not always realistic; often, particularly in areas where man has intervened, these landscapes should be considered potential.

The succession of these levels according to altitude is presented in **Figure 1**.

In the brief description that follows we refer to the aspects of plant life that play a significant role in the landscape of each altitudinal level considered. For the relative distribution on the slopes of the volcano we recommend you refer to the map of vegetation on Etna, on a scale of 1:50,000, drawn up by E. Poli and others.

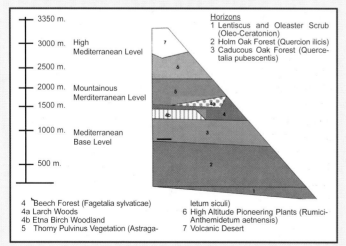

Horizons
1 Lentiscus and Oleaster Scrub (Oleo-Ceratonion)
2 Holm Oak Forest (Quercion ilicis)
3 Caducous Oak Forest (Quercetalia pubescentis)

4   Beech Forest (Fagetalia sylvaticae)
4a Larch Woods
4b Etna Birch Woodland
5   Thorny Pulvinus Vegetation (Astragaletum siculi)
6   High Altitude Pioneering Plants (Rumici-Anthemidetum aetnensis)
7   Volcanic Desert

MEDITERRANEAN BASE LEVEL

This level extends from sea level up to an altitude of 1,000 to 1,200 metres and beyond (up to 1,400-1,500 metres).

Along the rocky coastline there is a narrow strip of halophilic vegetation (Crithmo- Staticion), characterised by a few scattered grasses, including the sea-fennel (Crithmum maritimum), perfectly adapted to the salinity of the environment.

After leaving this zone, now very fragmented because of the intense human presence, the essential elements of the plant landscape are represented by crops. Citrus fruit orchards dominate the whole area and follow the course of the Simeto river inland.

These evergreen crops, in distinct contrast with the highly dry Mediterranean character of the territory, have long since replaced the forests or scrub-forests (Oleo-Ceratonion) that once characterised the landscape on the lower slopes of Etna.

This is the most southerly plant landscape in Italy, distinguishing the hotter and dryer, almost North African, climate.

Above this level, beyond an altitude of 300-400 metres, the landscape is still heavily influenced by man: here we find prevalently vineyards, olive and almond groves. On the old lava substrata of the western side the landscape is dominated by the growing of pistachios, which stretch right down to the Simeto river, while on the eastern side, which is more humid, it is mostly characterised by hazelnut growing.

This is the area of holm oak (Quercion ilicis) forests that characterise the typically Mediterranean landscape, corresponding to a hot, less arid climate but with great scarcity of water in summer.

Just a few deteriorated pieces of holm oak forest remain, situated particularly on the western and northern slopes, where they grow up to and beyond an altitude of 1,200 metres.

The upper horizon (called sub-Mediterranean or supra-Mediterranean) is characterised by the forest of deciduous oaks (Quercetalia pubescentis), represented by various entities (such as Quercus pubescens, Quercus virgiliana, Quercus congesta, Quercus dalechampii). At higher altitudes, where the climate is cooler, we find another oak with caducous leaves, the Adriatic oak (Quercus cerris), a species that is widespread on the eastern slopes, where it forms large forests.

The forests of deciduous oaks have partly been replaced by chestnut woods and by cultivation in the form of orchards and vineyards.

Next to these forests, or in their place, we also find the forests of larch pines (Pinus laricio), a plant of tertiary origin native to mountainous areas of the western Mediterranean, which are situated at an intermediate altitude between the oaks and the beeches, creating a landscape of its own covering, in particular, old lava flows. This is a dry type of forest in less damp areas than those where we find the higher and lower broad-leaved forests.

MOUNTAINOUS MEDITERRANEAN LEVEL

Above the zone belonging to deciduous oaks and up to the higher limit of forests (1,800-1,900 metres and sometimes up to 2,300 metres), we come to the level of beeches, typical of cool very damp mountain areas, once largely formed by dense forests, presumably of Fagus sylvatica beeches.

Today the environmental changes that have taken place because of volcanic activity, human activity and changes in the climate, which has become warmer and dryer, do not allow the beeches to occupy the level they originally did.

We should not forget that the beech forests on Etna are the most southerly in Europe and live in very precarious conditions, almost in contradiction with current environmental conditions.

Here and there, especially on the eastern side, the beeches are accompanied by the Etna birch (Betula aetnensis), a woody tree of particular value since it is believed to be native to Etna.

It is found on the upper limit of the tree line and forms pure colonies in the manner of low brush.

HIGH-MEDITERRANEAN LEVEL

Above the tree line the plant landscape changes considerably, becoming singular and exceptional. All forms of tree life disappear and we find conditions of life more suited to vegetation with thorny pulvinus (Astragaletum siculi), which is well adapted to the more rigid climate, colonising the black volcanic sands of the higher slopes of Etna erratically.

These pulvinus, made up of the holy thorn (Astragalus siculus), a species native to Etna, take on an important

role in the landscape, as well as in the ecology of the volcano.

They shelter and protect delicate plants, some of which are also endemic. Among these we find the Etna chickweed (Cerastium aetnicum) and the Etna violet (Viola aetnensis), both native species that colour the pulvinus of the holy thorn with a myriad of white and violet flowers in the late spring.

This is a type of vegetation typical of the volcano which has no equal in any other part of the world, even though the landscape may appear very similar to that of other high Mediterranean mountains.

Around 2,400-2,450 metres this vegetation reaches its climatic limit.

From here up to 2,900-3,000 metres, in areas not affected by recent eruptions, plant life is represented by very few species, almost all native ones, scattered here and there on the substrata of the highest part of Etna.

It is such a barren landscape that at first glance it seems to be totally devoid of plant life. This 'poverty' is accom-

Top: flowering broom.
Left: view of Cubania Wood.

49

volcanic landscape. From the brief descriptions above we can see the diversity and uniqueness of plant life on Etna, which lies over the non-biological landscape and at the same time is integrated with it.

The result is a landscape with volcanic peculiarities and aspects peculiar to Etna, thus playing an important role in the characterisation of the territory. If you then consider that this landscape includes elements from traditional activities of man around the volcano, harmoniously integrated with the natural environment, you can fully appreciate the significance of the Etna landscape overall. This landscape should be protected and existing areas that have been long neglected should be improved. This can be achieved through correct management of the land

panied by characteristics of inestimable value. These plants are almost all native and therefore contain a unique genetic variety, exclusive to Etna. Together they represent a group of high altitude pioneering plants (Rumici-Anthemidetum aetnensis), which are highly adapted to the difficult soil and climatic conditions at high altitudes on Etna. At their upper altitudinal limit these delicate little plants struggle tenaciously to survive the difficult conditions imposed by the volcano: lava flows, emission of vapours and gaseous emissions, hurling out of pyroclastic materials.

Very often the plants succumb to these harsh elements but the seeds soon begin to germinate again and the plants take root once more, until the forces of the volcano eventually demonstrate their total superiority over the fragile and undefended plants. This is an ecologically very interesting zone, contested between life in a strictly biological sense and the life of the volcano.

Above this area, beyond 3,000-3,050 metres, up to the summit, we find the volcanic desert, where the intense activity of the volcano reigns supreme, making the survival of plant life impossible.

THE LAVA LANDSCAPE

When describing the main aspects of plant life on Etna we must also make a brief mention of the numerous groups of pioneering plants on the lava flows, which allow us to study the colonisation and development of plant life on new lava substrata.

The presence of some species of pioneering plants is of particular significance for the landscape, for example the lichen Stereocaulon vesuvianum, which covers wide areas of lava with its silver grey colour; the dock (Rumex scutatus), a robust suffruiticous plant that nestles in the rocky ravines and in July tinges them with the red of the tiny polygons of its fruits; Etna broom (Genista aetnensis), which in June brightens the black lava with its abundant yellow flowers, a typical characteristic of the Etna

in the context of the Etna Nature Park, which must reconcile the need for the preservation of unique values and the necessity for compatible development and responsible benefits.

Emilia Poli Marchese
Institute of Biology and Plant Ecology
University of Catania
Article and altitude plan taken from
"Etna Mito d'Europa", Maimone Editore - Catania 1997.

Right: birches in winter.

SANTA MARIA DI LICODIA: ARCHAEOLOGY AND ART

It is just a few kilometres from Ragalna to **Santa Maria di Licodìa**.

This area is particularly lovely and charming. Over 400 hectares of the municipality are in the Etna Park and the volcano has had a lasting effect on this place, allowing the formation of many woods and numerous caves. The wildlife is very interesting and includes foxes and birds of prey (this is particularly good news for **bird-watchers**).

Considerable archaeological evidence has been found in various localities around the town (**Poggio dell'Aquila**, **Pietra Pirciaria**, **Mendorlito**, **Luppino** and **Mancuso**) from various periods, demonstrating that the territory of Santa Maria di Licodìa was inhabited in ancient times. Some researchers even claim that this was the site of Inessa, a Sican city, the name of which was changed to Aetna by the tyrant of Syracuse, Gelon.

The history of the modern town is closely linked to the Benedictine monastic order. In 1143 the lords of Paternò donated the monastery named after Santa Maria di Licodìa, from which the town took its name, to the Benedictines, granting them the licence to build a hamlet.

The Normans also contributed indirectly to the foundation of the town, granting the monks the land on which the Monastery was situated. The Monastery became an important abbey and the town gradually grew up around it.

You should pay a visit to the **Abbey of Santa Maria di Licodìa**, a typical example of a church-fortress, with the characteristic black and white striped embattled tower, which has now become the emblem of the town.

The ancient complex now houses the Town Hall and the **Cathedral**. The facade of the Cathedral was renovated at the end of the last century during the relaying of Piazza Umberto I. Inside the Church you can see numerous valuable wooden statues, some of which are of notable historical-artistic value; the most beautiful paintings include a 16th century 'Annunciation'.

The **Cherub Fountain** is also worthy of note. It is of Aragonese origin, but was renovated in the late 1700s and is characterised by numerous masks and a series of blind arches supported by elegant columns.

It is interesting to visit the various **archaeological zones** around Santa Maria di Licodìa. In particular, apart from the areas already mentioned, we suggest visiting the archaeological area at **Civita**, where the remains of a Hellenistic age village have been found (5th century BC).

Moreover, just outside the town you can see the remains of a **Roman Aqueduct**.

PASTIMES

Santa Maria di Licodìa is a suitable place for those who have a more demanding palate and prefer simple genuine tastes.

The town is noted for its intensive farming and the production of high quality citrus fruit, in particular oranges of the **'sanguinella'** variety (blood oranges), and of **muscat**, a particularly spiced variety of grape from which exquisite wine is obtained.

The olives are also excellent and used to make a lively and tasty **extra-virgin olive oil**.

You should try the broad bean *'macco'*, sausages, vegetable fritters, rabbit, dishes that can be best appreciated if accompanied by excellent local **red wine** (if you can, take some bottles away with you). If you prefer to eat a sandwich and drink some good beer, you can head for the **pub Van Gogh** in via A. Moro.

The local cakes are also very good, the best ones being the almond and pistachio pastries, the nougat, the 'cassate' and the ice-creams.

If you want to buy souvenirs, keep an eye open for the **artisans' workshops**, where you can find objects in **wrought iron**, **lava stone**, **wood** and **pottery**.

Now here is a small list of events for those who love traditional festivals and street carnivals. 16th July is the Feast of Our Lady of the Carmel; on 21st and 22nd August there is a **Band Meeting** in the streets; from 28th to 30th August the **patronal Feast of Saint Joseph** takes place; from 4th to 12th September the **Craft Fair** is held with displays, sales and entertainment; in November the **Olive Oil Festival** takes place; 8th December is the **Feast of Our Lady of the Immaculate Conception**, celebrated in Piazza Umberto I.

RESTAURANTS-PIZZERIAS

- L'ABBAZIA: via Cavaliere Bosco -Vigne area.
- L'ULIVO: via Aldo Moro.
- MIRAGE: via Cavaliere Bosco, 72 -Vigne area (tel. 095 620329). Restaurant-pizzeria.
- PARADISE: SP, 229 (tel. 095 629497). We recommend the rigatoni 'alla Paradise'.

Right: view of the town centre and Benedictine Monastery.

BIANCAVILLA: BEAUTIFUL CHURCHES

Continuing along the SS 284 road you come to **Biancavilla** after just a few kilometres.

The first historical documentation of the existence of the town dates back to the late 1400s and is connected to the presence of a group of Albanian refugees that settled on land owned by the Moncada family, on the present day site of Biancavilla. This explains the name given to the place in the 1500s: Casale dei Greci (Farmhouse of the Greeks).

From the 1600s onwards a dominant social class began to emerge and laid the bases for the formation of a rich illuminated bourgeoisie in the following century.

In the 1800s the town was the scene of revolts during the uprisings of 1848 and 1860. A more recent episode shows the tenacity and determination of the local people, who, in the years following the Second World War, invented the so called 'on the contrary strike'.

The state had ordered farmers to leave some public owned land but the farmers not only refused to follow these orders

but took over other land that had been left untended. Confronted with such popular resistance, the government gave in and granted the land to the hard-working farmers.

Biancavilla has a very interesting architectural heritage, largely connected with the name of the famous architect Carlo Sada, who designed, among others, the sumptuous Bellini Theatre in Catania.

In Piazza Roma stands the **Cathedral**, dedicated to Our Lady of Charity, with baroque style elements created by Sada, who was also responsible for the restoration of the high bell-tower, decorated with sculptures and with a spire covered with majolica.

Inside, in the three naves separated by archways, you can admire 18th century paintings by Tamo da Brescia and the altar of Our Lady of Charity.

Also in Piazza Roma is the **Church of the Rosary** with a facade by Sada. Inside you will be struck by the profusion of floral decorations and stuccoes.

The work of the gifted architect can also be recognised in the **Church of Our Lady of the Annunciation**. This was built in the 1600s but altered in the following century, when Sada supervised the renovation of the facade. Inside you can admire frescoes by Tamo da Brescia.

Very near the Church of Our Lady of the Annunciation archaeological digs have brought to light a **Sikel necropolis**.

Before we move on to trips out of town we recommend stopping off at the **Belvedere** of Biancavilla, from where you get a breathtaking view over the Erei mountains and the surrounding towns, thanks to the position and altitude.

Just outside the town, to the north, you should visit the **Hermitage of Vadalato**, situated inside a cave that opens out onto a shaded clearing, a pleasant place to visit on a hot summer day.

To the south of the town, on the other hand, near the junction with the SS 575 road, you will find the **Cave of Scilà**, a lava cavity of great charm and beauty (for those who enjoy **hiking** the cave could be the destination for a lovely walk).

Top: Etna seen from Biancavilla. Left: Cathedral or Pontifical Basilica of Our Lady of Charity in Piazza Roma.

FOOD AND FEASTS

The traditional love of the local people for their land still produces its fruits today (all to be tasted!): **oranges**, **prickly-pears** (white, red and yellow), **almonds**, **apples**, **grapes** and **olives**. Don't forget to try the local **wine**, with its intense and strong flavour, and the **olive oil**.

Dairy products are also excellent and fresh, particularly **cheeses** and **ricotta**.

If you want to try local specialities, we recommend the **restaurant Le Grotte**, near the Cathedral in a natural cavern, the **Caffè Scandura** and the **bar-confectioner's Portici**, both in via Vittorio Emanuele.

If you want to buy sovenirs, you should visit the workshops in via Vittorio Emanuele, which sell **pottery** objects and the shop run by signor **Alfio Stissi** in via C. Colombo (**wrought iron**). For street maps, maps of the province and, obviously, books head for the **bookshop Greco** in Via Vittorio Emanuele.

The local festivals are very interesting, both the religious ones and the profane, and take place throughout the year in Biancavilla. From 28th to 31st January the town renews its devotion to **Don Bosco**.

During Easter the death of Christ is dramatised and performed in public. The rites begin with the traditional visit to the sepulchres on **Holy Thursday**; the next day at dawn the **Good Friday** procession gets under way as the simulacrum of Our Lady of Sorrows is carried around the streets of the town, while in the evening the **Way of the Cross** itself begins; on Easter Sunday the **Festival of Peace** takes place and involves the meeting between the statues of Christ Resurrected and Our Lady. Moving on to the summer you can enjoy the **Biancavillese Summer**, a review of music, drama, dance and cabaret in July and August, and the **Feast of Our Lady of Charity**, on the fourth Sunday of August. In October there is the **Patronal Feast of Saint Placid and Our Lady of Charity** from the 1st to the 7th and the **Olive Festival** towards the end of the month. Finally, there are illuminations and cribs throughout the Christmas period, from 16th December onwards.

RESTAURANTS-PIZZERIAS

- BEAUTY GARDEN: contrada Don Assenzio SP 80 (tel. 095 688802). Very refined traditional cuisine. The cuoricini 'Beauty Garden' are excellent.
  - DEL SOLE: via C. Colombo, 343 (tel. 095 688514). Restaurant-pizzeria.
  - IL CAVALLINO: via Vittorio Emanuele, 104 (tel. 095 686826). Restaurant-pizzeria. Excellent saltimbocca.
  - LA LANTERNA: Viale dei Fiori, 141 (tel. 095 981330). Characteristic restaurant offering home cooking and pizzas.
  - LA TIPICA SICILIANA: Viale Dei Fiori, 168 (tel. 095 983976). Traditional dishes and exquisite pizzas.
  - LE GROTTE: Piazza Verdi, 13 (tel. 095 982500). Restaurant-pizzeria. We recommend the liver 'alle Grotte' and Simeto eels.
  - VILLA HOLIDAY CLUB: contrada Poggio Mottese (tel. 095 688749). Restaurant-pizzeria.

Top: Cathedral bell-tower. Left: Etna covered with snow.

PIANO MIRIO BARRACKS (1,600M) - MONTE FONTANELLE - MONTE DENZA (1,812M) - FOREST NURSERY - BIANCAVILLA WOOD

BIANCAVILLA: 2nd ITINERARY ROUTE
Duration : 2 and a half hours
Total distance: 8 km
Difference in height: 200 metres

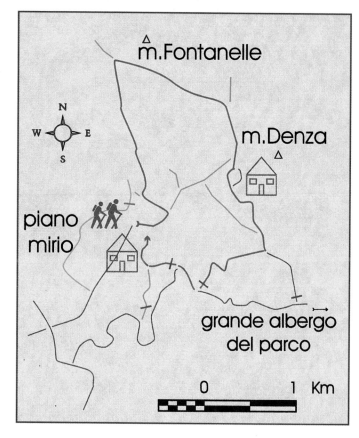

From the well known Nicolosi-Etna road (SP 92) take the turning for Adrano at Monte S.Leo. This is a pleasant secondary road that winds through orchards and chestnut woods, offering sudden glimpses of a lovely view up the western slopes and over the Simeto Valley. Once you pass the turning for the Etna Grand Hotel carry on for about a kilometre until you come to a junction where the road suddenly turns down to the left past an altar dedicated to Saint John Bosco. Here you must go up to the right along a narrow road that has recently been surfaced.

Alongside this road some lay-bys have been created to allow you to park your car.

As soon as you begin to walk you come to the Piano Mirio barracks (base point n°2 of the Etna Park, currently undergoing renovation), you go past this (following the signposts for itinerary 2.1) towards the lava flows of 1610 and Monte Fontanelle.

The route winds through ancient pine forests that have colonised the lava flows, renewing the eternal alternation between life and death, thanks to an old pathway made in the public owned forest.

After a short stretch along the side of Monte Fontanelle, climbing up the slope through the woodland, you come back onto the forest track that bends its way up to the 'ring road' of Etna, the high mountain route.

Don't miss an old shepherd's building near Monte Fontanelle, a characteristic *pagghiaru 'n petra'*, which is situated on an abandoned stretch of the same track.

Once you reach the track you have to go down southwards in the direction of Monte Denza, until you come to a tarmacked stretch. Here it is advisable to go up towards the forest hut of the same name, which is usually closed but offers excursionists a large picnic area equipped with tables and benches.

You then go down onto the high mountain route (where there is an altar dedicated to Saint John Gualberto) and you continue through old woodland until you reach a sign-posted turn off for the forest nursery from which you reach the tarmacked road that leads to the Etna Grand Hotel from the provincial road to Adrano.

At this point you must go downhill for more than a hundred metres along the tarmacked road until you come to a track (closed by an obvious barrier) on a hairpin bend that heads off into the wood. You continue along this rough track for about a kilometre until you come to a second gate situated right in front of a small house with a water tank.

Here you can climb up through the Biancavilla wood along the bed of a seasonal torrent, a detour that is particularly suitable for children because it is an enjoyable walk with little rocks they can climb on and jump from.

Moreover, you will be able to see all the particular rock formations created by water erosion.

If, however, you do not have enough energy for this detour you can continue straight on to the nearby Piano Mirio barracks, just below which you will find your car.

Left: Piano Mirio.

ADRANO: A THOUSAND YEARS OF HISTORY

From Biancavilla you continue to follow the SS 284 road and, after a few kilometres, you arrive in **Adrano**.

From the point of view of nature Adrano is one of the most interesting towns around the foot of Etna. It has not suffered any recent lava flows and so there are a lot of woods and luxuriant vegetation, thanks also to the vivifying presence of the Simeto river and numerous other natural springs. **Hiking** is possible here, not only in the Etna Park, but also along the Simeto, among citrus fruit groves, gorges, waterfalls and petrified lava flows.

The territory of Adrano is also extremely interesting from an archaeological point of view. Thanks to digs carried out it has been demonstrated that man (homo sapiens) was already present here during the Palaeolithic age. Areas of settlement have been identified near the Simeto river, at Mendolito, where Bronze age evidence has been uncovered.

In 400 BC the tyrant of Syracuse, Dionysius, subjected the settlement of Mendolito and transferred its inhabitants to Adranon, a little further north, a city that he himself had founded. The ancient roots of present day Adrano can therefore be traced back to the Syracuse colony of Adranon, which reached the height of its splendour in 300 BC under Timoleon.

The Romans were the first to darken the bright history of Adranon and the Vandals completed the job by sacking the city in 455 AD. The place started to flourish again with the arrival of the Arabs. They changed the Byzantine name of Adranion into Adarnu, made a lot of innovations, especially in agriculture, and built a tower. Under the Normans the city changed name again, to Adernio, and continued to prosper. Yet another name was imposed under the Swabians and Angevins, Adernò. This name remained until 1929, when the present name was adopted.

THE ROCK OF MARVELS

The **Castle** of Adrano stands in Piazza Umberto I. It was probably built as a watchtower by the Saracens, was restored and enlarged by the Normans and altered again by the Swabians. It stands out above the solid 16th century bastion that surrounds it with its stout quadrangular structure. The most interesting rooms are on the ground floor, where you can easily see the Arab architectural styles and where the armoury was originally situated; the first floor almost certainly used as a reception hall, although it is difficult to picture the original layout of the rooms; the rooms on the second floor were the private quarters of the inhabitants of the Castle, as is shown by the presence of a chapel.

Top: the Castle. Left: the town seen from the Castle terrace.

Inside the Castle you can visit the **Art Gallery**, which houses works of art from the 16th to the 20th century, the **Craft Museum**, which displays objects of a mostly religious nature, and the **Archaeological Museum**. The latter was set up in the late 1950s and brings together artefacts from Prehistoric times and the Greek, Roman and mediaeval periods. We particularly draw your attention to the artefacts from the Neolithic civilisation of Stentinello, those of the pre-Castelluccian and Castellucian age found in burial caves and the beautiful bust, probably depicting Demeter, found in the district of Santa Maria di Licodìa.

The **Cathedral**, dedicated to Our Lady of the Assumption, stands very near the Castle. The present appearance of the building dates back to the 1500s and is the work of the architect Mariano Smiriglio.

The cupola is of more recent construction, attributable to the 18th century. The interior has three naves divided by lava stone columns and you can see a 15th century crucifix, paintings by Vazano and a beautiful 16th century polyptych of the Antonello school.

The ex-**Monastery of Saint Lucy**, in via Roma, was set up in Norman times on the orders of Countess Adelasia, who came to power after the death of Count Roger, but the com-

plex, with its two hundred metre long facade, was rebuilt at the end of the 16th century. The adjacent church, on the other hand, was restored in the 18th century by the architect S. Ittar and Prince Biscari.

In front of the Monastery is the **Municipal Park** or Victory Garden, one of the prettiest public parks in the province.

Another monastic building is to be found in Piazza Sant'Agostino, where you will see the Convent of Saint Augustine with the adjacent 16th century **Church of Our Lady of the Annunciation**.

Moving on to Piazza San Nicolò you can admire the **Church of Saint Nicolò Politi**, which was built in the late 1600s but was destoyed by the terrible earthquake of 1693. Today the facade is in clear neo-classical style.

In via San Pietro stand numerous holy buildings worthy of note.

The **Church of Saint Peter**, characterised by a portal in lava stone, dating back to the 13th century; the **Church of Saint Francis** containing a wooden crucifix of the 17th century by Brother Humble of Petralia; the **Church of the Saviour**, with a 16th century bell-tower; the **Church of Saint Sebastian**, which houses the Christ at the Column, a 17th century wooden statue sculpted by R. Terranova.

In Adrano there are also some public buildings and private houses worth visiting. We suggest the 16th century **Palazzo dei Bianchi**; the 18th century **Palazzo Ciancio**; the 18th century **Palazzo Russo** and **Palazzo Guzzardi**; the **Municipal Theatre**, of 18th century origin but with a liberty style facade.

Archaeology enthusiasts should make a few excursions out of town.

Near Adrano stands the so called **Saracen Bridge**, which spans the River Simeto with its four arches.

In **contrada Mendolito**, about 5km from the town, you can see the remains of the city destroyed by Dionysius, the tyrant of Syracuse. You will easily recognise the city gate, reinforced by two towers.

In contrada Sant'Alfio is the **necropolis of Adranon**.

Top: Church of Saint Chiara. Left: Church of Saint Lucy.

GOOD NEWS

Adrano is very much a town for gourmets and the typical local dishes show great respect for culinary traditions accompanied by a skilful touch of imagination. Among the local specialities we can mention the risotto with orange, the dishes made with mushrooms, the mandarin cake, the lamb made with candy, must-cake with prickly-pears (prickly-pear cream mixed with grape must, chopped almonds, orange peel, flour or starch). Equally exquisite, though not the result of skilled cooking, are the dried figs and prickly-pears stringed on reed sticks.

We are sure that by now you will be licking your lips, so without hesitation we will supply you with the addresses of some restaurants and confectioners' where you can taste these and other specialities: **Holiday restaurant** in contrada San Giuseppe di Calcerana (the caserecce Holiday are excellent), **Di Primo restaurant** in vicolo Platania (excellent rabbit), **bar-confectioner's Cafè De Flore** in via Spampinato, **bar-confectioner's Spitaleri** in Piazza Umberto (pistachio pastries and ice-creams), **Jolly bar** in Piazza Umberto (exquisite ice-creams).

If, however, you cannot resist the temptation of biting into a good sandwich and drinking a frothy beer you can head for the **pub Discesa del Papa** in contrada Capici, the **pub The Eagle** in via Casale dei Greci, the **beer-hall** and **sandwich bar La Bottegaccia** in via Garibaldi.

If you feel like buying some souvenirs we recommend the **market** that takes place every Tuesday and Friday in contrada San Leo. Here it is possible to make purchases of any kind: from vegetables to cheeses, from shoes to T-shirts, from costume jewellery to ornaments.

For books and maps we recommend: **Cartolibreria 55** in via Gesù e Maria.

And now we will deal with the local festivals.

On Christmas Eve there is the **Performance of the Living Crib** in the main square.

On 19th March the **Feast of Saint Joseph** takes place during which the devotees of the Saint organise meals in their houses with the participation of some young girls called 'virgins'.

During the Easter period there are some very charming rites. On **Holy Thursday** the procession of Christ at the Column takes place; **Good Friday** sees the procession of Our Lady of Sorrows and, in the evening, the procession of the Dead Christ; at midnight between Saturday and Sunday the rite of the **Resurrection** is held in the Cathedral during which a large 18th century tapestry is hoisted onto the apse; Holy Saturday sees the dramatisation of the **Way of the Cross**; on **Easter Day** there is the meeting and procession through the streets of the town of the simulacrums of Christ, Our Lady and the Angel; also on Easter Day, at midday in the square in front of the Cathedral, there is the performance of the **'Diavolata and Angelica'**, a holy play dating back to 1752. The last day of the month is the **Feast of Saint Alfio** during which there is a parade of Sicilian carts pulled by sumptuously harnessed horses and ancient musical instruments are played. In the months of July and August the **Adranita Summer** takes place, a review of music, drama, dance and cabaret. Finally, you should not miss **The Flight of the Angel**, which takes place as part of the celebrations in honour of **Saint Nicolò Politi** in early August. The performance consists of a child dressed as an angel 'flying' from the top of the Arab-Norman tower as far as the Saint's carriage.

RESTAURANTS

- DI PRIMO: vicolo Platania, 34 (tel. 095 7691555). In the centre of Adrano. We recommend the pasta 'alla siciliana' and the stuffed rabbit.
- HOLIDAY: contrada Calcerana (tel. 095 7601021). Mountain specialities. Exquisite caserecce Holiday.
- TUCCIO: via Catania, 204 (tel. 095 7698726). Local cuisine.

PIZZERIAS

- EL MUNDIAL: via IV Novembre, 45 (tel. 095 7690174).
- IL RUSTICONE: Piazza Armando Diaz, 31 (tel. 095 7690936).

Top: performance of the Diavolata and the Angelica.
Left: Municipal Park.

PIAZZALE MONTE GALLO - PIANO FIERA (1,500M) MONTE PALESTRA MOUNTAIN HUT (1,920M)-MONTE ROSSO - MONTE NESPOLE - MONTE GALLO

ADRANO: 3rd ITINERARY ROUTE
Duration : 3 and a half hours
Total distance: 13 km
Difference in height: 420 metres

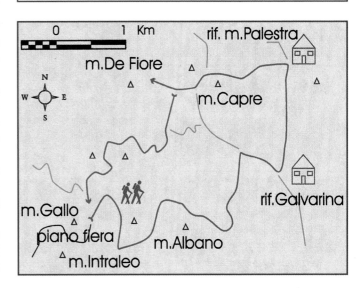

The upper western slopes of Etna have been managed for decades by the Forestry Service and constitutes a large part of the 29,000 hectares of publicly owned land incorporated into the Etna Park.

The square facing Monte Gallo (marked on the IGM map as Piano Fiera) is a perfect point from which to begin excursions by bike or on foot into the area we are about to describe because it allows you to start from quite a high altitude.

To reach it you have to follow the provincial road from Adrano to Monte San Leo (this is a little higher up than Nicolosi along provincial road 92 to Etna-south) and look out for the signposts to Monte Intraleo.

Among all the possible circular routes in this vast area the best to take is the one that starts from the square and follows a forest path that starts on the right, no more than fifty metres from square.

You walk through thick woodland climbing quite steeply (at a certain point the track splits into two but the two paths join back together a little further on).

Just after Monte Albano a pathway on the right leads to Monte Fontanelle.

You continue walking through the wood until the track joins the one that comes up from Monte Gallo via Monte Nespole. You carry on uphill and after a few minutes come to the very popular Galvarina forest hut (1,850 metres). At this point the itinerary continues northwards along a track as far as the next forest hut at Monte Palestra (or Poggio La

Caccia). From here a sign-posted pathway begins and takes you through a lovely area made up of old lava flows colonised by Corsican pines.

The route has several climbs and descents and passes Monte Capre (here you can see the interior of an old crater) and then suddenly drops down towards Monte Rosso, where it comes to an end when it meets a forest track. At this point you can make a detour towards Monte De Fiore, the most recent eruptive complex on this side of the volcano, dating back to 1974.

To reach it follow the sign-posted pathway that leaves from the southern side of Monte Rosso, remembering that you will go down about a hundred metres in altitude and on your return you will have to climb back again to reach the original departure point.

Otherwise you can climb directly along the forest track that you meet between Monte Capre and Monte Rosso in order to reach a junction situated about 700 metres away and from here you turn right and quickly go downhill to Monte Gallo, passing by Monte Nespole, thereby completing the circular route without ant further detours.

"OASI DEL SIMETO" NATURE RESERVE

If you are in the province of Catania and you want to get an idea of what the coastal landscape in the south of the province was once like, then you have to visit the Oasi del Simeto Nature Reserve, the last remaining piece of one of the largest wetlands in Sicily, which was once formed by the Biviere lake of Lentini, the marsh of Catania and the marsh of Lentini.

Visitors cannot, however, expect to find the Oasis in completely unspoilt natural condition because of the negative influence man has had on the area (especially in the form of illegal building); just a few stretches of river and of the estuary of the Simeto have kept, in part, their original natural landscape appearance.

The Reserve is about 10km south of Catania and was set up in 1984 to protect one of the most important wetland areas in Europe for bird life and for dune and marsh plant life: it covers an area of about 1,850 hectares and stretches for about 8km along the coast and 2km inland.

As well as the estuary of the Simeto river, it includes typical marshlands and the Gurnazza and Gornalunga ponds.

The Reserve owes its existence to the Simeto, the longest river in Sicily which is born from the convergence of three torrents coming from the Nebrodi mountains (the Cutò, the Martello and the Saracena).

The waters of the Simeto, before arriving at the mouth, flow for about 113km through some of the most beautiful countryside in Sicily, in which the intense colours

of the natural vegetation and the crops contrast with the dark volcanic soil. Before reaching the flat final stretch near the sea the river flows through lovely gorges, such as the Cantera, a deep gorge dug by the river in the basalt rock of Etna.

The entrance to the Reserve can be reached from Catania along the SS 114 road towards Siracusa at the Primosole bridge. Here you can find guides to accompany you in the Oasis. One of the itineraries begins

at the entrance to the Reserve and follows the left bank of the river: if you follow it as far as the coast and then turn northwards you can get to the old loop of the Simeto, which is now completely separated from the river itself due to the straightening that the latter underwent in the 1950s in the final stretch. This meander maintains

its own mouth and continues to exist today thanks to the supply of water that largely comes from the underground water bed and partly from the torrents Jungetto and Buttacento and some canals.

This stretch of the Simeto river is about 1.5km long: it is the most important environment in the Reserve because the separation from the main river has, paradoxically, kept it free of interventions that alter the flow of water. This means that it has maintained an environment suitable for hosting the animal and plant species typical of marshlands and which have become very rare in Sicily.

The plant species found here include the Cattail and the Marsh Reed; both these species form a thick cloak of vegetation offering cover for many species of birds, some of which find the ideal environment for breeding. If you continue northwards you come to some brackish pools behind the dunes called 'Salatelle': these are small pools about 1 metre deep that can completely dry up in summer.

If at the entrance you follow the right bank as far as the coast and then head southwards, you come to the lakes of Gurnazza and Gornalunga, brackish pools, the second of which is fed by the Benante canal and is home to numerous species of birds all year round. The peculiarity of this part of the Reserve is that, apart from the normal bodies of water, in winter and spring several swamps form and the plants growing in them attract many species of migratory birds that stop off here.

From the top: mouth of the river Simeto, a stretch of the river.

The importance of the Simeto Reserve from the point of view of nature is also due to what remains of the coastal sand dune system, a unique environment that was once widespread all over the region.

The sand dunes have an ecosystem of their own, characterised by particular plant and animal species suited to life in an extreme environment where the high temperatures, high salt concentration and lack of water caused by the inability of the sand to retain it, all make life very difficult indeed.

Among the plant species present here we find the 'Salsola kali' and the 'Agropyron junceum', plants that are called 'pioneering' because their roots are capable of holding the sand together and helping to create the dunes. We can also find the Sea Lily (Pancratium maritimum) with its highly fragrant flowers.

In such a difficult environment insects are the animals that are best adapted to survival.

One of these is the 'Pachipo', a small coleopteran (with a black upper body and brown lower body) native to Sicily; the 'Aplidia del Massa' is a small beetle less than a centimetre long native to the Reserve.

BIRD LIFE

What strikes you most when you visit the Simeto Nature Reserve is the presence of numerous species of birds.

The variety of colours, shapes and sizes of the birds in this particular environment offer a gratifying spectacle for naturalists, enthusiasts and the simply curious.

If you visit this area in autumn and spring and you bring a pair of binoculars and a guide to bird watching (necessary equipment if you want to know which species you are observing), you will not be disappointed.

In a relatively very small area it is possible to observe 80% of the species present in the whole of Sicily.

If you do not have this equipment don't despair, because even if you cannot identify the species you are observing you can still enjoy the sight of dozens of ducks suddenly lifting up into flight, forming a single flock in which the wing beats of each individual is synchronised with all the others.

You will still be able to identify some species that can be seen in nature documentaries, such as the unmistakable Flamingo with its characteristic bright pink colour on its wings, neck and very long legs.

The importance of the Reserve from the point of view of nature is also due to the presence of certain aquatic bird species.

These species nest along the estuary of the Simeto and in very few other sites in Sicily.

This is true of the Mallard, an elegant duck, the male of which has a bright green colour with metallic reflections on its head and neck and a reddish-brown

breast; the female, on the other hand, is speckled brown all over.

This species builds its nest very near the water, often at the base of the thick marsh vegetation; the female lays about 10-12 green-grey eggs. Mating in this species, as in other species of ducks, happens in a particular way; sometimes several males try to mate at the same time with a single female, almost causing the poor female to drown.

Another rare nesting species in Sicily is the Night Heron, a bird belonging to the heron family with a rather squat

From the top: specimens of Little Egret, Shelduck, Flamingos.

shape and rather short legs for a species living in a marshland area.

It nests in colonies, generally in large bushes and trees; at the mouth of Simeto, on a small island situated in the centre of a pool at Torre Allegra, 45 nests were identified in July 1993, a very high number for a single site in Sicily.

Other species of heron that nest here are the Grey Heron, the Little Egret and the Squacco Heron; the latter species is different from other similar ones, such as the Little Egret, because of the presence of a long drooping crest of feathers and differences in certain parts of the body (the reddish head, neck, back and breast) and nested in Sicily for the first time at the mouth of the Simeto.

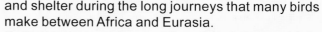

During spring it is possible to see a gracious bird swimming elegantly, almost giving the impression of moving without making any movement: this is the Great Crested Grebe, a species with an unmistakable silhouette characterised by a pointed beak, a long thin neck and a body half immersed in the water.

During the mating season it has red plumes on the sides of its head, which, apart from its dimensions, allow us to distinguish it from other species of Grebe. All the species of Grebe are expert divers, able to catch fish at great depths.

The Great Crested Grebe also nests at the mouth of the Simeto.

Most of the birds that can be found in the Reserve are, however, species passing through that take advantage of this favourable environment in order to stop off during their migrations; wetlands such as this are very important because they are situated along the main migration routes and are therefore suited to supplying food and shelter during the long journeys that many birds make between Africa and Eurasia.

During autumn and spring, therefore, it is possible to observe typical aquatic birds, such as the Cormorant (with flocks that sometimes number more than two hundred individuals), the Shelduck, a brightly coloured duck, the Shoveler with its characteristic spoon shaped bill, the elegant Glossy Ibis with purple, bronze and green reflections in its plumage. In the areas where there are pools and along the coast near the 'Salatelle' it is possible to observe many species of limicolous birds, so called because they feed on aquatic invertebrates which they find by searching the mud bottoms with their long beaks.

Among these species there are frequent sightings of the Redshank with its typical red legs and long red beak with a black tip, of the unmistakable Avocet with its characteristic long upward-pointing beak, of the Curlew Sandpiper and the small Little Stint whose flocks are often formed by hundreds of individuals, concentrated in certain areas in a frenetic search for food, and of many other species.

If you happen to see a small brightly coloured bird (upper body blue and emerald green and reddish lower body) diving into the water from a projection and returning there with a small fish in its beak, you are privileged to see another gracious guest of the Reserve, the Kingfisher.

During your visit to the Reserve, however, you should not limit your attention only to what happens on the ground and in the water because if you look up into the sky you could spot another important guest that often spends all winter here: the Marsh Harrier.

This is a bird of prey, the undisputed predator of this ecosystem; its presence in this environment, since it is at the top of the food chain, demonstrates the wealth of life present here.

If, during your visit, you happen to catch a glimpse of its dark silhouette (and it is not unusual) hovering with slow wing strokes above a thick reed bed and then diving into it to capture the small mammals, marsh birds and amphibians on which it feeds, you will certainly be satisfied with the time you spent in one of the last remaining wetlands in Sicily.

Antonino Di Maggio

Top: specimen of Kingfisher.
Left: the river at dawn.

BRONTE: FROM THE SIKELS TO THE ENGLISH

Following the SS 284 road from Adrano, you reach **Bronte** after about 14 kilometres.

This cheerful town is situated on the western slopes of Etna at a moderate altitude (above 700 metres), giving it a particularly pleasant climate in summer and a marvellous view. In particular, against the ever present and ever changing background of the volcano you will see thousands of hectares of highly fertile farmland, thanks to the volcanic soil, which have allowed the development of a profitable agricultural economy. The most famous product of this economy, exported all over the world, is undoubtedly the pistachio.

Using Bronte as a base you can make numerous excursions to places of outstanding beauty and of great historical and natural interest (for example the lava flow of 1651).

It is assumed that the first inhabitants of this area were the Sikels, whose presence here is demonstrated by burial chambers dating back to the 8th century BC. Archaeological research has also ascertained that the Greeks and Romans passed through here. The Arabs were the first to fully take advantage of the fertile land around present day Bronte. They brought with them innovations in agricultural techniques and planted the first pistachio trees. During the Middle Ages Bronte, along with other hamlets in the area, was under the jurisdiction of the Benedictine Monastery of Maniace. Charles V, in the early 1500s, granted Bronte the dignity of a town with administrative functions and placed the other hamlets under its control. As a logical consequence the town became enriched with public, religious and private buildings.

Historically the name of the town is linked with the so called "events of Bronte" which happened during Garibaldi's epic expedition. Following bloody clashes between the richer and poorer classes Garibaldi sent General Bixio to Bronte and the latter put an end to the riots by having the rioters (members of the 'dura lex sed lex' movement) shot.

Just over twelve kilometres from Bronte you will find the

Nelson's Duchy or Castle, which can be reached along the Bronte-Maniace provincial road. The site on which the Castle stands was originally occupied by the Abbey of Santa Maria di Maniace, which was built on the orders of Queen Margaret in honour of the Byzantine General who succeeded in defeating the Arabs. Despite the ravages suffered at the hands of man and of nature the abbey was transformed into a fortified residence and offered to Admiral Horatio Nelson by the Bourbon King Ferdinand IV in 1799 in recognition of the help given to him in reclaiming power. Nelson's descendants made further changes to the building and renovated the old abbey **Church** with three naves. The most beautiful element in this church is the superb Norman portal, richly decorated with grotesque anthropomorfic figures in relief. The Duchy is situated in a natural park of great beauty which is freely open to the public. Also outside the town, in contrada Piana

Top and left: panoramic views of the town.

Cuntarati, you will find the old **Lombardo Farm**, which stands on the site of a Norman building. The premises of the farm have been appropriately restored and now house the lovely **Museum of Local History and Civilisation**.

In the town of Bronte, on the other hand, there are several buildings to visit, mostly of a religious nature.

In Piazza Leone XIII stands the 16th century **Cathedral** dedicated to the Holy Trinity. At the baroque style altar you can see the lovely 16th century wooden crucifix and 18th century frescoes.

In Corso Umberto you can admire the rococo facade of the **Capizzi College**. The College was founded in 1744 and for more than a century represented the most important cultural institution for the ruling class in Sicily. Among its illustrious pupils we can mention the writer Luigi Capuana. The premises of the College still house a **Library** which contains books that belonged to the Jesuits until the suppression of religious orders in Sicily.

Also worthy of note are the **Sanctuary of Our Lady of the Annunciation**, home to the valuable group of marble statues of the Annunciation attributed to Gagini, and the **Church of Our Lady of Succour**, which houses another valuable work by Gagini.

PISTACHIOS TO BE PROUD OF

The famous Bronte **pistachios** are of very high quality and really must be tasted to be appreciated, natural, toasted or in one of the numerous forms offered by local gastronomy. Indeed, pistachios are used as the main ingredient in many recipes for first and second courses, as well as in cakes and ice-creams of course.

Pistachio ice-cream is the pride and joy of the town. Pistachio cakes can be found at the **confectioners' Meli** and **Conti Gallenti** both in via Umberto, **Di Vincenzo** in via

Messina and **Al Caprice** in Viale della Regione. You should also try the local dairy products, fresh and genuine or tastily matured. In particular, we recommend the **pecorino cheese**, which can purchased from all the grocery shops or directly from the producers. If you want to try for yourself the delicious local cuisine we suggest two **restaurants**. **La Tavernatta**, in Viale A. Grassia, serving meat roulades with vegetables and delicious desserts; **Parco dell'Etna**, in contrada Borgonuovo, with a varied menu made from genuine ingredients, including first courses with mushrooms, pistachios, asparagus and other fresh seasonal produce (the Parco dell'Etna also organises guided trips up Etna, even on horseback).

Top: Capizzi Royal College.
Left: Cathedral.

A good alternative place for dinner is the **pub-pizzeria Pub 1860** in via Umberto.

It is, in a certain sense, obvious and legitimate that the symbol and pride of the town should have a festival dedicated to it. indeed, in the second week of October the green nut is celebrated with the **Pistachio Festival**, displays and tasting of local pistachio dishes.

At the end of May there is another opportunity to taste local delicacies: the **Spring Festival** includes displays of crafts and tasting of local produce.

Summer, on the other hand, is given over to culture and entertainment. On 25th July there is **Etna Jazz**, a travelling review of jazz music; in July and August **Brontestate** sees music, drama, cabaret and fashion; in August **Rock Evolution** offers rock music in Piazza Cimbali.

RESTAURANTS-PIZZERIAS

- AL SIMETO: contrada Serra (tel. 095 692032). Restaurant-pizzeria. Try the home-made starters and the fresh fettuccine with pistachio.
- CRISTAL: contrada Cantera (tel. 095 7722399). Restaurant-pizzeria. Delicious penne with pistachio and mutton.
- DA ZIO VITO: cortile Aida, 8 (tel. 095 691837). Trattoria-pizzeria.
- DON CICCIO: contrada Serra (tel. 095 7722916). Restaurant-pizzeria. We suggest the pasta with pistachio and the pasta 'alla Don Ciccio'. Booking essential.
- ETRUSCA: Viale Kennedy, 41 (tel. 095 692575). Lovely restaurant with garden. Mediterranean cuisine, highly skilled chefs.
- IL PALIO: Viale Regina Margherita, 128 (tel. 095 693131) Restaurant-pizzeria.
- L'ANGOLO PICCANTE: via Borsellino, 1 (tel. 095 693730). Restaurant-pizzeria. We recommend the home-made pasta with local mushrooms and the lamb with pistachio.
- LA TAVERNETTA: Viale A. Grassia, 3 (tel. 095 692789). Specialities include roulades with vegetables and pistachio pancakes
- OMNIBUS: via Umberto, 329 (tel. 095 7724347). Restaurant-pizzeria-pub. Particular attention for dishes made with fish and pistachio. Good choice of wines and beers.
- PARCO DELL'ETNA: via Carlo Alberto Dalla Chiesa - contrada Borgonuovo (tel.095 691907). Hotel restaurant. Try the pennette with pistachio, the pasta with asparagus, the risotto with mushrooms, mutton, lamb and goat.

HOTELS

- PARCO DELL'ETNA ♥ ♥ ♥: via Carlo Alberto Dalla Chiesa - contrada Borgonuovo (tel.095 691907 fax 095 692678). Chalet at an altitude of 910 metres. With restaurant and bar.
- LA CASCINA ♥ ♥: contrada Piana Cuntarati (tel. 095 7721991 fax 095 77221035). With resaurant-pizzeria (excellent local charcouterie and pistachio specialities).

Top: pistachio orchards and in the background Bronte and Etna.
Left: Capuchin Church.

NELSON'S DUCHY

It is interesting to visit a corner of Sicily that belonged, until recently, to members of the English nobility: the Duchy of Bronte, on the western slopes of Etna, once belonging to Horatio Nelson, the hero of Trafalgar. Bronte was given to the English Admiral by King Ferdinand IV of Bourbon to thank him for having saved his life and his throne: he had been forced to leave Naples by revolutionaries and had found refuge in Palermo. Here, he managed to reorganise and, with Nelson's help, returned to power.

The accounts of the time tell us that Nelson repressed the revolt ruthlessly. Today all that remains of the Duchy is the castle of Maniace and surrounding grounds, about eighteen kilometres north of Bronte, on the border of the province of Messina. The castle was originally an abbey and has been purchased by the local authorities to be turned into a museum and tourist attraction. Currently it is undergoing restoration, so it is probable that by the time this guide is available it will be possible to visit the whole

castle, as well as the ruins of the abbey, the courtyard and the park.

According to an ancient legend, still known to the old people of the area, it was written in the book of destiny that Sicilian Bronte would one day fall into the hands of an Englishman. According to the prophecy, some say that on the death of Queen Elizabeth I her body was taken away by a host of devils and carried across the Channel, France and Italy, as far as Sicily, where it ended up in the crater of Etna. While falling, a shoe came off one of her feet, just as happened to the philosopher Empedocles, and fell to the ground near Bronte, on the Calanna rock.

The fable does not end here. It goes on to say that Admiral Nelson was approached by a mysterious woman during his investiture in the Royal Palace in Palermo and she gave him a casket. Inside was the Queen's shoe, which Nelson decided to give to his lover Lady Emma Hamilton. This gesture was not appreciated by the mysterious woman, who, on the eve of the Battle of Trafalgar, appeared to Nelson again to reproach him and to announce his imminent death.

This is the legend. Nelson was pleased to have received the Duchy but never bothered to visit it. His heirs, however, never failed to administer it and to spend their holidays there. After Nelson's death it passed to his brother William, an Anglican priest, who kept it for thirty years. He was succeeded by his daughter Charlotte, wife of the Viscount of Bridport.

Under her signoria the Duchy of Bronte was the scene of one of the most painful episodes in Sicilian history. It took place in 1860, when Garibaldi and his men reached Palermo. A group of peasants rose up against the landowners and, after spiralling violence, the result was a massacre. Garibaldi sent Bixio to Bronte and he had the ringleaders of the revolt arrested and shot.

This episode is recounted in a very biased account by Giuseppe Cesare Abba in his 'Da Quarto al Volturno'.

A more detailed and accurate account was published in the early 1900s by the local researcher Benedetto Radice. In the English Duchy relations with the peasants were always difficult. Nelson's heirs only allowed limited social reforms in the very last years of their presence in Sicily.

Under the Facist regime the Duchy was confiscated as 'enemy property'. After the war it was returned to the Bridports, Nelson's heirs.

Matteo Collura

Extract from "*Unknown Sicily*" - Rizzoli 1997

PIANO DEI GRILLI (1,150 M)-MONTE EGITTO-MONTE SCAVO (1,700 M)

BRONTE: 4th ITINERARY ROUTE
Duration : 7 hours
Total distance: 18 km
Difference in height: 550 metres

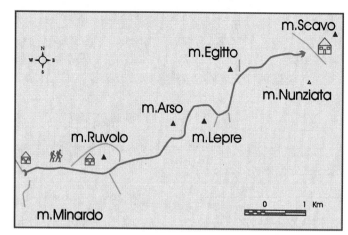

From Catania you follow the SS 284 road towards Randazzo enjoying the gradual changes in the appearance of the volcano. Just after passing the town of Bronte, you turn right into the new industrial zone and then continue along a road paved in lava stone that crosses the 1651 lava flow, passes Monte Paparia and finally arrives at Piano dei Grilli, where you can leave your car in front of an old forestry service barracks. The itinerary begins with a gentle climb along the track leading uphill. From this plateau you can see various craters, from the nearby ones, such as Monte Minardo and Monte Ruvolo, right up to the ones on the summit. This side of the volcano is characterised by wide open grasslands, dotted here and there with lovely Etna gorse bushes and, higher up, with huge isolated oak trees, clinging to the occasional craters. At the foot of Monte Ruvolo keep to the right and

you will see on the side of this crater a recently built mountain hut, still closed, and nearby a lovely example of 'pagghiaru 'n petra'. You then come to the first significant junction where you continue uphill, while by going right you can reach the base of Monte Tre Frati, where there is an old water tank. The track crosses the lava flows of 1763 passing alongside Monte Arso and Monte Lepro, where you find the second junction. Turn left towards Monte Egitto and, after a few hundred metres, on the right you will notice another splendid example of 'pagghiaru 'n petra' with its own sheep pen. Once you reach Monte Egitto, where the forest track ends, take the path (marked by yellow posts) that passes to the east of the mount, crosses the lava flows of 1651 and 1832 and finally brings you to the foot of Monte Scavo (where there is a forest hut open to walkers, with a water tank). The return is by the same route.

Caves on Etna

One aspect of the volcano Etna that should not be forgotten is the presence of numerous cavities that exist all over its slopes: the only volcanic caves in the whole of continental Europe.

It must be stressed that these caves, while being natural phenomena like the better known karstic ones, are very different from the latter because they are formed, along with the rock that contains them, during the lava flows of a volcanic eruption. Consequently, it takes a relatively short time for them to form, a period of one week to a few months.

Karstic caves, on the other hand, are created by the chemical-physical disintegration of calcareous rock and take a significantly longer time to form, even millions of years.

On Etna we find two principal types of volcanic caves: lava tunnels (or lava flow tunnels) and caves in fracture. The latter are prevalently vertical in shape, so special

caving equipment is necessary in order to explore them.

Lava tunnels are what remains of channels, now solidified, through which the lava flowed internally and which later emptied because of drainage or because of erosion of the bottom.

These tunnels are often very easy to explore as they are usually made up of a main channel, sometimes very wide and long (even several hundred metres), and conserve an interesting morphology, such as: sections of varying geometry; remelting stalactites on the roof (commonly called dog's teeth); lateral curling rolls formed by the rapid drainage of the lava flow; shelves and sills sticking out from the walls (very evident in caves on three levels) formed by a sudden slowing down of the lava flow.

Inside the caves on Etna, particularly those formed following the eruption of 1983, an important and previously unknown phenomenon of concretion of minerals was discovered, giving rise to coloured stalactite and stalagmite structures of great visual effect. Unfortunately, they are of very short duration, since their formation is due to the presence of concurrent factors (inside a cave that is still hot) that no longer exist after a few months.

There are more than two hundred volcanic caves on Etna today and new ones are continually discovered, mapped and registered by pot-holers from Catania.

Many of these caves were already known in ancient times and have often given rise to popular fantasies and numerous legends, such as the one of Prosperine's abduction, linked to the

---

Top: lava flow tunnel.
Right: Cassone Cave.
Facing page top: summit craters Monte Nuovo and Monte De Fiore. Bottom: Three Level Cave.

Church Cave in the territory of San Giovanni Galermo; others were lived in by prehistoric men or used as burial places: this is shown by the discovery of numerous human skeletons, vases and fragments from the Castelluciano period in the Nuovalucello I Cave, situated inside the Archbishop's Seminary in Catania, above the ring road; others were used as places of meditation: this is true of the Saint's Cave, situated at an altitude of 1,043 metres in the Adrano district, which according to legend was the refuge of Nicola Politi, a 13th century Saint, who fled here during a spiritual crisis after abandoning his bride on their wedding night. Others were used as snow grottoes, in other words places where snow was stored during winter and then removed and sold in the valleys in summer: this is true of the Snow Cave, later called the Cave of Thieves, situated at Piano delle Donne (1,550 metres) at Km 19 of the Fornazzo-Piano Provenzana road (Mareneve road).

Certainly the most famous cave on Etna is the Gelo (Ice) Cave, situated at an altitude of 2,043 metres. It was formed during the eruption of 1614-24 (the longest in recorded history) and contains a spectacular glacier that is present all year round.

Finally, here are some more detailed descriptions of how to reach two famous beautiful caves that are easy to explore with an electric torch and a helmet to protect your head.

The first one is the Cassone Cave, which is suitable for visitors who do not want to make any effort to walk, since it can be reached by car.

Leaving from Zafferana Etnea along the SP 92 road, after about 10km, you reach a large flat open area (on the right) called Piano del Vescovo.

You continue to climb for about 500 metres and imme-

diately after the first hairpin bend to the left you will see the entrance to the cave on the right-hand side of the road (1,400 metres).

It is a lava flow tunnel that originated during the 1792-93 eruption and is 300 metres long with a difference in height of 25 metres.

The deepest part of the cave is easily accessible and it gradually widens and becomes more interesting, above all because of the variable geometry of the sections, which are oval, ogival, triangular and keyhole shaped. There are also some morphologies, mentioned before, remelting stalactites, stretches of lava 'ropes' and some roots here and there of plants growing above the roof of the cave, determined to survive despite the harshness of the volcanic rock and managing to find what little moisture they need through the fissures.

If, however, you want to accompany your visit to a cave with a pleasant walk through the woods, pretty countryside and across lava flows, we recommend the Lampioni (Raspberry) Cave.

To reach it you have to take the Mareneve road that climbs from Linguglossa towards Ragabo Pine-Wood.

When you reach the Brunek mountain hut (1,400 metres), you turn right along an unsurfaced road and after about 1.7 km the road is barred at the point where Zone

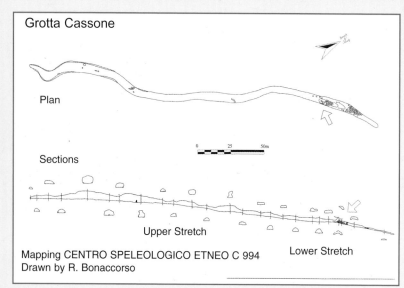

Grotta Cassone

Plan

Sections

0   25   50m

Upper Stretch

Lower Stretch

Mapping CENTRO SPELEOLOGICO ETNEO C 994
Drawn by R. Bonaccorso

Top: Ice Cave.
Facing page bottom: Raspberry Cave.

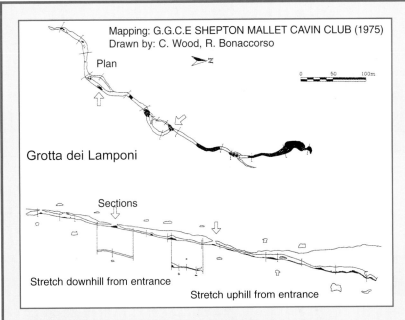

Mapping: G.G.C.E SHEPTON MALLET CAVIN CLUB (1975)
Drawn by: C. Wood, R. Bonaccorso

Plan

Grotta dei Lamponi

Sections

0   50   100m

Stretch downhill from entrance

Stretch uphill from entrance

Raspberry Cave, although the entrance is about 30 metres further up, on the lava flows of 1614-24, called Passo dei Dammusi.

This itinerary can be linked to the classic tour around Etna from south to north along the high mountain route, on the western slopes of the volcano.

The Raspberry Cave (1,745 metres) is a lava flow tunnel about 750 metres long. It has two entrances, with raspberry plants growing in one of them, hence the name. It is, therefore, easier and more interesting to walk along the stretch between the two entrances and then continue up the tunnel until it is completely blocked.

In this final part you need a strong torch and we advise the use of a protective helmet. The cave is of considerable dimensions and has sections of great variety, ending in a large ellipse in the deepest part of the tunnel.

A of the Park begins on the high mountain route. From here you put on your backpack and continue on foot (access for vehicles must be authorised).

The route is very pleasant and you cross fragrant woodland, the lava flows of 1923, 1911 and 1947 and get a spectacular view of the Alcantara Valley.

After about 5km you come to a junction (1,612 metres), where the right fork leads down to a Forestry Service building and the fenced-off entrance to the Palombe Cave.

Continuing straight on at the junction, on the other hand, after about 2km you come to a place right in front of the

For more detailed information contact
CENTRO SPELEOLOGICO ETNEO
(Etna Caving Centre) in via Cagliari, 15
95127 CATANIA Tel/Fax 095/437018
E-mail: csemail@tin.it
or the GRUPPO GROTTE C.A.I. CATANIA
(Italian Alpine Club Caving Group)
in Piazza Scammacca, 1 Tel 095/7153515

Giuseppe Garozzo

MANIACE: THE ADMIRAL'S FEUD

Just over ten kilometres from Bronte, a short distance from Nelson's Duchy, stands **Maniace**, which can be reached along the Bronte-Maniace provincial road. The name of this recently created municipality is linked to the old abbey of Santa Maria di Maniace, which, in turn, was so called because of the wish of Queen Margaret, who had it built in honour of the Byzantine General who managed to defeat the Arabs.

The town stands in a green valley, already well known for its fertility during the Arab domination. It was sparsely populated for centuries and at the end of the 18th century it became part of the feud that Ferdinand IV donated to Admiral Nelson, who helped to restore the fortunes of the area.

Two good reasons for visiting Maniace are the **patronal Feast of Saint Sebastian**, which takes place on the third Sunday in January, and the **Peach and Pear Festival** from 6th to 8th August, which includes tasting of these succulent fruits in the town square.

RESTAURANTS

• LA CONTEA: Corso Margherita, 69. Family run trattoria where you can try the local cuisine. we recommend the pork and lamb cooked in traditional ways.

FARM HOLIDAYS

• NELSON: via Dispensa, 7 (tel. 095 690806). Accommodation available in rooms or apartments. Excursions on horseback. Restaurant and sales of local produce.

Top: fruit trees in blossom.
Left: meadows at Maniace.

MALETTO: PRETTY LITTLE TOWN

Just six kilometres separate Bronte from **Maletto**, a small town situated at high altitude (more than 900 metres) on the north-western slopes of Etna.

It is surrounded by charming mountain scenery, thick woodland alternating with lava landscapes characterised by the presence of old volcanic cones, while at lower altitudes the countryside is gentler thanks to the presence of vineyards and orchards.

Given the nature of this area and its great beauty, Maletto is a good base for walks and longer **hikes** in the mountains. If you are interested in the latter we particularly recommend

excursions to Monte Scavo and Monte Maletto (1,780m and 1,770m respectively), old extinct craters from which you can enjoy marvellous views.

If you are fond of **bird-watching** we suggest a trip to the **Saracena Valley**, which is characterised by the presence of the Saraceno river and several ponds and numerous species of aquatic birds.

Although legend has it that the name Maletto comes from that of a not clearly identified Princess Maretta, in reality the town was founded in the late 13th century by the Count of Mineo Manfredi Maletto. The Count had a castle built, of which only a few ruins still exist, around which the original town grew up. Apart from various cataclysms and volcanic eruptions, the history of the town is tied to the powerful Spatafora family, the undisputed masters of Maletto from the 15th century until the abolition of feudalism.

The ruins of the mediaeval **Castle**, built by the founder of the town, are situated on a hilltop in the town centre. Other buildings of historical-monumental interest in the town are the **Church of Saint Michael Archangel**, which still maintains part of its original 16th century elements, the **Church of Saint Anthony Abbot**, dating from the 18th century, and the **Cathedral**, built in the late 19th century.

The area around Maletto is interesting from an archaeological point of view. At **Tartarici** tombs and caves have been discovered, while at **Rocca Calanna** megalithic remains from prehistoric times have been identified.

Now let's put aside nature, art and archaeology and change the subject completely.

The pride and joy of Maletto is undoubtedly its **strawberries**. The town has become famous all over Italy for its production of this delicious fruit.

There are also a lot of **pistachios** produced here and these often end up in the local cakes as one of their main ingredients (you can buy excellent pistachio cakes at the **confectioner's Orefice** in Piazza IV Novembre).

The local **cheeses** and **ricotta** are also exquisite. If you want to purchase these or other local produce just head for the grocery shops or go directly to the local farmers and shepherds.

On March 19th the town celebrates a religious festival: the **Feast of Saint Joseph** sees the traditional preparation of the *'sfilateddi che ciciri'* and rice 'crespelle' with honey.

In the second half of June the people of Maletto pay homage to the driving force of the local economy by holding the charming **Strawberry Festival**, including a display and market of strawberries and other local produce, tasting, folklore, drama and music.

In July and August another enjoyable event is organised: the **Malettese Summer**, with reviews of music, drama, dance and cabaret. In October the **Grape Festival** is held.

RESTAURANTS

- DA ZINO: SS 284 - contrada Tartaraci (tel. 095 699234). Restaurant-pizzeria. We recommend the home-made starters, the fettucine and the maccheroni with 'ferla' mushrooms.
- FONTANA MURATA: SS 284 (tel. 095 698196). Home-made starters, pasta cooked in paper and speciality grills.

Bottom: panoramic view of Maletto.

PAPPALARDO HOUSES (1,220 M)-MONTE MALETTO MOUNTAIN HUT-1975-76 LAVA FLOWS (1,800 M)-MONTE SCAVO (1,700 M)

MALETTO: 5th ITINERARY ROUTE
Duration: 5 and a half hours
Total distance: 14 km
Difference in height: 580 metres

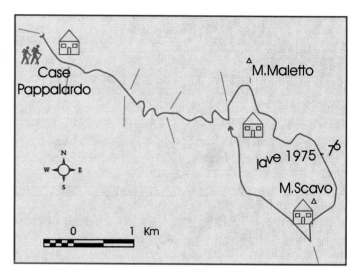

From Catania you head for Randazzo along the SS 284 road. After passing the turn off for Maletto, a small town on the north-western slopes of the volcano famous for its wonderful strawberries, you continue for another kilometre before turning right, firstly downhill, along a narrow road that passes a spring.

The cart-track you are now following runs between high drystone walls that alternate with small vineyards and sparse woodland composed of holm oaks and common oaks; after about 700 metres the cart track joins another wider one, that merges from the left.

You leave your car in front of a gate that blocks access to the public owned forest and continue on foot until you come to the small group of Pappalardo houses and their water tank after a few minutes.

At first the route runs through holm oak woodland, which

then opens up to give you a view of the summit craters.

Alongside the pathway the vegetation is at first characterised by replanted cedars of the Atlantic variety and then, further up, by a wood of Corsican pines. Once you reach the high mountain route, you turn left, following it for about a hundred metres, and then move off to the right where the track climbs up towards the Monte Maletto mountain hut. Here you can stop off, rest and refill your water bottles; nearby you can visit the Vanette Cave.

After you start walking again you find that the track is blocked after a little more than a kilometre because of one of the branches of the 1975-76 lava flow, which ran across it. The path that now lets you cross the lava flow also lets you enjoy views of the steep slopes leading up to the summit craters and the final stretches of trees, at an altitude of 2,250 metres, above all beech trees that bend right over, almost parallel with the ground, given the difficulties of survival at such high altitudes.

At the same time their presence on Etna represents a limit of latitude, indeed it is impossible to find these trees at lower latitudes, given their preference for colder climates.

Leaving behind Monte Maletto, the view down into the valley includes Monte Nunziata, the Monti De Fiore and Monte Egitto.

This is the highest point on the itinerary, before re-entering the wood and then returning onto the track that leads to Monte Scavo. At the foot of this mountain you can take advantage of the welcoming hut before starting off again, back down the same track used to climb up, taking you back to your departure point.

THE BEECH WOOD OF MONTE SPAGNOLO

RANDAZZO: 6th ITINERARY ROUTE
Total distance: 3 hours
Total distance: 11 km
Difference in height: 290 metres

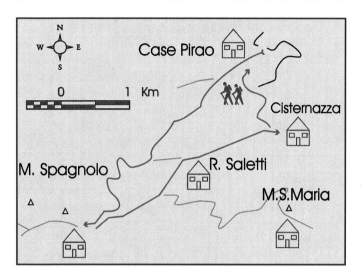

In the United States they call them "colour trips", trips to take a look at the colour shades of autumn, when the immense maple forests of North America 'catch fire' and take on all possible tones of yellow and orange.

Here on Etna you can make a more limited, but no less exciting, "colour trip" on the northern slopes of Etna around Monte Spagnolo, where you can find the most beautiful beech wood on the volcano. Throughout autumn, from September onwards the wood that stretches from the 1981 lava flow as far as the Sciara del Follone and westwards as far as the Monte Pomiciaro area is transformed in preparation for the first snows.

If you want to 'dive' into this sea of colours, we recommend leaving from the Pirao Houses area, which can be reached from Maletto by turning onto the panoramic road to Linguaglossa before arriving in the town of Randazzo; once you have passed the obvious lava flow of 1981 you take the first tarmacked road on the right, which climbs up the mountain.

After about three kilometres you come to a start of a forest track from where you can see the Pirao Houses, situated a little higher up on a panoramic knoll. You can leave your car in front of the gate and start along the track on foot. From here you begin a pleasant circular walk that lets you admire the splendid autumn colours of the Monte Spagnolo beech wood. In an hour and a half you climb up from an altitude of 1,150 metres at the car park through interesting vegetation, characterised above al by large broom bushes.

After turning right at a sign-posted junction, you pass the 1981 lava flow in the middle of which you can see some characteristic 'petracannuni' (tree trunks covered by fluid lava that take on the appearance of "cannon barrels" once the wood has rotted), until you come into the shade of large secular beech trees (1,450 metres).

This wood is one of the few that have been subjected to very few interventions and can be considered one of the most valuable zones of the whole Etna Park from the point of view of its unspoilt natural environment.

According to some experts access should be completely closed off, at least in a large area of the wood, in order to completely conserve the environment intact and to be able to observe the unfolding developments of nature. We warn you in advance that if you come to this area the Monte Spagnolo Barracks - marked on all the maps - has been abandoned and is no longer fit for use.

If it rains unexpectedly your only choice is (if you are a small group) to take shelter in the small rustic lava stone building, renovated years ago by the Sicilian Regional Forestry Service and situated right in front of the barracks. All around you stretches the beech wood along with some reforested areas of trees not really native to Etna, planted years ago by the Forestry Service.

In order to enter the main part of the wood you have to follow the pathway that branches off to the east, about fifty metres before the ruins of the barracks. In this way you can cover several hundred metres in this extraordinary autumn scenario, until you reach the impressive lava flow of 1981.

A specially created pathway guides among the explosive cones and effusive cracks as far as the eastern edge of the lava flow, where you will come across dried tree trunks that were not burnt despite the intense heat.

Beyond the black lava there is another stretch of beech wood and a little further on (about 200 metres from the lava flow) you go back onto the high mountain route.

At this point you have to go down to the left in order to quickly reach the Saletti mountain hut (1,374 metres), which has become one of the favourites with walkers in recent years. In front of the hut there is a drinking fountain connected to the water tank, tempting you to take a refreshing pause.

You carry on downhill turning right, so leaving the high mountain route and therefore heading for the Cisternezza (an obvious circular building at an altitude of 1,342 metres situated at the end of a short detour made by the cart track to the east, very near Monte Collabasso), which can be reached in about 20 minutes from Saletti.

At this point you have almost completed the circular route. There are still some hairpin bends on the forest track before you catch sight of a clear narrow road on the left that goes down towards the Pirao Houses. In order not to make mistakes just remember that the latter turn off is situated no more than twenty metres from the point in which the tarmacked road ends.

Overall the circular route is about 11 kilometres long and can therefore be comfortably completed in 3 hours, plus the time you wish to take to stop and admire the various natural beauties of the environment.

RANDAZZO: ONE IN THREE

Following the SS 284 road you arrive in **Randazzo** after about a dozen kilometres.

It has a pleasant climate, due to its position at a moderate altitude of about 700 metres, and an unspoilt luxuriant natural climate, making it a very popular tourist destination, also because it is the nearest town to the volcano. If you enjoy **excursions**, **hiking**, **bird-watching** or **horse-riding** you will be spoilt for choice about where to go (if you want to go on a guided excursion, contact the local CAI office, via Umberto 189 tel. 339 6399399).

The origins of Randazzo are quite confused and the hypotheses made regarding them seem to be quite improbable. We will limit ourselves, therefore, to the two most probable ones. According to some people Randazzo can be traced back to the Greek city of Rinacium but, despite the finds of Hellenic artefacts, it should be remembered that many experts identify Rinacium with Geraci (in the province of Palermo). The other hypothesis, prudently supported by the historian Amari, says that the name of the town comes from that of Randaches, governor of Taormina in Byzantine times.

The foundation of the present town can be attributed to the Normans, who first began to build public and private build-

ings here. Randazzo was almost immediately divided into three districts: the Santa Maria district, inhabited by the Normans called Latins, that of San Nicola, populated by Orthodox Christians called Greeks, and that of San Martino, where the Lombards lived. Under the Swabians, thanks to Henry VI and the great Frederick, Randazzo took on the role of a fortress-town. It was Frederick II that had the Church of Santa Maria built and brought Randazzo into the circle of state owned towns. The War of the Vespers, despite its bloody battles, marked the beginning of the economic and artistic rise of Randazzo. Indeed, the Royal Family lived in the town with their noble Sicilian court and turned the town into a real artistic jewel. It was the Bourbons, with their policy of repression, that brought an end to Randazzo's long period of splendour.

Although the town has been constantly exposed to the dangers of damage or destruction by Etna, given its nearness to the volcano, it has survived natural calamities quite well, as is shown by its respectable architectural heritage. The only serious damage was that caused during the Second World War.

UNDER THE ARCHES OF TIME

Rather than visiting Randazzo, you should 'walk' it. Indeed, the ideal thing to do is to stroll around without any particular destination, letting yourself be charmed by the outlines of old ephemeral noble buildings, by the black of the lava stone with which the principal monuments of the oldest part of the town were built. This part of town has a cosy pleasantly old-fashioned atmosphere with its mediaeval layout of narrow covered streets.

However, although our natural advice would be to start from via Umberto, the main street in Randazzo, and to wander around aimlessly, we cannot resist the temptation to head for the most beautiful places and monuments in town.

Examples of mediaeval streets can be found in **via Frisauli**, characterised by the presence of arches, and **via Degli**

Top: two-mullioned window in via degli Archi.
Left: Church of Santa Maria.

Archi, which owes its name to the numerous round-headed arches.

In Piazza Basilica stands the **Basilica Minore**, also called the Church of Santa Maria. The Church was built in the early XIII century using lava stone that characterises the black facade, with the splendid bell-tower in the centre, on which you will notice the elegant white decorations and the round-headed arches of the portals and the windows. The present appearance, however, has been strongly influenced by the renovations undergone over the centuries after its construction. The cupola is an 19th century addition by the illustrious architect Venazio Marvuglia. The interior has three naves and contains works of art of great value, including two paintings by Velasquez and a 10th century

enlivened by the two-coloured effect created by the lava stone of the semi-columns. The exterior of the imposing apses is beautiful with their embattled towers. Inside the three naves, divided by columns, you can see notable works of art, including a 16th century multi-coloured sculpture by Antonello Gagini depicting Saint Nicholas.

Right opposite the Church of Saint Nicholas is situated the statue of the Cyclops Piracmone, locally known as Old Randazzo.

Piazza Municipio is overlooked by the Town Hall, which is situated in the premises of an ex-convent, of which you can see the characteristic cloister, and the **Swabian Castle**.

The Castle has been recently restored and was once part of the 14th century city fortifications, which consisted of eight towers, of which the Castle is the only surviving element, and of the city walls, which still stand in some places. You can see an example of these in a stretch that includes the Gate of Saint Martin, in the district of the same name. Inside the Castle you can visit the Paolo Vagliasindi Archaeological Museum and an interesting **Sicilian Puppet Collection**, constituted by paladins of the cycle of the 'Chanson de geste'.

The **Paolo Vagliasindi Archaeological Museum** collects together material largely from the district of Sant'Anastasia, a few kilometres from Randazzo. The artefacts displayed in the Museum are mostly vases of Corinthian, Ion-

fresco. The baroque style main altar is also very interesting.

Near the Cathedral is the "**Tribonia**", a viewpoint from where you can admire the wonderful view of the Alcantara Valley. In the ancient district of San Martino, once inhabited by the Lombards, stands the **Church of Saint Martin** with an austere facade, flanked by a superb Gothic style bell-tower in lava stone with elegant white windows in its embattled structure. Inside the three naves there is a precious ivory reliquary from the late 14th century.

In Piazza San Nicolò stands the great **Church of Saint Nicholas**, built in the 13th century, with an appearance that can be traced back to the 16th century restoration and the renovations of the following century. The white facade is

ian and Attic production. The most important piece in the collection is a wine vase, called 'oinochoe Vagliasindi', dating back to the late 5th century BC.

There are two other museums in Randazzo that are certainly worth visiting. At the Santa Giovanna Antida Institute, in Piazza Roma, you will find the **Civic Natural Science Museum**.

This museum was set up in 1983 and brings together various collections of great historical-scientific inportance. There is the splendid Priolo ornithological collection, one of the richest in Europe, which also includes birds that are now extinct on the Island. There are also very interesting collections of minerals, fossils, lepidopterans and coleopterans.

At the Church of Santa Maria della Volta, in Piazza San Nicolò, you can visit the **Farm Tool Collection**. The Museum exhibits numerous everyday and ornamental objects. There is a very good reconstruction of the phases of wine production.

RECOMMENDED EXCURSIONS

Walks on Etna and in the Nebrodi mountains are not the only possible excursions to be made around Randazzo. There are really a lot of destinations but here we will limit ourselves to two easy excursions for people who love visiting historical places and those who prefer the open air life.

Heading towards Cesarò on the SS 120 road you come to **Murazzo Rotto**, a small renaissance period village of great charm, just two kilometres from Randazzo, and, a little further on, the **Gurrida Lake**, a depression of alluvial origin, which is filled seasonally by the waters of the Flascio river following the blockage caused by a lava flow. Nearby, lovers of bird-watching can engage in their favourite pastime on the banks of an artificial lake, crowded with migrating birds that stop here to rest.

SOMETHING FOR EVERYBODY

Local cuisine uses genuine ingredients (such as 'ferla' and 'porcini' mushroom varieties, wild asparagus, cheeses, charcuterie, extra-virgin olive oil) to produce really delicious meals that are always accompanied by good locally produced **wine**.

In order to try genuine Randazzo cuisine head for the **trattorias La Trottola** in via Basile, **San Giorgio e il Drago** in Piazza San Giorgio, **Veneziano** in via Dei Romano, the latter offers home cooking, home-made pasta and exquisite roasts.

If you prefer a good pizza you can eat at the pizzerias **La Ginestra**, in via IV Novembre, and **La Fontana**, in via Romeo.

For cakes we suggest the almond pastries to be found at **Arturo**, **Caffè del Corso** and the **bar-confectioners' Arturo Facondo** (which is also a **pub**), **Pippo Facondo** all in corso Umberto, **Lo Presti** in Piazza Vagliasindi (excellent almond pastries), **Musumeci** (delicious ice-creams).

If you want to buy **handmade souvenirs** the best thing to do is to stop off at one of the many workshops in the centre of town: objects in **lava stone**, **pottery**, **wood**, **copper**, **wrought iron** (one of the 'experts' in pottery is undoubtedly **Arcidiacono** and "il momento" run by Di Stefano for artistic ceramics). There is also a large picturesque **market** held every Sunday morning in Piazza Loreto.

If you have green fingers we suggest a visit to the **Russo Nursery**, on the edge of town if you are coming from Maletto, selling plants of every kind, including those typical of the local area, such as the pistachio.

As regards accommodation we suggest three places to satisfy varying requirements.

Hotel Scrivano, in Piazza Loreto, completely renovated with full facilities and a restaurant.

Farm holiday centres L'Antica Vigna and **Vallebruna**, in contrada Montelaguardia. These are two neighbouring farms.

At the Antica Vigna you can stay overnight, even in winter, and buy naturally grown produce.

At Vallebruna you can make excursions on horseback or by mountain-bike. There are also facilities for tennis, basketball and volleyball.

The **Pirao Houses Mountain Hut Club** is on the ESA road at an altitude of 1,000 metres. This a departure point for excur-

From the top: artefact displayed in the Vagliasindi Museum, mediaeval alleyway, near Randazzo.

sions up Etna and into the Nebrodi mountains. A restaurant service and tasting of local cheeses are available on request. Open from April to September.

FESTIVALS AND SPLENDOUR

The calendar of festivals and events in the town is rich and varied and includes religious, secular, cultural, naturalistic and gastronomic celebrations.

We begin with the month of December and the **Christmas in the Streets** festival. This includes a living crib, novenas in dialect, the lighting of 'zucchi', huge bonfires of wood.

Also in December there is the **Parks Festival**. This event is organised by the Etna and Nebrodi Park Authorities and the municipality of Randazzo, who lay on trips on horseback and

by mountain-bike, as well as entertainment in the town centre. On the first Sunday in June the **Feast of Our Lady of the Annunciation** is celebrated in Piazza Loreto.

In the last week of July the **Mediaeval Festival** takes place in the town centre. There is a re-enactment of the story of Bianca di Navarra, concerts, round tables, exhibitions and mediaeval feasts.

On 15th August **'A Vara** is a solemn procession of the triumphant carriage of the Assumption with real-life characters.

Also in August the **Randazzese August Festival** sees events of various kinds throughout the month.

On the third Sunday of September the **Feast of Our Lady of Sorrows** is celebrated in Piazza San Pietro.

In October the **Grape Harvest Festival** includes entertainment and tasting (you must try the grape juice and must-cake).

RESTAURANTS - TRATTORIAS - PIZZERIAS

- BRISTOL PARK: contrada Calderaro (tel. 095 924068). Restaurant-pizzeria. We recommend the mushrooms and the panzotti with pistachio.
- CASTELLO ROMEO: via Montelaguardia (tel. 095 921126 - 921433). Restaurant-pizzeria in a beautiful setting. Try the maccheroni 'Villa Romeo' and the pizza 'del Castello'.
- IL SOGNO: contrada Statella (tel. 095 7991627). Restaurant-pizzeria. Mushroom based specialities. Home-made starters, fresh maccheroni with mushrooms, barbecued meat.
- LA FONTANA: via Romeo, 44 (tel. 095 923621). Pizzeria.
- LA GINESTRA: via IV Novembre, 66 (tel. 095 7991864). Restaurant-pizzeria. Exquisite pasta 'alla boscaiola', pappardelle with mushrooms, rabbit 'alla cacciatora'.
- LA TROTTOLA: via G. Basile, 44 (tel. 095 921187). Trattoria-pizzeria. Local cuisine. Very good home-made maccheroni.
- SCRIVANO: via G. Bonaventura (tel. 095 921433). Hotel restaurant. Traditional Randazzo dishes prepared by the able chef. Excellent mushroom and pistachio specialities. We recommend the falsomagro (stuffed meat roll) 'alla randazzese' with pistachio, ham and wild fennel.
- TRATTORIA SAN GIORGIO E IL DRAGO: Piazza San Giorgio, 28 (tel. 095 923972). Local cuisine. Try the rabbit.
- TRATTORIA VENEZIANO: via Dei Romano, 8 (tel. 095 7991353). Very refined cuisine. Try the mushroom salads, the tagliolini with wild asparagus, the roast 'provola' cheese. Good choice of wines.

HOTELS
- SCRIVANO ♥ ♥ ♥: via Bonaventura (tel./fax 095 921126). Hotel right in the centre with car park, garden, bar and restaurant.

FARM HOLIDAYS
- L'ANTICA VIGNA: locality Montelaguardia (tel. 095 924003 fax 095 923324). Restaurant with naturally grown produce. Sales of must-cake, wine, oil, fresh and dried fruit. Excursions on foot and on horseback. Children's playground, tennis court and table football.
- VALLEBRUNA: locality Montelaguardia (tel. 095 924046 fax 095 923324). Also a residence.

Top: Feast of Our Lady of the Assumption.
Left: Mediaeval Festival.

The Mediaeval festival in Randazzo

Every year since 1995, in the last week of July and the first week of August, the Mediaeval Festival has been held, characterised by an impressive historical parade. The young people of Randazzo re-enact the visit to Randazzo by the vicaress of the kingdom, which took place in 1411.

The event is dedicated to Queen Bianca of Navarra, one of the most important figures in the Aragonese period and, apart from the folklore and simple historical re-enactment, it aims to reassess the image of a courageous woman whose memory has survived for centuries in silence and great humility. The costumes, music, songs and dances faithfully reproduce those of the historical period that is

represented; even the shape of the clothes is taken from 15th century iconography. There are over a hundred characters in 15th century costumes, representing the court with the Queen, the ladies-in-waiting, the knights and the pageboys; the common people with the musicians, the jesters, the dancers and the minstrels; the soldiers with their armour, trumpets and drums.

Dancing, trumpet blasts, drum rolls, musicians and jesters bring the festival to life and all contribute to creating a magical and electrifying effect that infects all those present. There is also a gastronomic side to things. Mediaeval banquets are held in Piazza San Nicola and in the cloister in Piazza Municipio. The menu is full of surprises. You can rediscover flavours of long ago: ginger, rose water, cloves and green pepper. The numerous dishes on offer include lasagne with herbs, wild boar sausages, 'biancomangiare', hare, rabbit and roast suckling-pig cooked on a spit in the square.

Such a full programme as this has made the festival one of the most interesting historical re-enactments in Sicily. The festival is organised by the Sicularagonensia Association in conjunction with the Municipality of Randazzo and has the aim of bringing together the development of tourism in the town and showing off its historical and artistic heritage.

Giuseppe Gangemi

HAMLETS OF ETNA

The origin of the hamlets is lost in the dim and distant past, so in some cases it is not possible to talk of definite and verifiable facts, however it is interesting and fascinating to quote an extract from "Le Zolle Hisoriche Catanesi" by Giovanbattista Guarneri, who died in 1665. "…Cham and Sena his wife and his sons and daughters, including Saturno and Zanelot, as well as Giganti, Ciclopi and Lestrigoni came to Sicily…They occupied the land at the foot of the mountain, stayed there, built accommodation, hunting-lodges, small bare stone houses…" But what remains in the Etna area as evidence of the presence of ancient settlements? The area, in particular the southern foothills, is full of natural volcanic cavities.

Some of them open up on ancient lava flows and were lived in by prehistoric man: the Petralia Cave, which lies under the *leucatia-liardo-de logu road*, for example, is 700 metres long. Here in 1990 precious evidence from the Bronze Age was found, along with utensils and pottery from the Castelluccio culture; the Nuovalucello I Cave; the four caves of the Immacolatelle complex and the Micio Conti Cave in the S. Gre-

gorio district, with prehistoric evidence, are just a few of the examples that have remained miraculously intact as proof that these places were inhabited in far-off times.

Moving on to more recent times, hamlets followed the same historical trends as the city: the Greek period is testified to by cinerary urns and tear-bottles found in 1872 at Monte Serra in Viagrande; the Roman period is represented by the Roman spas (Tammusi) in Misterbianco and Mascalucia, by the artefacts found on the hill known as Windmill Hill at Trecastagni, decorated funereal urns in terracotta, Roman tear-

Right: detail of San Giovanni La Punta Cathedral.

bottles and coins; then, in the Trinità district of Mascalucia, in 1800, a huge mosaic floor, clay columns and lead gargoyles of the Roman period were found.

Mascalucia was called Massalargia, from the Latin 'massa' (village) 'largia' (gift), indeed it was donated by the Emperor Constantine to the Holy See: the Romans called aggregations of people 'masse' or 'stationes'. These lands, or villages, so rich and fertile, were greatly contested over the centuries and passed repeatedly from the Papacy to the Royal Treasury and vice versa.

In 962 Otto I promised to restore the lands to the Pope as soon as the Saracens had been thrown out of Sicily.

The Normans succeeded in chasing out the Saracens and in 1091 Count Roger granted the Bishop of Catania Ansgerio a huge area of land, including, apart from the city, the hamlets, the wood and also other lands, Aci, Paternò, Adernò etc.. As a result of this donation the Bishop had all the prerogatives and powers typical of Kings and Princes in their domains.

Certain information regarding Viagrande can be traced back to 1124, when a church was built in the Rinazzo district. The ruins remained in existence until recently. Trecastagni certainly existed in 1302, as is shown by the inscription on the Bianco bell in the Church of the Bianchi Confraternity.

In the district of Catia, in S. Giovanni La Punta, on the heights of S. Basilio, there existed a small Byzantine basilica, destroyed in the earthquake of 1329.

Later, in 1410, the Benedictines built a church dedicated to Saint Nicolò on the western side of the heights and this became a parish in 1418.

The oldest written document referring to Pedara dates back to 1388 and is a bull by which the Bishop of Catania authorised the construction of the first parish. In the 'Rationes Decimarum' of the Vatican archives for the year 1308 the church of Saint Nicholas in Mascalucia is already mentioned as a parish. The latter is a very interesting hamlet.

In 1337, after the death of Frederick of Aragon, Queen Eleanor, his wife, wished to live a solitary and religious life and took up residence in the district called Le Guardie, today known as Santa Spera.

A Papal bull of 1446 declared the church of 'de Tribus Monasteris' (Tremestieri) a parish.

So far I have mentioned just a few of the centres that make up, together with others, the so called 'hamlets of the city of

Catania', in an attempt to show a certain homogenous evolution of these hamlets.

But how many people lived in these rich and contested places? And how many lived in the city? Well, it may seem incredible but the ratio between hamlets and city has remained almost unchanged for a thousand years. Not only!

The ruling class and many aristocratic families lived in the places of production, undoubtedly in those days agricultural and food production, while they had somebody representing them in the City Senate, if not they personally then a relative, and in all the public structures of Catania.

Pippo Di Lorenzo

President Italian Archeology Club S. Giovanni La Punta

Top: town centre and Mascalucia Cathedral bell-tower.

81

THE CUISINE OF THE PEOPLE OF ETNA

The cuisine of the people of the Etna area, which has spread over the millenniums along the Ionian Sea coast and up the sides of the fiery-spirited mountain, avails itself of numerous dishes that could be defined as tempting.

While the populations of Trapani and Palermo were initially submitted to the influence of the Phoenicians, the people of the Etna area, Messina and Syracuse underwent the more cultured influence of Greek colonisation. With the arrival of the Greeks, the bearers of a more advanced civilisation, the Ionian populations of Catania, Messina and Syracuse inherited not only their alphabet, stolen by the Greeks from the Phoenicians, but also the gastronomic habits of the new arrivals. Moreover, Etna cuisine, compared to others, took advantage of the vegetables and vines growing on the volcano, and this is still the case today. The lava scoriae, along with the fertile ground, have a beneficial effect on the produce of the earth and give it an extra touch in terms of flavour and appearance.

In Roman times the Plain of Catania became the granary of Rome, thanks to the abundance and quality of its spelt and wheat, from which various types of flour were obtained.

The Arabs brought to Sicily new techniques for the raising of irrigation waters. The people of Etna began to exploit the snow and rain that fell on the volcano above the height of 3,000 metres. The water reserves were channelled into the '*gebbie*', from here into the '*saie*' and finally raised by the '*zenia*', all Arabic words, still used in local dialect, to indicate irrigation techniques. Under the Arabs the Etna area was given over to lemon and orange groves, like the 'Golden Valley' of Palermo, and rice was introduced. Rice is still the main ingredient of '*tummula di risu*', a local Christmas and New Year dish, for which I will give a quick recipe at the end.

The great love of the people of Catania, as far as cooking

is concerned, is fish, generally preferred to meat. They have a passionate love for '*masculini*', fresh anchovies from the Gulf of Catania; a classic starter is small anchovies cooked with bitter lemon and then served with garlic, oil, salt, parsley and chilli pepper.

These anchovies are also used to make '*pasta ca nnocca*', that is 'with the bow', Catania's answer to Palermo's pasta with sardines. The bow is made up of gutted anchovies, with their heads removed, cooked with peas, tomato sauce and wild fennel.

However, the true symbol of Catania's cuisine is '*pasta alla Norma*', with tomato sauce flavoured with basil and garlic, with plenty of grated salted ricotta cheese on top of slices of fried aubergine placed on the pasta, along with large leaves of raw majore basil.

Other typical local dishes are the 'dark' pasta with cuttlefish ink, in which the concentrated tomato sauce, when cooked, is mixed with the black cuttlefish ink, giving it an unmistakable sharp taste; the ancient '*pasta 'a Milansia*', in other words with breadcrumbs and salted anchovies, simple to prepare, and which takes us back to the Middle Ages, when the Lombards came to Randazzo to teach the art of silk manufacture. '*Pasta 'a Milansia*' was and is served with lightly toasted breadcrumbs and mixed with small pieces of salted and boned anchovies, half-cooked in oil with garlic (the garlic of Randazzo is ideal, with its unique fragrance and fleshiness); raw chopped parsley is an optional extra.

Christmas '*schiacciate*', derived from Spanish 'empanadillas', are typical of the Etna area: two round pieces of bread dough, baked and stuffed with melted tuma cheese and pieces of salted anchovy. The salted anchovies are also present, from Christmas to Saint Joseph's Day, in '*sfince*', pancakes of soft raised dough, fried with oil and lard, enclosing pieces of salted anchovy or sifted sheep's ricotta.

These are some of the specialities of local rotisserie, to

Top: 'biancomangiare'. Left: anchovies in orange.

which we should add the rice 'arancini', filled with ragù sauce, peas, onion and fresh pecorino cheese.

In the last twenty years restaurants have been opened on the slopes of Etna serving excellent seafood risottos, sometimes along with mushrooms, asparagus or other wild vegetables, and seafood salads with octopus, prawns and squid, dressed with garlic, oregano, oil, salt, chilli pepper and lemon juice. However, it must be said that in places such as 'La Grotta' run by Don Carmelo, 'Il Molino' in S. Maria la Scala, 'La Scogliera' run by the Tripodo family and 'La Grotta Azzurra' between Ognina and Canizzaro the seafood salads and soups are a different thing altogether.

You can also find good original Etna cuisine in the restaurants 'Poggio Ducale, 'Rigoletto', 'Siciliana' (all in Catania), 'La Pigna' and 'Paradiso dell'Etna' (San Giovanni La Punta) and 'Parco dei Principi' (Zafferana Etnea), the best known restaurant for tasting Etna mushrooms.

With regard to sauces we should mention that the 'salmoriglio' sauce has two versions: white and red. White salmoriglio is exquisite both with meat and fish and is obtained by beating boiling water and extra virgin olive oil with a fork.

Once you have a light delicate mixture, you add salt, pepper, parsley leaves and chopped garlic, oregano and lemon juice. 'Pollo alla diavola' (spicy chicken) flavoured with white salmoriglio is excellent. Red salmoriglio is served with barbecued meat and fish and is obtained by mixing tomato pulp, barbecued with skin and seeds removed, with olive oil, pieces of garlic, oregano and parsley.

Delicate veal meatballs roasted between two large lemon leaves and served with red salmoriglio are excellent and are served today as an original starter.

The prime meat dish in Catania remains 'falsomagro', that is a large thick slice of veal or beef which is richly stuffed - with boiled eggs, strips of lard and caciocavallo cheese, minced meat on slices of mortadella - and then rolled up and tied with kitchen string.

This braise can then be put in the 'gran ragù della festa etnèa', a sauce made of tomato conserve, lightly fried meatballs, chunks of sausage and pork rind.

Also worthy of note are the artichokes 'a fucuneddu', in other words cooked on an iron stove (in the open air).

They are whole roasted artichokes wrapped in layer after layer of breadcrumbs, grated cheese, cloves of garlic, parsley, pieces of anchovy and extra virgin olive oil.

Just a quick mention for the sweet side of Etna cuisine, which can be fully appreciated from the small pastries, 'granite' (those in Riposto are excellent) and ice-creams. In this area in the past ice-cream was made using snow from Etna, then Procopio de' Coltelli of Acireale made ice-cream famous in Paris during the Age of Enlightenment.

Now, as promised, here is the Christmas recipe for 'tummula di risu'.

Cook the rice 'al dente' in a good broth of chicken and 'nuzza', in other words turkey. Make a layer of rice about 5 cm thick in a buttered baking tray sprinkled with breadcrumbs and then cover the rice with pieces of boiled turkey and chicken, soft salami, Parma ham and cinnamon. Cover it all with slices of tume cheese, fresh pecorino cheese and mozzarella. Onto this pour plenty of 'gran ragù della festa etnèa' sauce with pieces of boiled egg yolk. Put on another layer of rice with chicken livers, moistened with a mixture of beaten eggs, grated parmesan or caciocavallo, salt, pepper and crushed parsley.

Then put into the oven at 180°. As soon as there is a golden crust on top, the 'tummula' is ready to be served. It can be cut into slices or served with more ragù sauce. Have a good meal!

Pino Correnti

Top: almond pastries. Right: pasta 'alla Norma'.

CASTIGLIONE DI SICILIA:
DATING BACK TO PREHISTORY

A little more than twenty kilometres along the SS 120 road separate Randazzo from **Castiglione di Sicilia**.

Castiglione di Sicilia is a picturesque hill town on the northern slopes of Etna and offers visitors one of the most varied landscapes in the province of Catania.

It is half way between the mountain and the sea and has become a tourist destination for those looking for a relaxing nature holiday. Luxuriant woodland, lava caves and farmland on which man has intervened to plant vines and fruit trees are the main attractions of the town, which is the departure point for exciting excursions onto one of the most interesting parts of Etna from a natural and geological point of view.

Considerable archaeological evidence found in the Castiglione area confirms man's presence here since prehistoric times.

The first definite traces of a settlement in the area of the present day town can be dated to the 5th century BC, according to some researchers. It is sure that under the Byzantines the site was of some importance, as is testified by the small holy building called 'Cuba', still the subject of extended research.

Present day Castiglione was founded by the Normans, who, after having thrown out the Arabs, began to build around the castle and to construct defensive walls.

The town was named Quastallum, in a clear reference to the castle, and began to assume a certain importance in the zone, also thanks to its privileged strategic position.

This importance was undoubtedly already well established in the 13th century, so much so that Frederick II decided to grant the town certain fiscal and administrative privileges.

The Aragonese changed the name Castellum into Castellione, probably just another word for castle, which has also been interpreted as castle of the lion.

The Aragonese were followed by the powerful family of the Pirrone Gioeni family. After a long period of decline, in the 17th century the town freed itself of feudal ties and became prosperous once more, numerous holy and civil buildings were put up, also thanks to the presence of an active and influential bourgeoisie.

FROM THE CASTLE TO THE CAVES

One of the most fascinating monuments in Castiglione is the famous **'Cuba'**, dedicated to Saint Domenica, a small Byzantine church with three naves dating back to the 8th-9th century, the remains of which can be found about two kilometres out of town.

What distinguishes the Cuba, and justifies its name, is its characteristic quadrangular shape with false cupola.

The building is of considerable architectural and artistic interest, being one of the few examples of Byzantine cubes still visible in an area that

Top: the Alcantara River and town of Castiglione. Left: view of Castiglione di Sicilia.

certainly contained numerous of them. Apart from the attention it receives from researchers, the Cuba is worth visiting because of its charming location and characteristic style.

The history of Castiglione is, however, mainly linked to three fortified structures of which there are remains of one kind or another.

The **Lion Castle** stands out on the high rock on which it was built with its compact structure, with lovely two-mullioned windows inserted on the second level. An ogival opening that is still present was the entrance to the Castle and could be defended from enemy attacks through a loophole.

The rock housed the residence of the feudal lord and his family and numerous facilities. Near the Lon Castle are the few remains of the so called '**Castelluzzo**', a structure that was entered by a stairway cut out of the rock. The third fortification, the '**Cannizzo**', which stands on a hill, is constituted by a cylindrical tower from Norman times, used as a watchtower.

The **Basilica of Our Lady of the Chain** was built in the 1700s but has been restored several times over the centuries. The 18th century facade, which is decorated with statues and characterised by a small portico, is the work of Baldassare Greco. Inside it has a Greek cross layout and is decorated with 19th century stuccoes. Here you can see the beautiful statue of Our Lady of the Chain, sculpted in the 16th century and usually attributed to Giacomo Gagini.

The **Church of Saint Anthony Abbot** is characterised by its concave 18th century facade, flanked by a massive bell-tower. The interior has a single nave and you can see numerous works of a certain importance, including the baroque confessional into which the pulpit is unusually inserted.

The **Cathedral** is dedicated to Saint Peter and is attributed to the Normans, even though its present appearance is the result of numerous alterations over the centuries. Inside it is worth looking at the 19th century meridian by the astro-

nomer Zona, canvases by Tuccari and the valuable 17th century wooden crucifix.

We also advise you to visit the **Church of Saint Benedict**, inside which you can admire a valuable canvas by D'Anna, situated on the main altar, depicting the Virgin; the small pretty **Municipal Park** behind which stands the **Church of Our Lady of the Carmine**, completely rebuilt in 1659 at the same time as the construction of the **Convent of the Carmelites**, which was completely renovated in the 1980s.

Finally, you should take a stroll through the mediaeval **Santa Maria district**, characterised by stairways, small houses and alleyways.

Those who are attracted by the beauties of nature as well as artistic-monumental ones are advised to make some excursions.

The **Grotta del Gelo** (Ice Cave) is particularly interesting, so called because it has a constant layer of ice on the walls, as is the **Grotta dei Lamponi** (Raspberry Cave), almost 700 metres

Top: altar and apse of the Basilica of Our Lady of the Chain. Left: the Cuba, dedicated to Saint Domenica.

long, and the **Grotta delle Femmine** (Women's Cave). If you enjoy hiking or bird-watching you should head for the **Alcàntara River**, which is situated in an area of outstanding natural beauty and is home to numerous species of mammals and birds.

A LITTLE OF EVERYTHING

The local cuisine uses simple ingredients, intelligently transformed into exquisite and imaginative delicacies. You should try the fresh maccheroni in rabbit sauce, the 'caponata', the pastry delicacies made from ricotta (such as *'sciauni'*) and nuts.

These and other dishes can be ordered in the restaurants and numerous bars and confectioners' in the town. In particular, among the **restaurants** we recommend **Club La Cuba** in contrada Sciambro, **Le Chevalier** in Piazza Lauria, **Belvedere d'Alcantara** in via A. Coniglio.

If you are fond of cheese you should head for **Alcantara Formaggi**, in via Federico II, where you can buy genuine tasty local cheeses, including excellent ricotta and delicious pecorino.

You can find lovely nut, almond and pistachio cakes in via Regina Margherita, where we suggest stopping off at the **Caffè President** and the **Bar-Confectioner's D'Amico**.

Another peculiarity of Castiglione is its **wines**, as strong as the volcano and as generous as the land. If you are interested in tasting or purchasing some you can try the **Boccadifuoco Estate of the Marquises of Anfittia**, a famous wine producing concern in via Pietramarina (tel.0942 986404), which produces high quality wines, including Turì red and Etna red.

Souvenir hunters should keep an eye open for the **artisans' workshops** in the town, especially those making objects from **wood**. In via Regina Margherita you can visit the workshop run by signor Finocchiaro, which produces **pendulum clocks**.

Just ask around to find one of the many women who sell their beautiful **embroidery** work.

It is not difficult to find accommodation in Castiglione but we recommend the **Piccolo Golf Club Farm Holiday Centre**, on the SS 120 Km200 in contrada Rovittello. It is situated at an altitude of 650 metres above sea level in beautiful countryside, with a bar, restaurant, and a well kept golf course for those who enjoy a round.

To end with, here are some of the most important events in town.

During the Christmas period there is the **Crib within the crib**; on the first Sunday of May the **patronal Feast of Our Lady of the Chain** is celebrated; in August **Etnalquantara** is a review of music, drama and dance held in the streets; in October the **International Women's Open Golf Tournament** takes place.

RESTAURANTS

- BELVEDERE D'ALCANTARA: via Abate Coniglio, 42 (tel. 0942 984397). Restaurant-pizzeria. Try the home-made maccheroni in rabbit sauce.
- CLUB LA CUBA: contrada Sciambro. Restaurant-pizzeria.
- LE CHEVALIER: Piazza Lauria, 12 (tel. 0942 984679). Sicilian cuisine. We recommend the sardines 'a beccafico'.
- REVIVAL: via Nazionale, 2 - Solicchiata.
- KASTALIA: via comunale Mitogio (tel.0942 985090). Tourist menu. Try the pennette 'alla boscaiola', the maccheroni 'alla Norma', pork and onion grill.
- IL PICCIOLO: SS 120 Km 200 - contrada Rovittello (tel. 0942 986252). Hotel restaurant.
  Situated in an old mill. Sicilian cuisine, Etna wines, including the Picciolo Red Etna DOC produced with grapes from the vineyard alongside the hotel. Excellent pennette 'al Vecchio Picciolo'.

HOTELS

- IL PICCIOLO ♥ ♥ ♥ ♥: SS 120 Km 200 - contrada Rovittello (tel. 0942 986252). With 18-hole golf course "Il Picciolo Golf Club". Restaurant and bar. Rooms with lovely views. The Picciolo offers wine and food itineraries, "wine tours", and courses in Sicilian cuisine.

FARM HOLIDAYS

- AZIENDA AGRICOLA BOCCA DI FUOCO DEI MARCHESI DI ANFITTIA: contrada Verzella (tel. 0942 986404). Restaurant for groups on booking. From the starters to the dessert, everything offered to guests is produced on the farm. Wine production and tasting.

ICE CAVE FROM
THE PITARRONE BARRACKS

CASTIGLIONE: 6th ITINERARY ROUTE
Total distance: 6 hours
Total distance: 18 km
Difference in height: 550 metres

In the middle of an expanse of black stones, modelled by fire and by time, in the blinding sunlight of Sicilian mountains, there is a micro-glacier that has formed inside a cave and which has an irresistible fascination: it is a rarity, a goody offered to us by nature in order to continue amazing us. This is how to explain the success of the Grotta del Gelo (Ice Cave) and the irresistible fascination it has held for mountain enthusiasts for decades.

Once upon a time there was a much more practical reason for shepherds and woodmen to climb up to 2,000 metres and visit the cave: the search for water for themselves and for their livestock, especially at the height of summer when it was impossible to find this precious liquid, even in the woodland a little lower down. Still in 1981, when an explosive fracture opened up very near the Cave - putting its continued existence in doubt - the area in front of the cave was strewn with stone 'scifi' (containers), which were used by shepherds to melt blocks of ice and let their livestock drink. It is also said that during the Second World War grain 'smugglers' (who supplied the black market in Catania and district) used the paths high up on Etna, stopping off at the Ice Cave, so as to avoid checkpoints and reach their anxious customers at night.

The Cave has been closely monitored over a period of time to ascertain its state of health, especially considering the growing number of visitors and the gradual warming of the climate.

However, the glacier of the Ice Cave is still there, in spite of the fiery lava of Etna that surrounded it in 1981 and the consequent devastating earth tremors; despite the scorching summers and the poor winter snows that have characterised the final years of the 20th century. It has been modified and has adapted itself, as is appropriate to a living creature, and it is well worth taking the long walk to see it.

The itinerary suggested here is the classic access route from the north-eastern side, departing from the Pitarrone barracks (situated in the municipality of Castiglione). The latter can be reached from the Linguaglossa-pine wood road, turning onto a forest track (open to traffic for a short stretch) that starts right opposite the restaurant-hotel "Da Filippo". After a kilometre and a half of rough track you have to park your car in front of the Pitarrone barracks. Here, a barrier stops

you driving any further along the track, also known as the 'Etna ring road'. At first you walk through pleasant woodland, occasionally interrupted by wide lava flows that have run down this side of the volcano in recent times. Looking downhill you can see the Alcantara Valley unfolding with all its small towns (Castiglione, Moio, Roccella Valdemone and Randazzo a little higher up).

After about five kilometres you come to a detour leading to the Palombe (Wood-pigeons) Cave and the nearby forest hut. Another kilometre further on you arrive at a junction (to the left you head for the Timpa Rossa mountain hut) above which you will find the Raspberry Cave (a long lava tunnel that is easily accessible). To reach your destination you have to follow the signs (piles of stones and paint marks) that head off from the Raspberry Cave in a south-westerly direction across the beautiful lava flow of 1614-24: an unending mass of fluid, rope and tube lava, which in some places forms chaotic hills in an impressive variety of shapes, some of which even take on almost human forms. In this final stretch the route winds across wide terraces, separated from one another by short steps.

The pathway, however, is very clear and you just need to pay attention in the presence of fog or patches of snow that can make walking difficult.

The area in which the Ice Cave is situated is easily recognisable from the presence of thick deposits of ash and lapilli left behind by the 1981 eruption.

Finally, we remind you that, according to an ordinance of the Etna Park Authority, access to the cave is allowed in groups of no more than twenty people accompanied by a mountain guide, also because the descent in the bottom part of the cave requires a certain degree of technical skill and adequate equipment (ice crampons and/or pitons and ropes).

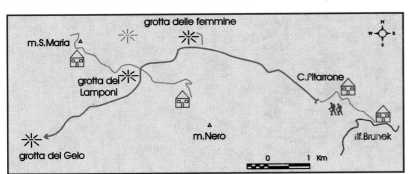

THE ALCÀNTARA RIVER

The Alcàntara river is just under 50km long in all and marks part of the border between the provinces of Catania and Messina. The river rises in the Nebrodi mountains, near Floresta, and flows into the sea near Taormina, crossing the territory of 15 districts in the two provinces.

There is a certain amount of confusion regarding the more ancient names of the river and its identification. We will now explain this better.

The Greeks are said to have called it 'akesine', that is 'healing river', but some claim that the Akesine corresponds, in reality, to the Fiumefreddo river.

The Romans are said to have called it 'onabala' or 'onobola', but some believe this was the name of a torrent that has nothing to do with the river in question. The Romans, however, are thought to have built a bridge across the river, something that seems relatively plausible.

Indeed, the Arabs, who always changed the names of the places they conquered according to the characteristics of the place, called the river 'Al Qantarah', which means bridge.

The fame of the Alcàntara, whose water is cold even in summer, is closely tied to the spectacular gorge, which is situated in the province of Messina, a visit that we strongly recommend and which we will deal with later. However, the gorge is only one stretch of the river. Throughout its length, the Alcàntara offers beautiful scenery and luxuriant vegetation, home to numerous species of animals.

At Fondaco Molta (Catania) there are water springs which feed the river in dry periods, indeed the Alcàntara has plenty of water at any time of year.

At Mitogio (Catania) there is a particularly lovely stretch with basalt rocks.

The river can be followed swimming, on foot or by canoe. However, canoeists should pay great attention and not venture out alone, counting on their experience and ability.

The Alcànatra does not have a regular flow, it is often winding and meandering, sometimes it forms small ponds and sometimes quite substantial waterfalls. We therefore underline the concept that **the river is very dangerous for canoeists**. It is a good idea to contact the Alcàntara Kayak Association (tel. 095 503020), which supplies information, equipment and guides and which has installed hand-ropes and other aids in difficult points to help the passage of canoes.

As we have already said, the most charming stretch of the river and the

Top and left: basalt rocks.

most interesting from a natural and geological point of view is the one in the province of Messina, called the Alcàntara **Gorge**. Here the water flows on a gravel bottom and the walls, which are five metres apart, are dark because made of lava.

The area is well equipped from a tourist's point of view. On private land there is a car park, snack bar and a picnic area. A small fee is payable for using the lift that takes you down into the Gorge. Alternatively, you can use the steps, situated about a hundred metres from the car park on the main road. You have to equip yourself with rubber boots, which can be hired on the spot, because at certain points the water is quite deep and the bottom is slippery.

The origin of the walls of the Gorge is clearly linked to a volcanic eruption of long ago, around which a legend has also been created.

Once upon a time two brothers, one of whom was blind, had to share out a large amount of grain. Obviously the sighted one divided it, using a 'mojo' (a cylindrical container with a convex bottom). As they say in Sicialian '*cu sparti avi a megghiu parti*' (he who shares out takes the best part) and the sighted one easily

deceived his brother, handing him the '*mojo*' filled on the less capacious side. To the blind one, however, it seemed full when touching it. Needless to say the dishonest one was unable to enjoy the mountain of grain he had accumulated. The grain and the thief were turned into a real mountain, or rather into the volcano Mojo, from which a terrible eruption came forth.

In reality the Alcàntara Gorge is nothing more than the result of an enormous lava flow from Mojo, the most unpredictable secondary crater on Etna.

The flow was made up of basic lava, more fluid than acidic lava and slower to solidify. It flowed along the Alcàntara, blocking the river, and reached the sea, where it created the small peninsula of Capo Schisò. The peculiarity of the Gorge is due to the fact that water erosion over the centuries has revealed the internal conformation of the thick basalt walls. They have a column structure with hexagonal and pentagonal prisms that are mostly perpendicular to the height of the walls. This geological phenomenon is determined by the cooling of the lava, which begins externally and gradually reaches the interior. The Alcàntara Gorge is one of the most spectacular examples of this phenomenon in Europe.

Top and left: Alcàntara Gorge.

LINGUAGLOSSA: IN THE SHADE OF LEAFY BRANCHES

From Castiglione di Sicilia you go back along the SS 120 road. After a little more than four kilometres you come to **Linguaglossa**.

Linguaglossa is a pleasant place to stay, both in winter and in summer. In the hotter months of the year the **Ragabo pine-wood** offers relief from the torrid heat and is a lovely place to take an invigorating walk.

Climbing further up, but still in the forest of Linguglossa, you can reach **Piano Provenzana** (altitude about 1,800 metres)

to the rebellious actions of its inhabitants. The name of the town is probably derived from the large tongue of solidified lava (Lingua Grossa) on which the town stands. Another interpretation, with the same meaning, is that it derives from the repetition of the same word; 'glossa' in Greek means tongue.

UNDER THE PROTECTION OF SAINT EGIDIO

Although the main tourist attraction of Linguaglossa is its natural environment, the artistic-monumental heritage of the town should not be underestimated.

The 17th century **Cathedral**, dedicated to Our Lady of Graces, stands in Piazza Duomo. Inside the three naves contain a splendid wooden choir, dating back to the early 18th century, with bas-reliefs depicting scenes from the life of Christ. Near the Cathedral you will notice the monument to **Our Lady of the Pine Wood**. The statue of Our Lady is the work of the sculptor E. Russo and is placed on a block of lava stone that formed during the eruption of 1566.

The **Church of Saint Egidio Abbot**, in via Sant'Egidio, is dedicated to the patron of the town and was built during the Angevin domination, but was considerably altered over the following centuries. Inside the Latin cross layout of the church you can see 16th century frescoes and a carving in the architrave of the portal belonging to the original church of a mermaid fighting two snakes, a symbol of the eternal struggle between good and evil.

about ten kilometres from the town, a departure point for exciting excursions up to the crater of the volcano, either using the ski-lifts or by off-road vehicle. In the winter the ski slopes offer experts and beginners alike the chance to spend a relaxing holiday combined with healthy physical exercise in a superb location.

Some researchers attribute the foundation of the first nucleus of the town of Linguaglossa to the Nassi who escaped the destruction of Naxos.

It is certain that Linguaglossa existed and enjoyed certain privileges at the time of Roger II, as is shown by historical documents. For a long time it was a possession of various feudal lords and passed from the hands of one noble family to another. The last feudal lords were the Bonanno family and they lost possession of the town in 1634, the year in which Linguaglossa became a free city, thanks

Top: Town Hall.
Right: Cathedral.

The **Dominican Convent**, in via San Nicola, is now home to the San Tommaso Holiday Home and is characterised by the wide colonnade on the facade.

Inside there are numerous works of art, the most interesting of which is the 18th century painting of Our Lady of the Rosary.

The **Church of Our Lady of the Immaculate Conception** and the adjacent **Capuchin Convent**, in Piazza Cappuccini, date back to the mid-17th century. The two buildings are home to some of the most important works of art in Linguaglossa. In the Church, on the high altar, you can admire the splendid 18th century tabernacle, expertly carved in wood by Pietro Bencivinni, and the beautiful group of wooden sculptures of Our Lady of the Immaculate Conception and the Saints, attributed to Brother Humble of Petralia, whose fame is linked to numerous crucifixes scattered around many Sicilian churches. The Convent is home to a library containing volumes from the period between the 16th and 18th centuries.

The **Church of Saint Francis of Paola**, in via Roma, was built in the 16th century but has undergone numerous alterations over the centuries.

Outside it has a lovely quadrangular bell-tower. The stuccoes decorating the single nave of the interior are 17th century. Worthy of note is the statue of Our Lady of Loreto, believed to be by Domenico Gagini. Also in via Roma, adjacent to the Church of Saint Francis of Paola, stands the beautiful **Town Hall**.

In the small square of the Annunziata, which opens out onto via Roma, stands the 17th century **Church of Our Lady of the Annunciation**. The clear facade is characterised by a two-coloured portal in lava stone and red marble and is flanked by a high bell-tower. There is a curious presence of murals on the outer walls of the building.

In the same square you will find the **Local Tourist Office**, which houses the Ethnographic Museum of the Peoples of Etna and some collections relating to the flora and fauna of the volcano.

The **Museum of the Peoples of Etna** brings together objects and utensils of everyday use linked to ancient and traditional activities.

The reconstruction of a small mill shows the various phases of wine production using traditional methods (open every day, on Sundays only in the morning).

Also worthy of note is the **Church of Saints Anthony and Vito**, especially because of its beautiful portal and the window above it, both in lava stone and from the 18th century. You should also pay a visit to the **Milana Park**, in via San Rocco, with its characteristic fountain decorated with Moors' heads in ceramics, and the **Villa dei Vespri Siciliani**, in Piazza Giardino.

WORKING UP AN APPETITE

The healthy air of Linguglossa, especially after a long walk through the woods, gives you an appetite.

The local cuisine comes to your aid with numerous speciali-

ties to tempt you, both sweet and savoury. Here they produce excellent **cheeses and ricotta**, which can also be bought directly from the shepherds.

We recommend you try the local **sausages**, flavoured with wild fennel seeds, and all the dishes made with **mushrooms**. The delicious hazel nuts are widely used to make **cakes** that are exquisite, though unfortunately very fattening! Try to resist them if you can. We recommend the bar-confectioner's-takeaway **Pino Azzurro** in Piazza Matrice 10.

Excellent **wines** are produced in Linguaglossa. The local wines can be purchased directly from private producers, just ask around, or from the **Vallegalfina** winery, at Km 2 on the Linguglossa-Zafferana provincial road.

There are numerous and varied chances of tasting the typical dishes of local cuisine, mostly outside the town in relaxing surroundings. Here are some suggestions: **Baita del Pino**, at Piano Provenzana, a characteristic wooden building with a name that gives it a mountain atmosphere, serving meat and mushroom based dishes; **Gatto Blu**, on the Mareneve road, which also caters for pizza lovers; **Monte Conca**, at Piano Provenzana, a quiet cosy trattoria serving tasty and substantial meals; **Trattoria del Parco**, in via Mareneve just outside the town, offering sausages and mushroom based dishes that are not to be missed.

You can also choose the accommodation best suited to your needs. If you prefer a farm holiday, you will certainly appreciate **La Casa degli Ulivi**, a farm in contrada Chiusa del Signore.

This family run farm is situated at an altitude of more than 500 metres above sea level and offers you the chance of staying in a quiet spot, not far from the ski slopes and places of great beauty. Guests are accommodated in a carefully restored liberty style building, a sort of small castle, with attractive well furnished rooms. From here it is also easy to get to the beach, just 10 km away. Guided excursions are organised, even on horseback. The cuisine is based on genuine produce, almost all from the farm itself and all grown using natural methods. If you prefer a typical mountain hut, we suggest: mountain hut-campsite **Clan dei Ragazzi**, on the Mareneve provincial road at Piano Donnavita. Situated in the green Ragabo pinewood at an altitude of 1,500 metres it offers accommodation in wooden chalets or in tents on the fully-equipped campsite. There is a restaurant for guests. It is very near the ski slopes. Various activities are organised for mountain enthusiasts, including excursions by mountain bike and on foot; **Brunek mountain hut**, at Bosco Ragabo. This hut is near the ski slopes, at an altitude of 1,400 metres, and offers accommodation in pleasant wooden building with a restaurant for guests.

The hut is the headquarters of the Italian Sleddog School and exciting trips are organised on sleds pulled by dogs. Numerous activities are on offer to make the best of your holiday in the mountains, as well as excursions on horseback and on foot.

FESTIVALS

The numerous interesting events held in Linguglossa throughout the year are an opportunity for getting to know the town and its inhabitants better.

From 29th April to 1st May there is a **Craft Exhibition**, allowing you to browse around in search of original objects.

July sees **Etna Week**, held from the 18th to the 25th. The town is enlivened from the centre to Piano Provenzana by the presence of artists who sculpt wood or paint multi-coloured murals in competition for the impromptu 'Wood engravings and brushes'. On the walls of many houses in

the town you can see the picturesque results of previous competitions, Mediterranean images with a touch of artistic inspiration. At the same time folkloristic displays are held, along with various other events, including the interesting 'Etna Pentathlon'.

The Sunday after 15th August is the day dedicated to the **Feast of Saint Rocco**. The celebrations include various events, such as the characteristic sack race.

On 1st September the **patronal Feast of Saint Egidio** is celebrated. The traditional procession of the Saint's statue through the streets of the town takes on a particular significance in Linguaglossa, as in many other towns around Etna. The celebrations end with a 'pledge' by the Saint to protect the town from the menace of the volcano, towards which the statue is pointed at the end of the procession.

Finally, in November we have the **Feast of Saint Martin** and the **Exhibition of Local Wines** with tasting of wine and local produce, folklore and displays.

RESTAURANTS-PIZZERIAS

- ANTONIO: via S. Nicola, 12 (tel. 095 647756). Pizzeria-restaurant-pub-beer-hall. Try the pizza with buffalo mozzarella.
- BAITA DEL PINO: locality Piano Provenzana (tel. 095 643479). In typical mountain surroundings, serving mostly meat dishes, excellent roasts and fresh mushrooms. Among the first courses we recommend the home-made maccheroni 'alla boscaiola'.
- ETNA: Piazza Stazione (tel. 095 643920). We suggest the maccheroncini 'Etna', escalopes with mushrooms, mixed grill.
- GATTO BLU: via Mareneve, 21 (tel. 095 643637). Restaurant-pizzeria with numerous mushroom based dishes. Specialities: ravioloni 'alla Parmentier' stuffed with meat, and the tasty sausages.
- LA PROVENZANA: locality Piano Provenzana - Etna nord (tel. 095 643300). Hotel restaurant. Home cooking. Try the penne 'alla Provenzana' and the mixed meat grill.

Top: Piano Provenzana. Left: nordic ski runs.

- LE BETULLE: locality Piano Provenzana (tel./fax 095 643430). Hotel restaurant serving mushroom based dishes and mixed grill with lamb and wild boar. Specialities: the chef's first course and the caserecci 'alle Betulle'.
- LE SCIARE: via Mareneve (tel. 095 643401). Cosy trattoria with tables in the shade of the trees in the wood in summer. Country cooking and full-bodied local wine. We recommend the fresh maccheroni with mushrooms, the pasta 'al ragù' and the goat.
- MONTE CONCA: locality Piano Provenzana (tel. 095 647922). Trattoria with home cooking serving filling mountain dishes. Numerous dishes with mushrooms.
- PINETA RAGABO: Piano Donnavita - locality Bosco Ragabo (tel. 095 647841). Restaurant-pizzeria-bar-mountain hut. We suggest the maccheroni 'Ragabo' (mushrooms, meat and spicy sauce).
- TRATTORIA DEL PARCO: via Mareneve, 27 (tel. 095 643037). From the menu we recommend the steaks, the sausages and the mushrooms, all washed down with excellent local red wine. Among the first courses we suggest the maccheroni 'alla boscaiola'.
- SCIARAMANICA: via Mareneve - km 2,9 (tel. 095 643007). An old mill with a warm cosy atmosphere, serving typical Etna produce and delicious pizzas cooked in a wood-burning oven. We recommend the lasagnette with mushrooms and the seasoned sausages. Also a pub-beer hall.

FARM HOLIDAYS

- LA CASA DEGLI ULIVI: contrada Chiusa del Signore (tel. 095 643593). With restaurant and stables. You can visit the farm animals and the fields with exclusively natural crops. The restaurant serves local dishes, home-made pasta, wild boar, venison and lamb.
- TENUTA SCIGLIO: contrada Vallegalfina, SP Linguaglossa - Zafferana - Km. 2 (tel. 095 933694). Vineyard and winery with tasting.

HOTELS

- HAPPY DAY ♥ ♥: via Mareneve, 9 (tel./fax 095 643484). Panoramic position, with bar. Telephone and television in rooms.
- LA PROVENZANA ♥ ♥: locality Piano Provenzana (tel. 095 643300). With restaurant, bar, self service cafeteria, souvenir shop.
- LE BETULLE ♥ ♥ via Mareneve - locality Piano Provenzana (tel./fax 095 643430). With restaurant, bar and ski lift. In summer excursions to the crater by jeep. In winter skiing.

CAMP SITES

- CLAN DEI RAGAZZI ♥: SP Mareneve - locality Bosco Ragabo (tel./fax 095 643611). With rooms, restaurant, bar, children's play area. Sleddog and excursions on horseback.

ROOMS FOR RENT

- CASA PER FERIE S. TOMMASO: via Tommaso Fazello, 2 (tel. 095 643272).
- VILLA REFE ♥ ♥: via Mareneve, 42 (tel. 095 643926). With garden and car park.

MOUNTAIN HUTS

- BRUNEK: locality Bosco Ragabo (tel. 095 643015). With bar and accommodation. At an altitude of 1,400 metres. Il custodian is sig. Enrico Emmi.
- NORD-EST: locality Piano Provenzana (tel. 095 647922). With bar and accommodation. At an altitude of 1,800 metres. The custodian is sig. Leonardo Pennisi.
- RAGABO: Piano Donnavita - locality Bosco Ragabo (tel. 095 647841). With restaurant and bar. The custodian is sig. Giacomo Mangano.

Right: north-eastern summit crater.

93

From Linguaglossa Towards "the mountain"

From the valley to the mountain. With an eye on the high smoking summit. A last glance at the world of men, at the sweat of the of those toiling in the vineyards, at the houses built with lava stone and hard work, before setting off into the land of the volcano, where man has always trod respectfully, sometimes with a sense of subjection, without ever having the courage to go and live there permanently. Let's start off then.

From Linguaglossa the road goes straight past the Circumetnea railway station (the place from which the pioneers of this mountain set off on their long excursions on foot) and heads straight for the enormous cone of the volcano.

After 3.8 kilometres you come to the junction with the so called panoramic road (a road built by the Agricultural Development Authority that leads to Randazzo and Maletto). You continue straight on past vineyards and small rural houses through an area that fortunately is almost completely free of holiday homes. You soon come to the first belt of woodland vegetation, composed of oaks.

At Piano Donnavita you arrive at the first picnic area set up by the Forestry Service, encouraging you to make a short stop. Further on you meet the very high and very famous Corsican pines that characterise this side of Etna. At Piano Pernicana (13.5 kilometres from the departure point, with cooking facilities) the trunks of these trees stick up like organ pipes. These trunks have been variously used for making masts for sailing ships, as a source of resin (as can be seen from the deep incisions made at the base of the trunks) and even the roots have been used because of their long burning effect that cheers up long winter evenings.

When you reach the restaurant-hotel "da Filippo", you will come to the beginning of the very famous high mountain route (the Etna 'ring road'), which goes around the volcano on three sides. Continuing along the Mareneve road, a little further on you come to the holiday centre run by the Provincial Council (presently undergoing renovation).

After a few more hairpin bends you reach the municipal road that climbs steeply up to our destination by car: Piano Provenzana. This very road was once used (long before the days of tourist traffic) to drag down (with the help of mules) long tree trunks to be used for various purposes.

Suddenly the horizon is filled by the huge plateau of Piano Provenzana and the outline of the summit craters (particularly the north-east crater).

You have now arrived at the Etna-north tourist area, which offers hotels, restaurants, souvenir shops and five ski-lifts for winter sport enthusiasts. Your ascent of the volcano does not finish here, however. You can carry on up to the summit on foot or in one of the jeeps available at the hotel "Le Betulle". The track that leads to the top begins right next to the above mentioned hotel (alternatively, the first part of the route can be covered by following the nature path laid down by the Park Authority, which begins behind souvenir shops and is signposted in yellow, see the description below). The first stretch of the itinerary is through woodland but the trees soon give way to expanses of pioneering plants that break out into multi-coloured flowers in early summer.

You climb up the mountain walking alongside the gorges that drop down to Piano Provenzana and the 'buttonhole' craters, which were active in the late 19th century (Monti 'Umberto and Margherita').

At an altitude of 2,800 metres you suddenly catch sight of Piano delle Concazze (covered with sand and lapilli) and the white outline of the volcanological observatory of Pizzi Deneri. For the last stretch the track moves onto the northern slopes (with views towards the Nebrodi mountains and the Eolian Islands, the peaks of which can be seen on very clear days) in order to go around the huge bulk of the north-east crater.

When the track comes to an end you are truly in the domain of the god Vulcan. In this area it is highly advisable to be accompanied by mountain guides in order to gain information about the activity of the summit craters and their dangers. If you are fortunate enough to be able to lean over and look into the abyss, you will be able to understand the 'Empedocles syndrome', the mystery, and at the same time, the irresistible fascination created by these huge chimneys that come up from the centre of the earth (the walk from Piano Provenzana takes about four and a half hours one way).

In winter Piano Provenzana is an attraction for skiing enthusiasts, both those who prefer downhill skiing and the growing number of Nordic ski enthusiasts, who can enjoy two circular routes that are also used for official competitions.

Moreover, you can also make Nordic ski excursions (outside of the official routes in areas without too steep inclines) and off slope downhill skiing (on untouched snow, in search of the more fascinating aspects of the mountain in winter).

PIANO PROVENZANA (1,800 M) - MONTE NERO (2,000 M) MONTE NERO MOUNTAIN HUT

LINGUAGLOSSA: 8th ITINERARY ROUTE
Duration : 2 hours
Total distance: 5.5 km
Difference in height: 200 metres

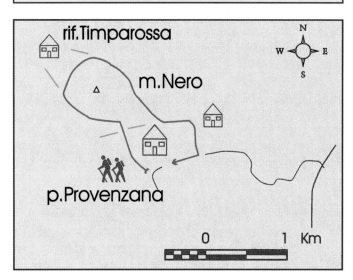

Behind the souvenir shops of Piano Provenzana you will find the beginning of the Etna Park path that leads towards Monte Nero.

It is marked by yellow signposts that initially guide you up a steep wooded slope.

After a few minutes of walking the route cuts across the track used by the off-road vehicles on their way up to the craters and crosses a fence, then continuing along a rough track that continues to climb through a thinly wooded landscape.

A little further on the trees disappear and you are suddenly confronted with the view of the wide plateau around Monte Nero.

The landscape here is dominated by volcanic material: large bombs thrown out by the nearby crater, stretches of fine sand and cracks from which the lava flowed out. Just outside the wood on the right you will see a sheep pen

situated in a tiny depression. The yellow signposts placed by the Park Authority now lead you to the higher side of Monte Nero in a narrow valley that separates it from Monte Timpa Rossa and from Monte Ponte di Ferro, inside which you can admire a beautiful lava flow now petrified.

Further on the pathway crosses the final clumps of beech trees and goes around Monte Nero to the north until it meets the narrow path that goes off to the left (north-westwards) and takes you to the Timpa Rossa mountain hut in fifteen minutes (see description of the 2nd stage of the GTE).

Continuing around the base of Monte Nero, you cross mounds of lapilli and sand and then go down to the eruptive fracture of 1923, where it is better to climb up onto one of the cones (made of fused scoriae) in order to admire the succession of so called 'buttonhole' hornitos (small ovens) that formed along the crack because of the intense explosive activity.

Beyond the 1923 fracture it is better to go along the rough track that crosses the whole plateau below Monte Nero and then enters a shady beech wood.

After about a kilometre in the thick wood, staying on the same track, you come to a large clearing on the edge of which there is a mountain hut run by the Province of Catania (open only to members of the Italian Alpine Club).

Continuing further on you come to the final downhill stretch, which gradually winds its way down to the eastern entrance to Piano Provenzana.

PIEDIMONTE ETNEO: LAND OF PRINCES

Just a few kilometres along the SS 120 from Linguaglossa you come to **Piedimonte Etneo**, a small hill town on the eastern slopes of Etna, which, along with the villages of Vena and Presa, is a quiet pleasant place to spend a holiday, especially in summer.

The pleasant climate, the luxuriant woodland and the chance to make wonderful excursions make it an attractive place both for those looking for a relaxing holiday and for those who intend to combine tranquillity with some **hiking**.

We would like to remind the latter that in the territory of Piedimonte there is a **volcanological observatory**, situated at an altitude of about 2,800 metres, almost on the summit of Etna.

The history of Piedimonte began in more recent times, above all if compared to that of the other towns around Etna, and is therefore free from the presence of the great dominators (Romans, Arabs, Normans, Swabians, etc.) who contested control of the Catania area with the sword and, according to the situation, even with the Koran or the Bible.

The town was founded by Ignazio Sebastiano Gravina Amato, Prince of Palagonia, who obtained permission to build in this area in 1687. In this way the original nucleus of Piedimonte (which was then probably called Belvedere) was born under the auspices and personal protection of its founder. It was soon enriched by the construction of the Cathedral (Church of Saint Ignatius) and the baronial palace before the end of the 17th century. Even after the death of Prince Ignazio the town remained under the control of the Palagonia family.

The urban development of the 18th century was due to the new Prince of Palagonia, Ferdinando Francesco, who encouraged the construction of new and important buildings and promoted communications and local transport, thus giving a boost to the town's economy.

The 'Etneo' added to the name of the town in 1862 was intended to distinguish it from the town of the same name in Campania.

The Cathedral, in Piazza Madre Chiesa, and the 18th century Church of Our Lady of the Immaculate Conception, in Piazza Umberto, are the most important holy buildings and those which house the most interesting works of art.

In particular, in the **Church of Our Lady of the Immaculate Conception**, adjacent to the **Convent of the Capuchin Fathers**, you can see valuable baroque altars in carved wood.

The **Cathedral** is dedicated to Our Lady of the Rosary and was built at the end of the 17th century. Outside it has a clear linear facade in classical style. Inside there are three naves divided by arches and you can see canvases and works of importance, including a 17th century painting by an anonymous artist which is of great interest because it shows some of the older buildings in the town that no longer exist. The marble altars along the walls of the lateral naves are jewels of workmanship.

In Piazza Roma, formerly Piano San Michele, the oldest part of town, stand the **Church of Saint Michael** and elegant **noble residences**.

A short distance away, in via Mazzini, you can admire the **Church of Saint Ignatius**, characterised by two twin bell-towers alongside the facade. It was built at the end of the 1800s on the same site as the first Cathedral of the town, dedicated by the founder to the same Saint.

Corso Vittorio Emanuele is the 'wide street' opened by Prince Ferdinando Francesco, son of the founder of the town, and is the most important street in Piedimonte. At the end of this street stand the so called **'pupa'**, two massive pillars that belonged to the **San Fratello Gate**, which has been partly demolished during this century.

Just outside the town, in the village of Vena, you can visit the Sanctuary of Our Lady of Vena, built in the 1500s, which is home to a very valuable icon depicting the Virgin.

GOOD NEWS

The driving force of the local economy is agriculture.

Left: view of the coast taken from Piedimonte Etneo.

are produced, both for eating and for making wine. The latter go to produce strong generous **wines**, such as the Etna Red DOC and give a boost to the business of some **Wine Cellars** we suggest you visit to taste and purchase the wine. Traditional cuisine can be found at the **restaurants Leonardi** and **Villa Pupa**.

The greedier among you should not hesitate to try the local cakes made with pistachio, hazel nuts or almonds and the traditional fried rice cakes with honey, which can be bought from all the bars and confectioners', including the **bar Centrale** and the **confectioner's Calì**.

The most important events in town also have a gastronomic element.

From June to September the Piedimontese Summer includes drama, shows and gastronomy in the streets.

On 31st July, in concomitance with the celebrations in honour of the patron **Saint Ignatius**, a **Festival of Seasoned Bread** is held, a chance to taste excellent home-made bread and delicious olive oil.

On 20th August, in the village of Vena, there is another **Festival of Home-made Bread**.

From 24th to 26th September the **Grape Harvest Festival** includes music, folklore, costumed characters, traditional grape treading, gastronomy and arts and crafts.

Finally, on 13th November the **Roasted Chestnut Festival** takes place.

RESTAURANTS

- LEONARDI: via Fossa Agliastro, 1 (tel. 095 648342). Restaurant-pizzeria. Typical Sicilian cuisine.
- VILLA PUPA: via Bellini, 143 (tel. 095 648371). With large characteristic hall and tree shaded garden. We recommend the sfogliatine with mushrooms, the home-made pasta, the grilled meat or fish.

This fact not only fills the wallets of the local people but also has some very tasty implications.

The local produce ends up on the table or in a bottle, to the joy of producers and visitors alike.

Since the territory of Piedimonte Etneo is partly at low altitude, the exceptional fertility of the lava soil allows all kinds of fruit to be grown, especially citrus fruits. Higher up, on the other hand, the thick woods bear hazel nuts and chestnuts. The local **mushrooms** are greatly appreciated, particularly the 'porcino' variety, and they constitute a tasty ingredient for numerous recipes, both for first and second courses.

The vineyards are the real pride and joy of Piedimonte. Grapes of very high quality

Top: the so called 'pupa', massive pillars once part of the San Fratello Gate. Bottom: Piazza Roma and the Church of Saint Felix.

WINE OF THE VOLCANO

Over the centuries wine has changed Etna. One day after another, one terrace after another, the farmers and more enterprising landowners planted vines and completely changed the appearance of the volcano.

What we see today is largely an manmade landscape, achieved through centuries of hard work by generations of labourers who, from 1700 onwards, were sent to extract 'red gold' from the higher slopes of Etna. In order to succeed they had to face a daily struggle with the harsh nature of the volcano; they had to till the ground, taking out the stones to uncover the fertile volcanic sand, rich in minerals.

For every plot of land reclaimed they had to labour hard and ended up with an enormous pile of stones, heaped in a corner forming artificial hills, evidence of their hard work and sweat (the "turette"). It is still possible to see them here and there on Etna today, in places where modern speculation has passed them by.

The poorer the land was, the higher the "turette" were, and they were sometimes used to make temporary shelters for the farmers.

The colonisation by winemakers continued for most of the 19th century with the impetus given by the market, which demanded strong dark red alcoholic wines, the type produced so well on Etna, and which could be easily transported overseas.

Napoleon also lent a hand by depriving the English of many of their traditional sources of wine supplies, foricng them to look elsewhere, including Sicily. The early 19th century was a happy period for the winemakers of Etna and they were confident enough to invest capital and labour to produce more and more 'red gold'.

Vines also began to be planted on the fertile sides of extinct craters without terracing, so when hoeing the labourers lined up and climbed the slope backwards, sinking into the volcanic sand.

Then came the time for terracing, built thanks to the patient work of master stonecutters. The mountainside was broken up into countless islands, connected by steps. Once the sunniest slopes had been tilled and planted only the higher ground above a thousand metres was left, where the snow lay for several months on the frost-hardened ground.

The unwelcome task of farming this land fell to the smallholders, who managed to tear away a small plot of land from the mountain and built a small millstone on it, each their own one, even though it was small, even though there was only a modest amount of grapes to be pressed, in typical individualistic Sicilian style, showing their atavistic wish to do everything by themselves, mistrusting the other smallholders.

The speed of deforestation and tilling of what was once called the 'Etna wood' was dictated by the ups and downs of wine prices: the higher the prices paid by traders, the greater the inclination to farm even marginal land.

This particularly happened around the 1880s, when phylloxera began to strike the vineyards of the north and Sicily seemed to become a paradise for vines. Then the Island was also struck by the merciless destruction of vines and Etna's vein of 'red gold' was exhausted.

Other plants replaced the vines and the 19th century terraces were put to other uses: at lower altitudes citrus fruits were introduced, particularly lemons in the Aci area, while higher up nuts gave new life to agriculture on the mountain.

The rest is recent history. A decree in 1968 established the Etna DOC production area, which extends around the mountain crossing the territory of 20 municipal districts, even though the traditional wine-producing areas are much smaller: you start from the vineyards of Biancavilla, passing through some of the outlying areas of Randazzo and the more famous wine producing areas around Castiglione di Sicilia (Solicchiata, Rovitello), until you arrive in the Milo district (with its exclusive superior white) and Sant'Alfio.

Etna DOC wine (red, white, rosé and superior white) has in truth been long neglected because of the enormous subdivision of the plots of land and it is only in recent years that a group of producers has emerged and come onto the market with a more professional attitude and better products.

Etna wine - particularly that produced by Giuseppe Benanti, Emanuele Scammacca del Murgo and Carlo Nicolosi Asmundo - now rises to previously unknown levels of refinement.

The 'dark alcoholic' liquid loved by English sailors is now a distant memory and the best bottles produced on Etna today are characterised by a refined bouquet for wines with a few years of maturing and by successful combinations with important international vines (especially Cabernet).

The traditional Etna varieites are not, however, neglected (nerello mascalese, carricante and catarratto) and this continues to guarantee the unique character and identity of the product.

Giuseppe Riggio

BEVACQUA HOUSES (1,010 M)
MONTE STORNELLO (1,150 M)

PIEDIMONTE ETNEO: 9th ITINERARY ROUTE
Duration : 1 and a half hours
Total distance: 3,6 km
Difference in height: 140 metres

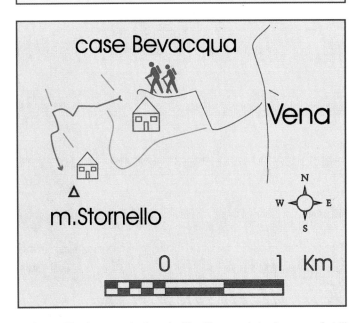

This is a short walk that takes you through the nut groves on the north-eastern slopes of Etna and lets you see the rural architecture that was once necessary to look after these orchards.

From Fornazzo you take the provincial road that leads to Linguaglossa. Just before reaching the turn off for Vena, you take a left turn into a steep cart track that brings you to the Bevacqua Houses after less than two kilometres; the only place you can go wrong is at halfway, where there is a fork in the road, and here you must go right. At first the landscape is characterised by chestnut trees, which gradually give way to hazel nut trees as you climb. You leave your car near the houses (which can be recognised by the large water tank past which the track passes) and continue on foot, after having admired the architecture of the pretty group of houses, with an adjacent storehouse, now without a roof, all of which give you an idea of the ancient balance in the relationship between man and the mountain. From here the view looking down takes in the Ionian coastline as far as Taormina and the coast of Calabria, while looking upwards you can see Monte Stornello, the Pizzi Deneri and the summit craters. You cross the large estate, coming across an altar, then other buildings, water tanks and millstones as you climb up. Until the early 20th century this area was full of vineyards instead of hazel nut trees. You go straight on past all the turnings in a westerly direction and then the route turns southwards. In a thick chestnut wood you will find a hut, perfectly cam- ouflaged in the vegetation, built with a certain degree of skill in lava stone. From here a faint pathway leads you up to the top.

Apart from the natural beauty of the countryside, this itinerary also causes you a certain amount of regret for the neglect and damage caused by vandalism that have led to the ruin of this important rural architectural heritage.

CALATABIANO: TWO CASTLES FOR ONE TOWN

From Piedimonte Etneo you follow the SS 120 road for a few kilometres until you reach the A18 motorway and head for **Calatabiano**. The town stands in the Alcantara Valley area, very near the sea, almost on the border of the province of Messina.

Nowadays this is an ideal location, a stone's throw from the sea and just a little further from the most amazing volcano in Europe, but it was once a cause for concern for the inhabitants. Indeed, in the past the area was subject to pirate raids from the sea and, as if this were not enough, the Alcantara was an ideal route for them to take towards the interior. During the Arab domination, therefore, as a means of defence and attack, a fortress was built ('kalat' is the Arabic word for castle and from this the town takes its name). The Normans then transformed it into a fully fledged **Castle**. Once it had lost its original purpose the Castle was subjected to numerous alterations that completely changed its appearance.

Calatabiano was built on its present site under the auspices of the noble Cruyllas family after the earthquake of 1693, which forced the inhabitants to move further downhill.

Clear evidence of the link between the Cruyllas family and Calatabiano can be seen in the coat of arms of the illustrious dynasty, which stands out on the portal of the Church of the Holy Crucifix and on the arch of the large hall situated at the entrance to the Castle.

The **Church of the Holy Crucifix** or of Saint Phillip was built in 1484, as is shown by the date inscribed on the facade, in late Gothic style. The facade is characterised by rich decorations in relief with floral and plant motifs and is flanked by the bell-tower topped by merlons.

Walking through the streets of the town you will occasionally notice elegant **portals** from noble buildings that have been incorporated into more recent constructions. You should also see the valuable 16th century cross kept in the **Cathedral**.

Near the beach of San Marco, just outside town, you will find the luxurious residence of the Gravina-Cruyllas family, known as the **Castle of San Marco**, which was built in the late 1600s. There is an attractive double stairway leading up to the first floor of the building, the noble floor, which still maintains its past splendour, despite the ravages of time.

The Castle is crowned by scroll decorations that run along the entire length of the cornice. The building is given the 'dignity' of a castle by the four corner cylindrical towers.

The name of the Castle, which then became the name used to refer to the district, is due to the presence nearby of a church dedicated to Saint Mark, of which only a few ruins are now visible. This was a meting place for al those who worked in the area in the service of the powerful family.

EXTRA INFORMATION

While you are in Calatabiano you should try the local cakes, particularly the superlative almond pastries.

The best ones can be bought at the **bar-confectioners' Silus** in contrada San Marco, **Brianni** in via Vittorio Emanuele (also try the 'martorana' fruit) and **Fortunato** in Piazza Vittorio Emanuele (taste the ice-cream as well).

If you are on the lookout for souvenirs keep an eye

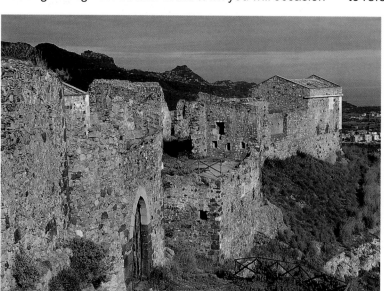

Top and left: the Norman Castle.

open for the **artisans' workshops**, particularly the one run by **signor Messina** in via Umberto, making objects in wrought iron.

If you keen on sunbathing or swimming you should head for the **beach of San Marco** mentioned above.

If you are in the area in summer we suggest you take part in the recreational and cultural activities organised along the San Marco coastline as part of the **Calatabianese August**.

Other enjoyable events organised in Calatabiano are almost all connected with gastronomy, so equip yourself with a napkin and get ready to eat at the **Ottobrata**, a fair, market and gastronomic event, at the **Roast Suckling-pig** Festival in February, the **Maccheronata** on 4th March in Pasteria and the **Medlar Festival** on the second Sunday in May.

On the third Saturday and Sunday in May the **Feast of Saint Phillip Syriac**, patron of the town, is celebrated. You really should not miss the spectacular 'race' of the carriage from the Norman Castle to the town if you are in Calatabiano at this time of year. There is a legend connected to this feast to which we would like to dedicate a few lines.

The Saint is depicted with a black face and this detail is explained by a story born out of popular imagination which has been passed down through the generations and whose origins are lost in the mists of time.

It is said that Saint Phillip was challenged and chained by Satan in the Castle of Calatabiano (which he certainly visited at some stage). He freed himself with the help of his faith and challenged Satan in return. The latter did not have the same luck and was thrown down a well.

From this uncomfortable position he begged Saint Phillip to set him free but the incorruptible Saint answered "mai" (never), a word mistaken by Satan as May (and so he still waits to be freed every year in the month of May when, however, the celebrations in honour of the town's patron take place).

Once Saint Phillip had eliminated the Prince of Darkness, he decided to complete his work of exorcism by chasing all the other demons to hell. He succeeded in his task but came back with his face blackened by the heat of the flames.

RESTAURANTS

- CASTELLO DI SAN MARCO: via San Marco, 6 (tel. 095 641181 fax 095 642635). Restaurant-pizzeria on the campsite. Typical Sicilian cuisine.
- IL PINO VERDE: via San Marco.

CAMP SITES

- ALMOETIA ♥ ♥: via San Marco, 19 (tel./fax 095 641936). With restaurant, bar and shop.
- CASTELLO DI SAN MARCO ♥ ♥: via San Marco, 6 (tel. 095 641181 fax 095 642635). With restaurant and bar. Open all year round.

FARM HOLIDAYS AND RESIDENCE

- GALIMI: via Pasteria 19/a - locality Galimi (tel./fax 095 641756). Lemon and mandarin production. Open from March to September.

Top and left: San Marco Castle.

View of Etna from Troina.

Etna from Biancavilla.

View of Etna from Sferro.

Etna seen from Libertinia.

View of Etna from Agnone Bagni.

Bronte with Etna in the background.

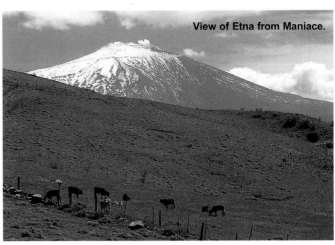
View of Etna from Maniace.

Calatabiano and Etna.

Etna seen from contrada Milia near Nicolosi.

View of Etna from Taormina.

SANT'AGATA LI BATTIATI:
DEDICATED TO THE SAINT

Very near Catania (7km), so much so as to become one of the favourite places for people from Catania to spend the summer, Sant'Agata Li Battiati was once one of the hamlets of Catania.

The name of the town was originally just Battiati. The reference to the patron Saint of Catania was added after the miraculous event which according to tradition was linked to the volcano and heavenly protection. During the terrible eruption of 1444, indeed, the town was seriously threatened by the lava that was approaching quickly and the help of Saint Agatha was invoked. The Saint's Veil performed the miracle and stopped the lava. Out of gratitude a church dedicated to the Saint was built and as a lasting memory of the event the name of the town was changed to its present one. The town was a feud of the Massa family of Castelforte. The most important monument is the above mentioned **Church of Saint Agatha**, the oldest in the town. It was built in the 15th century and, although it has been considerably renovated, you can still recognise some elements of the original construction. Other buildings of a certain interest, such as the **Church of Saint Thomas** and the **Church of Saint Lawrence**, display the style typical of Sicilian solar baroque. if you happen to arrive in Sant'Agata Li Battiati at lunch or dinner time, you

Right: lava stone arch. Bottom: Cathedral of Our Lady of the Annunciation.

can stop off to try the **local cuisine** at **Bella**, in via Bellini, or **Al Petite**, in via Umberto.

For dessert head for the **confectioner's Dolce Sorriso** or the **bar-confectioner's Orchidea**, both in via Umberto.

In August the town comes to life for the **Effetto Battiati** review, music, drama and cabaret in the streets. In the same month, on the 10th, the **patronal Feast of Saint Lawrence** is held. Finally, on 3rd and 4th October the grape harvest is celebrated with the **Grape and Wine Festival**.

RESTAURANTS - PIZZERIAS

- BELLA: via Bellini, 48 (tel. 095 212993). Pizzeria-restaurant. Excellent caserecci 'alla Bella' and speciality fish dishes.
- AL PETITE: via Umberto, 50.

PUBS - CLUBS - SANDWICH BARS

- A'CONCA: Piazza Chiesa Madre, 14.

HOTELS

- LA VILLETTA: via Bellini, 4 (tel. 095 212975). With restaurant, pizzeria and bar.

GRAVINA DI CATANIA: IN THE NAME OF THE PRINCE

The name of this town, which was originally a hamlet depending on Catania with the name of Plache, derives directly from that of Prince Girolamo Gravina Cruyllas, who was feudal lord here in the mid-17th century.

The building of greatest historical-artistic importance is the **Cathedral**, dedicated to the patron Saint Anthony of Padua, essentially characterised by the lovely 18th century bell-tower with spire.

Once the typical residences of the area were the 'dammusi', which were constructed with pumice-stone, which is still used today.

The atmosphere of Gravina is peaceful and pleasant, so it is worth taking a stroll and stopping off to taste some of the local dishes. If this is your intention, we suggest the **restaurant Rasula Alta**, in via Fratelli Bandiera.

If you would like a good cup of coffee or to try an exquisite cake, then head for the **bar-confectioner's Alexander**, in via Vittorio Emanuele, whose specialities are almond pastries and Sicilian 'cassate'; the **bar-confectioner's Alecci**, in via Gramsci; the **bar Santoro** in via Vittorio Emanuele. Don't leave Gravina without visiting **La Cantina**, in Piazza Etnea, where you will find a wide choice of Etna wines.

The customs and traditions of the town are on show on 13th June, the day of the **patronal Feast of Saint Anthony of Padua**; in September there are popular theatre performances in the Borsellino Park, as part of the **Gravinese September**; from 30th September to 4th October there is the **Exhibition and Market of Terracotta, Lava Stone and Wood** in the Borsellino Park; in October the **Arts and Crafts Exhibition** is held.

RESTAURANTS

- RASULA ALTA: via Fratelli Bandiera, 81 (tel. 095 417023). Restaurant of the Hotel Sport Rasula Alta.

PIZZERIAS

- LA LANTERNA: via Tiziano, 13 (tel. 095 416965).
- NORD EST: Piazza della Regione, 1. Pizzeria-fast food restaurant-bar-beer hall.
- SAIA: via S. Giovanni Galermo, 11 (tel. 095 393315).

PUBS - CLUBS - SANDWICH BARS

- ALBATROS: via Etnea, 419 (tel. 095 395598). Beer hall-sandwich bar.
- MONTANA: via Vecchia San Giovanni.

HOTELS

- HOTEL SPORT RASULA ALTA: via Fratelli Bandiera, 81 (tel. 095 417023 fax 095 417909). With restaurant and bar.

Top: view of Etna covered in snow.

MASCALUCIA: WHERE HORSES GREW

Situated on the southern slopes of Etna, Mascalucia is a pleasant place to stay in summer bercause of the favourable climate offered by its position at an altitude of 420 metres.

The name of the town is linked to the fact that in Mediaeval times horses were bred here, leading to the name 'maniscalcia', then corrupted to Mascalucia.

It was a feud of the Massa family in the 17th century and later of the Branciforte family.

The area around Mascalucia was also affected by the eruption of 1669, which threatened the town and destroyed many of those nearby.

Despite this the artistic-monumental heritage of the town is of a certain interest.

You should particularly visit the **Cathedral**, characterised by a beautiful lava stone portal, flanked by columns, and by the bell-tower with spire; the 18th century **Church of Saint Vito**, with a harmonious soberly decorated facade; the **Church of Saint Anthony Abbot**, built in the 15th century and still preserving the original white limestone portal.

Handicrafts are of some importance here, especially the production of **carpets** and **musical instruments**. An opportunity to browse and make some purchases is offered by the **Antiques Market**, which is held once a month, on the second weekend, in the municipal park.

Don't underestimate the gastronomic aspects of your visit to Mascalucia.

At luch or dinner you can try the specialities of the **local cuisine** in one of the welcoming and friendly restaurants in the town.

Al Mio Ristorante, in via SS. Crocifisso is a comfortable restaurant in an old farmhouse with a splendid view and offers a rich and varied menu of Sicilian and international cuisine; **Villa Cinque Re**, in Corso San Vito, with its elegant rooms and green garden, is a refined setting for equally refined cuisine. Receptions and dances are also organised.

For your stay in Mascalucia we recommend the **Trinità Farm Holiday Centre**, at Trinità, on the slopes of Etna, in an 18th century building typical of the Etna area, carefully restored respecting the original style.

Visits are organised to the ornamental park run by the same centre (typical Mediterranean and exotic plants), as well as excursions up Etna and to other places of natural beauty and interest.

Among the produce you should try are the sun-dried tomatoes, marinated cheeses, pasta Trinità (with grilled vegetables), chicken casserole with grapes and roulades in lemon leaves.

Moreover citrus fruits are grown here using natural farming methods.

The centre organises gastronomic meetings and botany and craft courses. The ski slopes are 25km away; the sea is 15km from here.

A short list of main annual events in Mascalucia will help to make your stay more pleasurable: in May there are numerous events linked to nature and protection of the environment as part of **Ecological May**; on the third Sunday of the same month the **Feast of Mompilieri** is held, in memory of Our Lady of the 'Sciara' or of Mompilieri, also celebrated in August; 15th June (and also 15th August) the **patronal Feast of Saint Vito** takes place; in September, the first Sunday of the month is dedicated to **Our Lady of Consolation**.

RESTAURANTS - PIZZERIAS

- AL MIO RISTORANTE: via SS. Crocifisso, 29 (tel. 095 7270004). Traditional Sicilian and international cuisine. Specialities include bread with aromatic herbs, with pistachio, with nuts and also with lemon.
- AL PORTICHETTO: via Pulei, 38 (tel. 095 7270007). Restaurant-pizzeria. Excellent meat and fish specialities. Wide choice of wines.
- CHAMPAGNE: via Roma, 116 (tel. 095 7274740). Restaurant-pizzeria. Try the casarecci 'alla boscaiola' and the agnolotti stuffed with mushrooms and served in 'montanara' sauce.
- MICHELANGELO: via Roma, 106 (tel. 095 7274662). Pizzas, maxi pizzas, also first and second courses.
- VILLA I CINQUE RE: Corso San Vito, 226 (tel. 095 7272941). A short distance from the centre of Mascalucia. Restaurant-pizzeria-reception hall with dances.

FARM HOLIDAYS

- AZIENDA AGRITURISTICA TRINITÀ: via Trinità, 34 - locality Trinità (tel./fax 095 7272156). With swimming-pool. The centre organises gastronomic meetings and courses of botany and crafts. Ski slopes 25 km away; beach 15 km away.

APARTAMENTS

- LOCATOURIST: via G. Sciuti, 24 (tel. 095 7914397).

SAN PIETRO CLARENZA:
A QUIET STOP OFF

About ten kilometres from Catania, on the southern slopes of Etna, stands **San Pietro Clarenza**.

The name of the town comes from that of the Clarenza family, who owned the feud. It then passed into the hands of other nobles, including the Massa and Reitano families. Under the latter it became a principality.

A small cosy town, San Pietro Clarenza is home to some noble buildings of a certain importance, which you can discover by wandering along the silent streets of the town. You should visit the **Church of Saint Catherine**, which was originally built in the 17th century.

They produce excellent **olive oil** here and this can be bought directly from the oil mills. Another 'souvenir' to take home, apart from the products of the flowering local crafts, is the **wine**, which you will easily find in the various wine cellars in town. You can try the local dishes at the **restaurant Caccetta**, in Piazza Marconi, with a menu to satisfy gourmets. Tasty pizzas of various kinds are served at the **pizzeria Catania**, in via Umberto I. If you happen to arrive here on 25th November, don't miss the **Feast of Saint Catherine**, dedicated to the patron of the town.

RESTAURANTS
• CACCETTA: Piazza G. Marconi, 1/a (tel. 095 529524).

PIZZERIAS
• CATANIA: via Umberto I, 196 (tel. 095 522433).

Top: fountain in the main square. Facing page: noble residence in the town centre.

CAMPOROTONDO ETNEO

The name of Camporotondo comes from its physical characteristics and the layout of the land on which it stands.

It was also once one of the hamlets depending on Catania and then became a feud of the Reitano family in the 17th century, becoming a marquisate under the same family in the following century.

The oldest buildings in Camporotondo were destroyed, as was the whole town, during the eruption of 1669. **Palazzo Signorello** is the most interesting building in town from an architectural point of view. You should also visit **Palazzo Natali** and the **Church of Saint Anthony Abbot**, in baroque style, dedicated to the patron Saint of the town, who is solemnly celebrated on 17th January. In September Camporotondo is home to artists for the **Impromptu Art Exhibition**.

If you are passing through Camporotondo stop off for a cup of coffee or refreshing drink at the **bar Anzalone**, in Piazza Sant'Antonio Abate, or at **Campisi**, in via Nazionale.

TREMESTIERI ETNEO: MILLS AND OLD LACE

Situated on the southern slopes of Etna, less than ten kilometres from Catania, **Tremestieri Etneo** is one of the favourite summer holiday destinations for the people of Catania, also because of its pleasant climate.

The name of the town was originally Trimosterium and seems to be connected to the dialectal expression used to refer to mills.

Tremestieri was also a hamlet dependent on Catania and, like other towns round Etna, was the feud of noble families, in this case the Massa family in the 17th century, and the Rizzari family later on.

The urban layout of Tremestieri still depends on the fact that the town was born as a small village on the road (the via Etnea) that climbs up from Catania towards the volcano.

There are some interesting religious buildings, mostly 18th century, including the **Cathedral**, and some noble buildings from the early part of the 19th century.

Tremestieri is a town of ancient traditions but with an eye on the future. There is still a great deal of love and attention, however, for traditional activities that have almost disappeared elsewhere. Many women in the town, for example, practise the ancient art of embroidery, or more exactly **pillow-lace**, and produce really refined works of art that you can admire and purchase during the **Pillow-Lace Exhibition and Market**, which is held in March.

The first Sunday after Easter sees the **patronal Feast of Our Lady of Peace**.

Sports enthusiasts follow with interest the **International Women's Tennis Tournament**, which takes place in August in various towns, including Tremestieri. Throughout the **Christmas period** numerous concerts and other events are organised in the churches.

RESTAURANTS

- FASANARO: via del Canalicchio, 21 (tel. 095 338729).
- IL VECCHIO OLEANDRO: via Etnea, 174 (tel. 095 7252131). Restaurant-pizzeria. Starters, first and second courses with mushrooms.
- PIRANHA: via Monti Sicani, 5 - Canalicchio (tel. 095 580113). Trattoria-pizzeria. Home cooking.
- VILLA DEL SOLE: via Garro, 41 (tel. 095 7411494).

PUBS - CLUBS - SANDWICH BARS

- CELTIC CLUB: via Gravina, 42.

SAN GIOVANNI LA PUNTA: BETWEEN THE VOLCANO AND THE SEA

San Giovanni La Punta is just 12 kilometres from Catania and was once a hamlet that depended on the city. Situated halfway between the coast and the volcano, it is the ideal place for those who want to spend a relaxing holiday in the countryside without missing out on the beach.

A popular legend explains how the town got its name through a miraculous event that happened at an unspecified time in the past.

According to tradition, on the site of the present day main square there once stood an altar (no longer in existence) dedicated to Saint John the Evangelist, around which the town had grown up. It is said that following an eruption of Etna the lava flow reached the town and suddenly stopped forming the shape of a point.

The inhabitants attributed this miracle to the Saint and named the town after him.

The historical origins of the town seem to be traceable to contrada Catìra, where, around a small now ruined church dedicated to Saint Nicolò, there once stood a town whose population later moved to the present site.

ON TIPTOE

To get to know the town take a stroll through the quiet narrow streets and visit the few but interesting monuments. You should see the **Church of Saint John the Baptist**, built in the 18th century, characterised by the imposing facade and the adjacent oratory; the **Church of Saint Sebastian**; the **Church of Our Lady of Graces**; the **Church of Our Lady of Loreto**; the **Villa of the Paternò Castello di Caracci**. In the centre there are also some elegant 19th century residences with gardens that help to enrich the parkland of the town. An absolute 'must' for a visit is the workshop constructing **Sicilian carts**, which are hand-made piece by piece, according to tradition, and painted by hand, bearing witness to a now disappearing art. Take advantage of your stroll to stock up on postcards to send to your friends or to choose a good book to read while relaxing. These and other things can be found at the **bookshop Di Lorenzo**, in via Roma, and at the **stationer's-bookshop Il Bosco**, in via della Regione.

Few people can resist good food, especially on holiday, and

it can also be a way of getting to know the 'character' of a town and its people better. Local cuisine is the result of various influences, adaptations and evolutions and says a lot about about the true nature of a population. The generous effusive taste of almond pastries and Sicilian 'cassate' from the **confectioners' Nicosia**, in via della Regione, and **Turrisi**, in via Roma, will help you make peace with the world; exquisite nougat, to try immediately or to take away as presents, and excellent ice-creams from the confectioner's **Tosto** and the above mentioned Nicosia. You can find excellent almond granita at the **Bar Balsamo 1937**, the oldest confectioner's in town, on the corner of via Etnea and Piazza Gabriele Allegra. The best known recipes of traditional Sicilian cuisine and refined dishes inspired by international cuisine can be found on the rich menu of the **Villa Grifoni**, in via Fisichella, just outside town on the road to Trecastagni, in the splendid setting of an old nobleman's house, tastefully restored. If you are looking for somewhere to stay in San Giovanni La Punta, which combines the comfort of a hotel with the opportunity to taste the specialities of local gastronomy, we recommend the hotel **Villa Paradiso dell'Etna**, peaceful and tranquil, on the slopes of Etna and only 15 kilometres from the centre of Catania, with about thirty rooms and four suites, all furnished with sober elegance and attention to detail. On the panoramic terrace you can have breakfast with the stupendous scenario of the volcano in the background. The parkland that surrounds the hotel offers the chance of relaxation to the hotel guests; the **Garden Hotel**, in the district of Trappeto, is also suitable for meetings, thanks to the convention hall. The restaurant of the hotel, **La Vecchia Quercia**, also houses guests on its large elegant terraces in summer. You can never really understand the spirit of a town without participating, along with the inhabitants, in the celebration of the most important events of the year. Here then is a short list of such events: in July there is the **Antiques Exhibition**; from 10th August to 4th September the events of the **Puntese Summer** are held; on 15th August there is the **Feast of Our Lady of Ravanusa**, a day when, according to local tradition, every family should eat anchovies and water melon; in September the Review of Art by Contemporary Sicilian Masters **PuntArte** is held; 27th December sees the **patronal Feast of Saint John the Evangelist**.

RESTAURANTS

- AL CALATINO: via Della Regione, 103 (tel. 095 7411727). Restaurant-pizzeria. We recommend the home-made maccheroni and spaghetti 'alla Norma'.
- GIARDINO DI BACCO: via Piave, 3 (tel. 095 7512727). Traditional cuisine and a wide choice of famous wines, mostly Sicilian. Shady garden.
- JUPITER: contrada Savoca (tel. 095 7177373). Restaurant of the Ares Hotel. In lovely countryside. International cuisine based on fish and meat. Also a pizzeria.

- LA PIGNA: road to Viagrande, 37 (tel. 095 7512409). Restaurant of the hotel Villa Paradiso dell'Etna. Try the pennette with pistachios and almonds, the mushrooms and the fish baked in salt. Piano bar three times a week.
- LA VECCHIA QUERCIA: via Madonna delle lacrime, 12/b – district of Trappeto (tel. 095 7177767). Restaurant of the Garden Hotel. Sicilian cuisine. With large terraces.
- REITANO: via Motta, 109 (tel. 095 7412369). Restaurant-pizzeria. Specialised in typical Sicilian cuisine.
- VILLA GRIFONI: via Fisichella, 63 (tel. 095 7412063). With a summer terrace. Sicilian and international cuisine. We recommend the fresh tagliatelle with flavours of the forest and the braised meat in fresh mushroom sauce.

PIZZERIAS

- TIFFANY: via Siracusa, 8 (tel. 095 7512403). Pizzeria-discotheque.

PUBS - CLUBS - SANDWICH BARS

- 15/18: via Roma.
- LAVORI IN CORSO: via S. Ten. Scalia, 51.

HOTELS

- VILLA PARADISO DELL'ETNA ♥♥♥♥: road to Viagrande, 37 (tel. 095 7512409 fax 095 7413861). With restaurant and bar. Panoramic terrace, meeting room, open-air pool and woodland. Piano bar three times a week and discotheque every Sunday. Air-conditioned rooms with mini-bar, safe, satellite TV and telephone.
- GARDEN HOTEL ♥♥♥: via Madonna delle Lacrime, 12/b - district of Trappeto (tel. 095 7177767 fax 095 7177991). With restaurant, swimming-pool, convention and meeting room.
- ARES HOTEL ♥♥♥: contrada Savoca - Trappeto (tel. 095 7177373 fax 095 7177859). With restaurant and bar. Air-conditioned rooms. Meeting and convention hall.

Right: San Giovanni La Punta Cathedral. Facing page: Cathedral of Peace in Tremestieri Etneo.

NICOLOSI: CHALLENGING THE VOLCANO

We begin our second itinerary around the volcano from **Nicolosi**, about twelve kilometres from Catania. Nicolosi is situated at an altitude of about 700 metres on the southern slopes of Etna and is place you have to pass through to reach many of the interesting areas of the volcano. Etna does not completely dominate the panorama, however, which also includes the twin outlines of the green Monti Rossi. The fame and fortune of Nicolosi, which was also well known by travellers of the 18th and 19th centuries, has always been linked to its particular geographical position, which has earned it the name of the Gateway to Etna.

Since it is very near Catania it is a favoured place for local day trips, but also as a holiday destination both for lovers of the mountains and **winter sports** and for simple tourists looking for a little peace and quiet away from the heat of summer. The history of Nicolosi is largely connected with the activity of Etna, which has often damaged or even completely destroyed the town with its lava flows.

The town first started to grow up around the Monastery of San Nicolò l'Arena, from which the town took its name, founded by the Benedictine fathers in the 13th century on the site of small holy building of the previous century.

The monks were forced to abandon the Monastery following the natural calamities that struck the town in the early 1500s and almost completely wiped it out. The town was then rebuilt on its present site in the 17th century and in the following century the inhabitants once again suffered the terrible caprices of the volcano. Despite this the town was again rebuilt on the same site, against the wishes of the feudal lords, the Moncada family of Paternò.

Other memorable eruptions placed Nicolosi in danger in 1883 and 1886. On both occasions the inhabitants of the threatened town and Dusmet, then Bishop of Catania, held a spectacular procession carrying the Veil of Saint Agatha, the statues of Saint Anthony Abbot, Saint Anthony of Padua and Our Lady of Graces, as far as the end of the lava flow that was threatening the town. In both cases, whether by miracle or coincidence, the lava came to a halt after a few hours. Despite the threat posed by Etna, Nicolosi has a significant number of old religious buildings, often built with the same lava that has poured out of the volcano.

In Piazza Vittorio Emanuele stands the **Cathedral** or the Church of the Holy Spirit. It was almost completely rebuilt after the eruption of 1669 and has a linear facade flanked by a bell-tower, partly made of lava stone, with a spire. Inside you can see a valuable wooden crucifix.

Also in the same square you will find the **Etna Volcanological Museum**, housed in the premises of the Town Hall. The display cases exhibit lava materials, minerals and fossils. There is also a very interesting collection of iconographies and illustrations relating to the history of the volcano. It is also worth visiting the **Church of Saint Anthony Abbot**, protector of the town, which has a structure dating back to the late Middle Ages. This Church is the only building that survived the disastrous earthquake of 1693. Nicolosi possesses other churches of a certain importance, all built or rebuilt from the 18th century onwards. Among these we particularly remind you of the **Church of Saint Joseph**, with a lava stone facade, and the **Church of Our Lady of Graces**, which originally dates back to the 16th century.

A few kilometres away from the town you can visit the **Benedictine Monastery of San Nicolò l'Arena**, built in the 13th century, from which Nicolosi took its name.

Outside the town it is certainly worth making an excursion to the nearby **Monti Rossi**, covered by a cloak of luxuriant green woodland that offers cool shady protection from the hot summer sun.

Near here you can also visit the **Cave of Doves** and the so called **Calvary**, a small hill, of obvious volcanic origin, on top of which a small chapel has been built. This is reached by climbing a lava stone stairway flanked by the Stations of the Cross. Finally, we remind you that the departure station of the **Etna Cable Car** is situated near the Sapienza mountain hut (for information contact **Sitas** in Piaz-

On this page: ski lifts and ski slopes. Facing page from the top: Cathedral, panorama of the snow covered town, town of Nicolosi.

za Vittorio Emanuele tel. 095 911158 / 095 914209).

FROM RESTAURANT TO HOTEL

Among the typical gastronomic specialities of Nicolosi the most famous are undoubtedly the **mushrooms**, especially the delicious fragrant ferula variety, basic ingredients for numerous recipes.

The local cuisine can be tried at the **restaurants La Ginestra** in via Gemmellaro, **Etna** in via Etnea, **Grotta del Gallo** in via Madonna delle Grazie, **At the Pines** in Viale della Regione, **Corsaro** in Piazza Cantoniera, **Il Cantuccio** in via Torino, **Antico Orto dei Limoni** in via Grotte, **Al Buongustaio** in via Etnea.

If you want to eat out in a **pub** you can head for **Titanic** in via Etnea, a restaurant-pizzeria-pub serving local cuisine based on mushrooms, and for **Vetus** in Piazza Vittorio Emanuele, a pub-sandwich bar. The local cakes are worthy of note and

worth tasting. The best cakes in Nicolosi can be bought at the **bar-confectioner's Vitale** in Piazza Oberdan (try the 'sciatori' covered in chocolate), the **bar-confectioner's Bonanno** in Piazza Vittorio Emanuele (also here there are excellent 'sciatori'), the **bar-confectioner's-sandwich bar Italia 90** in piazzale Funivia - contrada Cantoniera (excellent 'cannoli', pistachio cakes and 'cassate'). If you want to take away a **souvenir** of Nicolosi to remember your stay near the volcano you can try the artisans' workshops in search of objects in **lava stone**. In the same workshops you can also buy attractive **wooden** articles and refined **pottery**.

We make a special mention of **Santo Doca** in via Etnea, an elegant showroom for pottery and gifts. As far as accommodation is concerned, Nicolosi offers numerous possibilities to suit every need and every budget.

We recommend the **Gemmellaro Hotel**, via Etnea; **Hotel Biancaneve**, via Etnea; **Hotel Restaurant Corsaro**, Piazza Cantoniera Etna South; **Etna Campsite**, via Goethe-pineta

Monti Rossi; **Youth Hostel**, via della Quercia. Some of these merit a more detailed study.

The Hotel Restaurant Corsaro, recently rebuilt, is the nearest hotel to the crater of the volcano and is situated at the notable altitude of 2,000 metres; it offers an excellent restaurant service (traditional cuisine with local dishes) and the chance of excursions, also with guides, to caves, to the central crater and to the Astrophysical Observatory. The Etna Campsite is the ideal place for younger and more adventurous people who enjoy sleeping in a tent under the stars; it is a departure point for excursions up the mountain and is situated in a pretty chestnut wood, offering all the conveniences necessary for a carefree holiday. The Youth Hostel is particularly suited, as its name suggests, to young people or those who do not have any great expectations; generally, it is a cheap place for those who choose Nicolosi as the base for their excursions.

LET'S SANCTIFY THE FESTIVALS

Even if you only take a glance at the calendar of events in the town, you will immediately notice that almost every month in Nicolosi gives you the chance to participate in some kind of festival, whether it be religious, folkloristic, gastronomic, cultural or sporting. Normally from January to March (although the period is strictly dependent on the snowfall) the **Three Days on Etna** is held, an international skiing competition at the Sapienza mountain hut. In April there are folkloristic displays and tasting of local produce as part of **April in Festival**. In July and August **Etneadi** takes place, a review of music, drama and dance, cinema and cabaret; the events and shows continue throughout the hottest period of the year and are held in the most pleasant and characteristic parts of town. On 10th August the **Saint Lawrence's Night** is celebrated at the Sapienza mountain hut with music and a picnic. On 15th August the **patronal Feast of Saint Anthony of Padua** takes place, along with the **exhibition-market of crafts and folk-**

lore. Also in August you can attend the **International Women's Tennis Tournament**; the **National Basketball Display**; **Craft Exhibition and Fair**. In September the **Etna Race** is held, an uphill car race of national importance. September, October and November are the months that see the **Mushroom Market**. In October there is another event held in Piazza della Cisterna dedicated to these delicacies of local cuisine, the **Mycological Exhibition and Mushroom Festival**. In November the **Indian Summer** includes preparation and tasting of ricotta, exhibition-market of local agricultural produce and folkloristic displays. Last of all, in December, **Christmas in Nicolosi** includes concerts and cribs.

RESTAURANTS AND PIZZERIAS

- AL BUONGUSTAIO: via Etnea, 105/f (tel. 095 7915760). Try the caserecci with mushrooms with sausage and tomato, mixed meat grill with mushrooms.
- AL TUKANO: via Etnea, 75 (tel. 095 910884). Restaurant-pizzeria. Excellent mushroom dishes and seafood.
- ANTICO ORTO DEI LIMONI: via Grotte, 4 (tel. 095 910808). We recommend the pennette with pistachio.
- AT THE PINES: Viale della Regione, 55 (tel. 095 914033). Restaurant-pizzeria. The Special Locale pizza is very good.
- BELVEDERE: via Etnea, 110 (tel. 095 911406). Hotel restaurant-pizzeria. Very refined cuisine using local produce. Excellent mushroom dishes and desserts.
- CORSARO: Piazza Cantoniera (tel. 095 914122). Hotel restaurant. Fresh home-made pasta. Very good agnolotti with mushrooms.
- CRATERI SILVESTRI: Piazza Crateri Silvestri (tel. 095 914133 fax 095 7809149). Restaurant-bar situated at an altitude of about 1,900 metres. Home cooking. Delicious roasts, mushrooms and cooked meats.
- ESAGONAL: contrada Cantoniera (tel. 095 7807868). Restaurant-bar. Mushroom based cuisine.
- ETNA: via Etnea, 93 (tel. 095 911937). Restaurant-pizzeria. Fresh mushroom specialities.
- GROTTA DEL GALLO: via Madonna delle Grazie, 40 (tel. 095 911301). Restaurant-pizzeria. Traditional Etna cuisine

with interesting seafood dishes. We recommend the caserecci, the Mare e Monti risotto, the roast leg of veal.
- IL CANTUCCIO: via Torino, 1 (tel. 095 7914994). Restaurant-pizzeria. Sicilian cuisine with special attention to mushroom dishes.
- IL RIFUGIO SAPIENZA: contrada Cantoniera (tel. 095 911062). Mountain hut restaurant. Mountain cuisine. Roasted mushrooms, escalopes 'alla parmigiana', DOC Etna wines.
- ITALIA 90: piazzale Funivia - contrada Cantoniera (tel. 095 7807242). Restaurant-pizzeria-bar.
- LA CANTONIERA: contrada Cantoniera (tel. 095 914155). Restaurant-bar. Specialities with mushrooms and game.
- LA CAPANNINA: piazzale Crateri Silvestri (tel. 095 7808427). Restaurant-bar-souvenirs. Excellent spaghetti with pistachio and 'alla palermitana'.
- LA GINESTRA: via Fratelli Gemmellaro, 91 (tel. 095 914563). Restaurant-pizzeria. Etna cuisine. Exquisite risotto with mushrooms and risotto with broom. Refined wine list.
- PICCOLO MONDO ANTICO: via Garibaldi, 123 (tel. 095 914906). Typical Sicilian cuisine. Try the caserecci with mushrooms and sausage with mushrooms. Sicilian wines.
- SETTE PIÙ LA TEGOLA: Viale della Regione (tel. 095 914876). Restaurant-pizzeria.
- TERRAZZA DELL'ETNA: contrada Cantoniera (tel. 095 914353). Very near the cable car station. Mountain specialities.
- TITANIC: via Etnea, 187 (tel. 095 7916351). Restaurant-pizzeria-pub. Local mushroom based cuisine.

HOTELS

- BIANCANEVE ♥ ♥ ♥: via Etnea, 163 (tel. 095 911176 fax 095 911194). With restaurant, bar, swimming-pool, tennis court.
- CORSARO ♥ ♥ ♥: Piazza Cantoniera (tel. 095 914122 fax 095 7801024). With restaurant and bar.
- GEMMELLARO ♥ ♥ ♥: via Etnea, 160 (tel. 095 911373 fax 095 911071). With restaurant and bar.
- BELVEDERE ♥ ♥: via Etnea, 110 (tel. 095 911406). With restaurant and bar.
- MONTI ROSSI ♥: via Etnea, 177 (tel. 095 7914393). With restaurant and bar.

MOUNTAIN HUTS CAMPSITES AND HOSTELS

- SAPIENZA: contrada Cantoniera (tel. 095 7808226 fax 095 7809966). With restaurant and bar.
- CAMPING ETNA ♥ ♥: via Goethe - pineta Monti Rossi (tel. 095 914309). With swimming-pool, bar, volleyball, bowls, football, video-games, table tennis.
- OSTELLO DELLA GIOVENTÙ: via della Quercia, 7 (tel. 095 7914686 fax 095 7914701). At the foot of Etna.

Left: Monti Silvestri. Facing page: Philosopher's Tower (2,900m).

Nicolosi: the gateway to Etna

For once history leaves no space for doubt and interpretation: from the 18th century until the early 20th century the only access to the volcano was from Nicolosi. Only here, from the 1700s onwards, were there local people able to place their services at the disposal of travelling aristocrats and to take them up to the summit. Some guides have been immortalised by quotations dedicated to them by their clients in their travel diaries. Biagio Motta, called the Cyclops, for example, was depicted in two engravings by Jean Houel, now kept in the Hermitage. Roland de la Platière described how he "walked ahead with great steps, without saying a word, answering any questions briefly and precisely; he went, came and stopped where it was necessary, he had a good appetite, asked nothing and adapted himself to everything". Anyway, in those days Nicolosi was no more than a group of black stone houses that had grown up near the craters of 1669, not far from the historical Monastery of Saint Nicholas, a tiny mountain village inhabited by shepherds, charcoal merchants and carters for whom acting as a guide was an honour and an important source of income.

After the Cyclops, the job of guide in Nicolosi began to be passed on from father to son. Obviously, not all travellers felt the need to go right up to the summit of the giant mountain. In 1787 Goethe was content to climb the Monti Rossi just outside Nicolosi, the craters that caused the disastrous eruption of 1669: "I sat down to get my strength back and to contemplate the view. But I was no better off in that position – wrote the great German author – the wind was coming from then east, above the magnificent landscape stretched out below me, near and as far as the sea. The long coastline from Syracuse to Messina, with its bends and its gulfs, was laid out before my eyes, either fully visible or a little hidden by the coastal rocks.

The 19th century in Nicolosi was the century of the Gemmellaro brothers, Carlo, Mario and Giuseppe: they were versatile experts and enthusiastic promoters of the beauty of 'their' volcano and at the beginning of the century managed to collect enough funds to have a shelter built at the foot of the summit cone. They called it the "Casina degli inglesi" in honour of the British soldiers that provided the capital for the construction of the building. This important support facility for travellers visiting Etna gradually grew and at the end of the 19th century earned the praises of Gustavo Chiesi, a journalist and writer travelling through Italy: "The Italian Alpine Club - wrote Chiesi in 1892 - has scrupulously chosen the guides on Etna: they are all people of proven experience, courageous, cold-blooded in their difficult job, and treat strangers with courtesy, and absolute honesty".

The excursion to the summit followed a standard procedure: departure from Nicolosi in the afternoon on mule-back, through woodland that some visitors found disappointing when they compared it to the forests of central Europe. The first stop was made at the Cave of Goats, on the edge of the desert area. Here the excursionists could eat and rest for a few hours on straw mattresses, before leaving for the final hike up towards the summit in the middle of the night so that the guides could get their clients to the top by sunrise, so they could admire dawn from the crater: this spectacle was made famous throughout Europe by Patrick Brydone in his book "A tour through Sicily and Malta", published in 1773.

Finally, in 1936 the long awaited moment arrived when the road up Etna was opened. A long series of hairpin bends up to an altitude of 1,900 metres, the road changed attitudes to the volcano. No more tiring mule-back climbs, but fast drives up in motor vehicles, which began to carry up tourists to the edge of the desert area. The 1936 road was destroyed by the 1983 lava flow but has been worthily replaced by a lovely provincial road that largely follows the same route and twists its way gently up the slope of the volcano as far as the Etna-south tourist area. From here there is an efficient transport service by means of cable car and off-road vehicles in order to get up near the summit, at the Philosopher's Tower (2,920 metres). If you prefer to climb up on foot, you can follow the same route taken by the off-road vehicles (see the description of the fourth itinerary of the Cross-Etna Walk) calculating about three and a half hours of walking to reach the Philosopher's Tower.

Near the Sapienza mountain hut you can also make a short excursion to the summit of the nearby Monti Silvestri (the first craters you see from the cable car station looking east) formed at the end of the 19th century, or you can go down towards Piano Vetore (heading for the Etna Grand Hotel) and then go up the mount of the same name (accessible along convenient forest paths, 1,820 metres) from which you enjoy a lovely view both towards the summit craters and towards the coast. At the Etna grand Hotel the Park Authority has set up a base point for excursions where you can attend film shows about the protected area and get information on the routes.

The tourist area of Etna-south is also equipped with four ski-lifts (as well as the cable car) serving a ski slope that descends from 2,550 metres to 1,900 metres, with various possible intermediate stops.

Giuseppe Riggio e Giuseppe Vitali

PEDARA: TWICE IN THE DUST

Pedara is less than four kilometres from Nicolosi, a hill town situated at an altitude of about 600 metres on the south-western slopes of Etna.

According to some researchers the name of the town derives from the term 'lapidaria', which was used to describe the local hard stone used in the construction of many buildings in the zone. Other interpretations conclude that the name derives from the Greek city of Epidaurum, the place of origin of numerous settlers that moved to Sicily, or from the Latin 'apud aram' (at the foot of the altar) in reference to a small building dedicated to Jupiter, which was situated on Etna. In the past it was no more than one of the many hamlets that depended on the city of Catania.

The town has ancient origins, as is shown by the numerous archaeological finds (burial sites, coins, pottery) in the zone, dating back to Greek times. It is certain that the town had already developed in the Middle Ages, when, in 1408 to be precise, a violent eruption forced the inhabitants to abandon their homes.

The town was razed to the ground but, as with many other towns around Etna, it was rebuilt in the same place. The economic development of Pedara was rapid from the 17th century onwards. Under the dominion of the Pappalardo family the town began to grow and was enriched by prestigious new buildings. The Pappalardos were also responsible for the 18th century rebuilding of the town following the earthquake of 1693, which had destroyed it.

In the 1700s it became a feud of the Alliata family. It has been an autonomous municipality since 1817.

Top: panoramic view of the town. Bottom: Cathedral.

CHURCHES AND HISTORIC RESIDENCES

Pedara has an artistic-monumental heritage of considerable importance. There are numerous high-class residences in the town centre. In particular, you should see the 18th century **Palazzo Pappalardo**, in via Regina Margherita, which is appreciated for the elegant decorations of its facade and for its spacious atrium, and **Palazzo Di Giovanni**, in Piazza Don Diego, with its characteristic two-coloured portal with ashlar decoration. Other elegant baroque buildings can be seen in Corso Ara di Giove, the most important street in the town.

In Piazza Don Diego stands the **Cathedral of Saint Catherine of Alessandria**, preceded by a stairway in lava stone and wrought iron railings around the parvis and with a facade that was rebuilt in the 18th century.

The clear surface of the facade is characterised by pilaster strips that divide it into four sectors and black lava stone around the portals surmounted by windows. High up you will see the bell-tower, with a conical roof and showing the same alternation of black and white. Inside the three naves you can see 18th century frescoes by G. Lo Coco. In the oratory adjacent to the church you can admire the 16th century portal belonging to the original church.

You should also visit the **Church of Saint Vito**, built after 1693, with a facade including a portal in lava stone; the **Church of Saint Biagio**, from the end of the 17th century; the **Church of Saint Anthony Abbot**, decorated by golden stucco decorations; the **Church of Santa Maria della Stella**, dating from 1735. The

114

town is surrounded by mountains and luxuriant woodland and also has a lovely **Municipal Park** dominated by an ancient pine tree.

There are numerous possibilities for lovers of country walks around Pedara. In particular we recommend the woods in **contrada Tardaria**, easily reached by following the signposts.

EVERYTHING YOU WANT

The particular fertility of the lava soil around Pedara is used, above all, for the intensive growing of vines and fruit.

The **wine** is of high quality and can be bought directly from the producers of the area.

The **fruit conserves** are well known and greatly appreciated, especially those made from prickly pears.

If you want to try the specialities of the local cuisine, which often include mushrooms, we recommend the **restaurants Belladonna** in via Della Resistenza, **Grotta del Monaco** in via Pacinotti, **La Bussola** in Piazza Don Bosco. Do not underestimate the local cakes and pastries.

We particularly recommend the **confectioners' Pappalardo** in Corso Ara di Giove ('panzerotti' and 'cannoli') and **La Bussola** in Piazza Don Bosco (Sicilian 'cassate' and 'castagnole' with ricotta).

Some good news for lovers of night life: the **pubs Dizzy** and **Big Ben**, both in via Marconi.

The characteristic souvenirs of Pedara are objects in **lava stone** and **pottery**. If you want to purchase them you need only visit the various workshops in Corso Ara di Giove. It is worth taking a look at the splendid colourful woollen and cotton **carpets** by **Roberta Scicali** in via La Pira. If you are looking for maps or books you can head for the **bookshop Maccarone** in via Ammiraglio Toscano.

There are numerous events and festivals to enliven your stay in Pedara. 17th January is the **patronal Feast of Saint Anthony Abbot**, with the ritual blessing of animals and vehicles, sales of natural produce offered to the Saint. 25th March is the **Feast of Our Most Holy Lady of the Annunciation**. At the end of May or in early June the **Olive Tree Trophy** is awarded to the winner in the archery competition at the municipal stadium. In July and August **Pedarestate** includes drama, music and sport in the Belvedere park. At the same time of year the **Summer Fair** is held in the municipal park and in Piazza Don Bosco, an exhibition and market of crafts and local gastronomic products. The second Saturday in September and the three following days see the solemn **patronal Feast of Our Most Holy Lady of the Annunciation**.

From 23rd to 31st October **Meletna** is held to promote the tasty local apples.

In October the **Mushroom Festival** takes place in the municipal park and in Piazza Don Bosco. 25th November is the **Feast of Saint Catherine**.

In December **Christmas around the Yule Log** is held. It is also worth keeping an eye open for the programme of the **drama season** at the Don Bosco Theatre, organised by the Amici del Teatro company (performances from October to May).

RESTAURANTS

- BELLADONNA: via della Resistenza, 69 (tel. 095 916121). Hotel restaurant. Traditional cuisine and mushroom based specialities. Good wine list.
- ETNA CATERING: Piazza Don Diego, 39 (tel. 095 7801083). Restaurant-pizzeria-pancake house-confectioner's.
- GROTTA DEL MONACO: via Pacinotti, 5 (tel. 095 916772). Trattoria-pizzeria. Barbecued and mushroom specialities. Excellent pappardelle with mushrooms and mixed grill.

- LA BUSSOLA: Piazza Don Bosco, 4/10 (tel. 095 7800250). Typical fresh mushroom based dishes. We recommend the pappardelle 'alla Bussola', escalopes with mushrooms, pancakes.
- LE MIMOSE: via L. Capuana, 31 (tel. 095 915834). Mountain and seafood cuisine. Exquisite prawns au gratin and barbecued bass.

PIZZERIAS

- LA TETTOIA: Corso Ara di Giove, 129 (tel. 095 7800988).

HOTELS

- BONACCORSI: via Pirandello, 2 (tel. 095 915337 fax 095 915136). With restaurant and bar.

ROOMS FOR RENT

- BELLADONNA: via della Resistenza, 69 (tel. 095 916121). With restaurant, pizzeria, private car park.

Top: local artisans collect incandescent lava to make ashtrays and other souvenirs.

TRECASTAGNI: DEVOTED TO THREE SAINTS

A short distance from Pedara stands **Trecastagni**, a hill town on the south-western slopes of Etna.

The name of the town derives from the Latin expression 'tres casti agni' (three chaste lambs) used in reference to the three martyr Saints Alfio, Cirino and Filadelfo.

Historical sources and digs carried out in the area show it is probable that the Sicans, Sikels, Greeks and Romans all settled here.

Certainly the area was already well populated in the 14th century.

Until the mid-17th century it was one of the hamlets depending on Catania and shared the historical ups and downs of nearby Pedara, first as a possession of the Di Giovanni family and later the Alliata family.

Trecastagni is a popular place for summer holidays because of its pleasant climate and the lovely countryside.

A stroll through the streets of the town will help you to appreciate the quiet relaxing atmosphere of Trecastagni and give you an opportunity to get to know its artistic heritage.

In via Vittorio Emanuele, at the top of a double stairway, stands the **Cathedral**, built in the 1600s. Inside the three naves of the Basilica there is an alternation of dark and light, typical of Tuscan Renaissance architecture, in the surface of the walls and around the arches and windows. The apses are richly decorated with stuccoes.

It is also worth visiting the **Sanctuary of Saints Alfio Cirino and Filadelfo**, originally built in the 1500s. Inside there is a large collection of votive offerings, characteristic expressions of popular faith, which illustrate favours received from the Saints in the form of rustic paintings.

You should also visit the **Church of Our Lady of Succour**, founded in 1648, as can be seen in the coat of arms on the facade; the **Convent of the Franciscan Fathers**, a national monument, with its characteristic cloister; the **Church of the Proiette**, built in the early 1800s, once attached to a convent of enclosed nuns; the **Church of Saint Anthony of Padua**, in 17th century style, with 18th century frescoes.

A tour around the Trecastagni area is interesting both from the point of view of nature because of the presence of luxuriant **chestnut woods** that cover the hills and the superb landscapes, and from the ethno-anthropological point of view, because of the numerous **rural buildings** scattered around the countryside.

ONE FESTIVAL AFTER ANOTHER

Gourmets will definitely find things to their taste in Trecastagni.

You need only decide whether to favour sweet or savoury foods, so we will just provide you with a few addresses: **bar - ice cream parlour - confectioner's Garden**, in Piazza Gugliemo Marconi, 'cannoli', 'cassate' and excellent hot snacks (superlative rice 'arancini' and tasty pizzas). You can find delicious ice-creams of all flavours, particularly yoghurt flavour; **confectioner's Peccati di Gola**, in Corso Europa; **confectioner's - bar Sport**; **ice cream parlour - confectioner's La Castagnola**, in Piazza S. Alfio.

There is a wide choice of places where you can try the specialities of local and Sicilian cuisine in general, we particularly recommend a couple where the typical menu is combined with a characteristic and comfortable atmosphere: **Villa Taverna**, in Corso Colombo, and **Uliveto**, in via Perni.

You will find original 'volcanic' souvenirs from the **artisan's workshop** run by **Antonio Torrisi**, in via Crispi, where objects made from lava stone are made. Local artisans also produce wooden objects and traditional Sicilian carts.

However, the most beautiful and personal souvenirs that cost nothing and last a lifetime will certainly be your memories of your stay in Trecastagni and these will be richer and more intense if you share the important moments of community life with the friendly welcoming local people.

There are numerous and varied events throughout the year, religious celebrations, gastronomic festivals

Top: panorama of the town. Left: Trecastagni and Etna. On facing page: views of the town during the Feast of Saint Alfio, bottom: characteristic roofs of Trecastagni.

and cultural events. From 7th to 12th May you can attend the **Feast of Saints Alfio, Cirino and Filadelfo**, with the procession of the devotees called 'nudes' and a fair with stalls selling fresh garlic and mutton specialities. As part of the celebrations on the 10th the **Festival of Sicilian Carts** is held. Also in May, on the first Sunday after the 10th, the **Regional Folklore Festival** takes place.

In July there are events for music lovers, the **International Music Festival** from 9th to 31st in Largo Abate Ferrara, and the roving review of jazz music **Etna Jazz**.

August sees the Craft Fair, an exhibition of local arts and crafts.

October is dedicated to gourmets of all ages: the **Grape and Sausage Festival** with tasting, exhibition and folklore on the second Sunday of the month; the **Honey and Cake Festival** is held on the third Sunday of the month; the **Chestnut Festival** sees tasting of mushrooms, home-made bread, ricotta, honey and must-cake.

In November the traditional **All Souls Toy Fair** will make children happy.

Finally, on 6th December the **Feast of Saint Nicholas of Bari** is celebrated in honour of the patron Saint.

RESTAURANTS

- AL NUOVO MULINO: via Mulino a Vento, 48 (tel. 095 7806634). Restaurant-pizzeria. Mountain style cuisine. We recommend the manicaretti with mushrooms.
- ARCHI VERDI: Piazza Marconi, 35 (tel. 095 7806616). Trattoria-pizzeria. We suggest the caserecci with mushrooms, sweet and savoury crêpes.
- IL VITTORIALE: contrada Ronzini, 30 (tel. 095 7800795).

Restaurant-pizzeria-piano bar. Elegant restaurant with garden and swimming-pool. Sicilian and international cuisine.
- LA BAITA: via Ronzini, 57 (tel. 095 7808315).
- OSTERIA I SAPONARI: via Vittorio Emanuele, 126 (tel. 095 7809907). Trattoria-'yoghurteria'. Home cooking. Excellent 'caponata', 'parmigiana', fettuccine with mushrooms and asparagus.
- VILLA TAVERNA: Corso Colombo, 42 (tel. 095 7806458). Characteristic restaurant. Etna, Catania and Palermo specialities. We recommend the fish skewers and the sardines 'a beccafico'.
- ULIVETO: via Perni, 4 (tel. 095 7806988). In an old mansion with garden. Very refined traditional cuisine.

PIZZERIAS

- LA CASTAGNOLA: Piazza S. Alfio, 59/61 (tel. 095 7413669). Try the Deni pizza with tuma cheese, pork, onion and tomato.
- PECCATI DI GOLA: Corso Europa.

FARM HOLIDAYS

- PULVIRENTI: via G. Mameli, 22 (tel. 095 7807670-362635 fax 095 515902). Accommodation. Organised excursions on Etna. Sales of jam, fruit and vegetables produced on the farm.

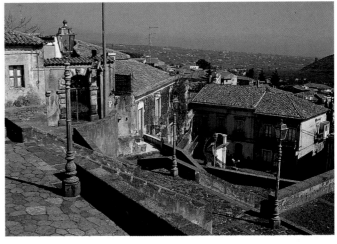

SAN GREGORIO: AT THE GATES OF CATANIA

Situated very near Catania (8 km), **San Gregorio** gained autonomy and its own identity only around the mid-19th century.

Even though it is an area that was already inhabited many centuries earlier, it was absorbed into the city of Catania, on which it depended administratively and with which it shared the ups and downs of history, until it passed into the hands of the Duke of Acicastello.

The small artistic heritage of the town shows evident signs of having undergone renovations over the centuries and particularly in the last century.

The most important buildings are the **Cathedral**, which still has a facade with clear signs of baroque style despite the renovations that completely altered its appearance; the **Church of Our Lady of the Immaculate Conception** and the **Church of Saint Phillip**, both of mediaeval origin but considerably altered.

If you are on holiday, in the breaks between one meal and another, there is nothing more relaxing to do than to read a good book.

If you have forgotten to pack one you can buy one at the **T.A.U. bookshop** in via Torino.

While you are sipping an aperitif at the **bar Strazzeri**, in via Colonna, you can decide in which restaurant you want to try the dishes typical of the local cuisine.

In the **restaurants La Collinetta**, in Viale Europa, and **Le Tre Caravelle**, in via Catira Savoca,

you can find delicious fish specialities; **'A Maruzzella**, in via Roma, and **La Locandiera**, in via Catania, will certainly satisfy your desire for pizzas and traditional cuisine.

If your visit to San Gregorio coincides with Easter, don't miss the **patronal Feast of Saint Gregory Magno** on Easter Monday.

An interesting annual event

for art lovers is the **International Art Exhibition**, which is held in July.

From the top: interior of the Cathedral, Town Hall, houses overlooking the square.

RESTAURANTS

- 'A MARUZZELLA: via Roma, 16 (tel. 095 7212190). At the entrance to San Gregorio. Home cooking and tasty pizzas. We recommend: pasta with fresh mushrooms, excellent pulses.
- LA COLLINETTA: Viale Europa, 69 (tel. 095 7211706). Restaurant-pizzeria. With panoramic terrace. Mostly fish dishes. Try the fish in sea water, baked in paper or in salt.
- LA LOCANDIERA: via Catania, 55 (tel. 095 7212816). Receptions, meeting room and buffet. Fish specialities and typical Sicilian cuisine.
- LE TRE CARAVELLE: via Catira Savoca, 2 (tel. 095 7177434). Fish and meat dishes. Interesting selection of wines, not only from Sicily. We recommend the linguine with 'neonato' or with sea-urchins and the baked fish with potatoes.

VALVERDE: THE TOWN AROUND THE SANCTUARY

The town of **Valverde**, a small pretty centre about ten kilometres from Catania, developed in mediaeval times around the Sanctuary of Santa Maria di Valverde, built in the mid-12th century and from which the town took its name.

It was one of the possessions of the Riggio and Gaetani families and of the Princes of Palagonia.

The **Sanctuary of Santa Maria di Valverde** is one of the most important buildings; it is preceded by a beautiful portico and has a lovely late 15th century portal. according to tradition it was built because of a miraculous event.

You should also visit the **Cathedral**, built at the end of the 17th century, inside which you can find a valuable painting of Our Lady of Valverde, and the 18th century **Palazzo Riggio**. Valverde is a farming town and one of the 'fruits' of this activity can be found and purchased in the various **wine cellars**. You will also find a wide choice of wines, local and otherwise, on the menus of the **restaurants Al Tavolo Verde**, in via Bellini, and **Casalrosato**, in via Fontana.

It is worth mentioning the events that animate the life of the town over the year, all inspired by religious traditions.

In January the **Feast of the Child of Brother Concetto** is held.

In May **Our Lady of Valverde** is celebrated and in memory of her apparition a procession takes place from the site of the miracle to the Sanctuary.

Our Lady of Valverde is also celebrated in August; as part of the celebrations there is an **Anchovy Festival**, with tasting of anchovy sandwiches and as much wine as you can drink.

In the district of Maugeri, in the first week of September, the **Feast of Our Lady of Graces** takes place.

RESTAURANTS-PIZZERIAS

- AL TAVOLO VERDE: via Bellini, 30 (tel. 095 524675). Traditional cuisine. Wide choice of wines. Specialities include stock-fish 'alla messinese' and tripe. Also pizzeria in the evening. Well-stocked bar.
- CASALROSATO: via Fontana, 84 – district of Casalrosato (tel. 095 524191 - 525882). Restaurant-pizzeria. Panoramic position. Traditional cuisine and well-stocked wine cellar. Try the pappardelle with mushrooms.
- L'ABAT JOUR: via Dante Alighieri, 37 (tel. 095 524087). Restaurant-pizzeria-piano bar (with the show man Fammy Lizzio)-disco pub-discotheque. Specialities include swordfish 'alla valdostana', aubergine roulades 'all'Abat Jour', Etna mushrooms.
- LA CISTERNA: via Maugeri, 41 (tel. 095 7211192). Restaurant-pizzeria. Specialities include tripe and stock-fish.
- PICCOLO PARADISO: via Maugeri, 2 (tel. 095 525368). Restaurant-pizzeria.

Bottom: the Augustinian Convent and the Sanctuary of the Madonna.

ACI SANT'ANTONIO:
LITTLE OLD WORLD

Aci Sant'Antonio is also a popular place for people from Catania to stay, especially in summer, because of how near it is to the city. The present day town was born and grew up around the church of Saint Anthony Abbot, after whom the town is named. The original town was seriously and irreparably damaged by various eruptions. In the 17th century it was one of the possessions of the noble Riggio family, who were responsible for rebuilding it after the earthquake of 1693, which seriously damaged the town.

The most important buildings in Aci Sant'Antonio all date back to the 18th century or were rebuilt in that period. You should see the **Cathedral**, dedicated to Saint Anthony Abbot and rebuilt in the early 18th century, which is characterised by a rich facade on two orders, decorated with numerous columns and surmounted by a thin bell-tower. Inside the three naves you can find frescoes by Vasta; the **Church of Saint Biagio**, characterised by a beautiful cupola; the **Church of**

Saint Michael; the 18th century **Palazzo Riggio Carcaci**, with an elegant portal standing out in the facade. Lovers of popular traditions will not miss the chance to watch the various stages of handmade building and decorating of **Sicilian Carts** in the workshop in via Tito, where you can watch skilful artisans at work, turning their work into real works of art. In November Sicilian carts have a **Cart Festival** dedi-

cated to them. In the same month the **National Prose Prize** is awarded.

Faith and folklore make up the inseparable combination that characterises the **patronal Feast of Saint Anthony Abbot**, on 17th January.

A popular event with the greedier is the **Festival of Seasoned Bread and Roast Chestnuts**, which is held in October in the district of Lavinaio, in Piazza Maggiore.

From the top: Cathedral, detail of the facade, cupola of the Church of Saint Biagio.

RESTAURANTS TRATTORIAS PIZZERIAS

- COUNTRY CLUB PANDA: via Giacomo Matteotti, 57 (tel. 095 7893233). Pub-pizzeria Only for members.
- LA PIGNA IN TESTA: Discotheque-pizzeria.
- LA REGGIA: via Torrente Fondachello-Monterosso (tel. 095 7893205). We recommend the caserecce 'alla Reggia' and the mixed grill cooked in earthenware saucepans.
- TRATTORIA DELLA NONNA: via Amari, 14 - Monterosso Etneo (tel. 095 7893715). Restaurant-pizzeria-pulse restaurant. Specialities include the excellent fresh pasta with mushrooms.
- VILLA MARGHERITA: via San Giovanni, 45 - Santa Maria la Stella (tel. 095 7651267). Restaurant-pizzeria. We recommend the caserecci 'alla Boscaiola' and the mixed grills.

ACI BONACCORSI: LAND OF LEMONS

Aci Bonaccorsi is a small town with a pleasant climate, very near the sea, and is therefore a popular place for summer holidays.

Once the territory around the present day town was the site of numerous landed estates. One of these was called Bonaccorsi and the town took its name from this in the 16th century.

The town developed, as you can still see, longitudinally along a main street that followed an ancient lava flow on the southeastern slopes of the volcano. It used to belong to the Riggio and noble Diana families.

The only buildings of historical-artistic interest are the **Cathedral**, decorated inside by 18th century frescoes, and the **Church of Our Lady of Consolation**, which incorporates part of a Romanesque style apse from the 11th century. You must not miss the two products that are the pride and joy of local agriculture: the fragrant **lemons** of the summer variety, a delicious ingredient for 'granite', sorbets and liqueurs, and excellent **wine**, which can be bought from the small wine producers in town.

You can find a menu with traditional dishes at the **restaurants Al Tipico** and **Slow & Quick**, both in via Garibaldi.

For dessert, forget about calories and give in to temptation

at the **bar-confectioner's Tiffany**, in via Garibaldi (almond pastries and ice-creams of all flavours), or at the **confectioner's Rapisarda**, in via Etna (almond, pistachio and mandarin pastries).

There are various colourful events throughout the year in Aci Bonaccorsi: the **Cheese Festival** takes place on the third Sunday in April, with tasting of typical Sicilian products; in May there is the **Festival of Cheese, Ricotta and typical Sicilian produce** on the 1st and 2nd; in the same month, on the second Sunday, the **Flower and Craft Festival** is held with a kite festival as well; on 2nd August there is the **National Firework Festival** and **patronal Feast of Saint Stephen**; in September the Feast of **Maria SS. Ritornata** is celebrated on the first Sunday of the month; finally, 26th December sees the **patronal Feast of Saint Stephen**.

RESTAURANTS

- SLOW & QUICK: via Garibaldi, 42/a (tel. 095 7899804). Restaurant - pub - sandwich bar - fast food. Typical Sicilian cuisine. Ice cream parlour - bar -hot snacks - tea room - video music.
- AL TIPICO: via Giuseppe Garibaldi, 59.

Top: Cathedral.

VIAGRANDE: ANCIENT TOWN OF THE NOBILITY

Viagrande is a quiet pretty town with a particularly pleasant climate and is visited by tourists mostly in the summer. Its position makes it an ideal base for those who want to spend time on the beach but would prefer to avoid the worst of the summer heat.

The name of the town is derived from the 'via magna', a road that led to Messina and along which the town began to develop towards the end of the 16th century. Originally it was a hamlet depending on Trecastagni. In the 1600s it belonged to the Di Giovanni family and in the 1700s to the Alliata family.

Walking through Viagrande it is not unusual to come across characteristic houses with interior courtyards, in accordance with a layout typical of Mediterranean culture and Arab culture in particular.

Viagrande has a number of interesting historical buildings and monuments that are worth visiting.

The **Cathedral**, rebuilt in the 1700s and dedicated to Our Lady of Itria, overlooks a large parvis with geometrical patterns in its paving. The linear facade has only one order with flat pilaster strips and portals in lava stone, decorated with columns. The interior has three naves, decorated with frescoes and stuccoes, and contains the remains of the patron of the town Saint Mauro Abbot.

You should also see the **Church of Saint Michael** and the **Church of Saint Catherine**, both 18th century.

The **Church of Saint Saviour** stands on the road leading to Monterosso and is notable because of its decorative elements, including the entrance arch in Moorish style.

In the town and the surrounding district there are numerous elegant summer residences of the nobility from Catania, who used to come here for their holidays, attracted by the climate and the lovely countryside around the town: **Villa Manganelli**, designed by the architect Carlo Sada, who also designed the Bellini Theatre in Catania, **Villa Paternò del Toscano**, **Villa Zappalà** and **Villa Biscari** are some of the most significant examples.

CUSTOMS AND TRADITIONS

The extensive vineyards that surround the town produce excellent grapes, used to make **wines** of renowned quality.

The **crafts** of Viagrande are based on two activities that are now in danger of disappearing: the construction and decoration of Sicilian carts of great beauty, and the working of iron using traditional methods. Do not miss the opportunity of visiting the workshops run by these artisans, living testimony to an age and a tradition that may soon become just a memory.

The specialities of local gastronomic tradition include **pizza 'alla siciliana'** (a fried pizza with cheese and anchovies) and the delicious **'pazientini'**, almond biscuits that take a lot of time and care to make, hence the name.

We suggest stopping off to try these and other delicacies at the **Gran Caffè Urna**, in Piazza Urna, a café of long and ancient tradition, once a meeting place for visiting nobles. You should try the excellent chocolate, strawberry and coffee 'schiumoni'.

The most important events in Viagrande are linked to the main occupations in town and religious festivals.

In January the town celebrates the **patronal Feast of Saint Mauro** for three days, during which horse races and firework displays are organised.

At the same time of year the traditional **Livestock and Agricultural Implement Fair** is held.

On 20th August, in Piazza Saint Mauro, you can see the entertainment organised as part of the **Show under the Stars**.

The grape harvest is an important moment for the whole community and is also the opportunity for meeting up and enjoying yourself; in September the **Grape Harvest Festival** takes place.

On 12th November the **Feast of Saint Martin** is celebrated.

In December a characteristic **Living Crib** is set up.

RESTAURANTS - PIZZERIAS

- BLUE MOON: via Giuseppe Garibaldi, 397 (tel. 095 7893011). Typical Sicilian cuisine. We recommend pappardelle with mushrooms and barbecued lamb.
- CAVIEZEL: via Manzoni, 20 (tel. 095 7901122). With a large terrace. Sicilian country specialities and, in winter, typical Nordic dishes, such as fondue.
- LE ZAGARE: via Umberto, 266 (tel. 095 7894177). Restaurant-pizzeria in Madonna degli Ulivi holiday village. On the slopes of Monte Serra. Mountain cuisine. Specialities include sedani 'del Villaggio'.
- LA REGGIA: via Torrente Fondachello - Monterosso Etneo (tel. 095 7893205 - 7893075). Restaurant-pizzeria. We recommend the caserecce 'alla Reggia' with mushrooms, smoked ham and Sicilian pesto.
- MARILÙ: via Garibaldi, 104 (tel 095 7901245). Pizzeria-bar. Restaurant only on booking.
- PICCOLO MONDO: via Garibaldi, 309 (tel. 095 7890936). Restaurant-pizzeria.

HOTELS

- VILLAGGIO MADONNA DEGLI ULIVI ♥ ♥ ♥: via Umberto, 266 (tel. 095 7894177 fax 095 7895570). Holiday centre. With restaurant, pizzeria-grill, bar, reception and congress hall, swimming-pool, tennis courts, bowls and football pitches. Rooms with air conditioning, TV and telephone.

Facing page: Cathedral.

SANTA VENERINA: LAND OF MILLS

Very near the beautiful town of Acireale, of which it was part until 1934, **Santa Venerina** is a pleasant holiday town, especially in summer.

The Santa Venerina area must already have been inhabited in Roman times, judging from the remains of buildings found in the zone.

The name of the town is probably derived from a well, called the Santa Venera well, which was situated near the hamlet.

The artistic-monumental heritage of the town, while not considerable, should not be underestimated.

We particularly mention the **Cathedral**, dedicated to the patron Saint Venera, inside which you can admire frescoes by Pietro Paolo Vasta and his son; the **Church of the Sacred Heart**, built in the late 19th century; the ruins of the **Byzantine Oratory** dating back to the 6th century.

Around the town, as in many other areas around Etna, there are numerous scattered rural buildings. In one of these buildings, a 19th century house in the Santa Venerina countryside, a **Mill Museum** has been set up. In the various rooms of the Museum you can see a reconstruction of farm activities, including a millstone and a wine cellar, you can also everyday tools, utensils and equipment collected from all over the Etna area.

Nearby there is also a pottery workshop, where you can watch traditional pot making using a potter's wheel. Moreover, the parkland in which the house-museum is situated offers the possibility of a pleasant rest in the country. The museum is open every day in the afternoon and also in the morning on Sundays and holidays.

SWEET MEMORIES AND DOC WINES

A place you must visit while in Santa Venerina is the confectioner's-bar Russo, in via Vittorio Emanuele, open since 1880. Beautifully wrapped cakes from the Russo confectionery can be sent all over the world. All the cakes are prepared using traditional methods and according to ancient recipes that are jealously guarded and passed on from father to son. The Russo confectionery is famous for its croissants with honey, 'mustazzoli', 'granite' and almond paste nougat.

In via Mazzini you can admire the workshop run by Alfio Fichera, an artisan who works with **wrought iron**.

Unlike numerous other towns around Etna, Santa Venerina does not use most of its abundant grape harvest for the production of wine but for **liqueurs**, which are widely appreciated.

One exception to this is Baron Emanuele Scammacca who produces the excellent Etna White DOC on his San Michele estate, as well as other less traditional wines, using only grapes from his own vines.

The **San Michele del Barone Scammacca del Murgo Winery** is open all year round and can be visited by appointment, also in order to taste the delicious wines free of charge.

In September the exhibition and market of Sicilian and Etna wines **Enoetna** is held in Piazza Roma.

In November the picturesque and entertaining **Feast and Fair of Our Lady of the Lamp** takes place, while the equivalent **Feast and Fair of Saint Sebastian** is held on the last Sunday in January.

On 26th August the **patronal Feast of Saint Venera** is celebrated.

RESTAURANTS

- LA LUMERA: via Princessa, 18 (tel. 095 953755). Situated in the hills, between the volcano and the Ionian sea coast. Traditional cuisine with a touch of imagination from the expert chef. We recommend the bourguignonne fondue.
- LA PERGOLA: Piazza Roma, 11 (tel. 095 953304). In the greenery of the Municipal Park. Typical Sicilian menu, with both meat and fish dishes. Specialities include caramel with mushrooms, pappardelle with mushrooms and mixed mushrooms.
- LO SCRIGNO: via Stabilimenti, 244 (tel./fax 095 953470). Restaurant of the hotel La Zagara. Home cooking. Excellent pulses and farfalle 'allo Scrigno'.
- RE BORBONE: Piazza Immacolata, 2 - Dagala del Re (tel. 095 954322). Typical Sicilian cuisine and dishes with mushrooms from Etna. Specialities include pappardelle with mushrooms and home-made maccheroni with pistachio.

HOTELS

- LA ZAGARA ♥ ♥: via Stabilimenti, 244 (tel. 095 953096). With restaurant, bar, TV in the lobby and car park. Rooms with air conditioning, telephone and TV.

Top: Cathedral and in the background Etna.

ZAFFERANA ETNEA: A DEEP SHADE OF YELLOW

Zafferana Etnea stands on the eastern slopes of Etna at a moderate altitude and is a good base for numerous excursions to other towns and the area around the volcano. It is surrounded by luxuriant woodland and is not very far from the sea, making it a popular tourist destination both in summer and winter.

The town originally began to grow up around a monastery dedicated to Saint James, in the valley of the same name, in the late Middle Ages.

The name of the town was originally Zafarana and is derived from an Arabic word meaning 'yellow', with reference to the presence of extensive areas of saffron and broom in the zone.

The heart of the town is the beautiful and panoramic Piazza Umberto I, where you will find the Cathedral, preceded by a lava stone stairway, and the elegant **Town Hall** in liberty style, preceded by a double stairway that has a bust of the painter Giuseppe Sciuti in the centre of it.

The **Cathedral** is dedicated to Our Lady of Providence and is characterised by an imposing baroque facade in white stone and by twin bell-towers, with a small cupola covering them and a crowning triangular tympanum. Inside the three naves you can admire a valuable painting by G. Sciuti.

It is extremely pleasant and relaxing to take a stroll through the centre of Zaferana, along its tidy quiet streets. Your walk is made all the more pleasant by the presence of bars and confectioners' where you can try fresh 'granite' and typical cakes.

You must pay a visit to the **Municipal Park** which has an amphitheatre that hosts numerous performances of great interest during the summer. The park offers you the opportunity of relaxing in the shade of its large secular trees.

It is worth going as far as the numerous **outlying districts** of Zafferana (Fleri, Pisano, Poggiofelice, Petrulli, Sarro) in order to appreciate the remains of ancient buildings, such as the so called 'Cisternazza', from the late 1600s, and the 'Fortino', what remains of a 17th century military construction.

If you are a nature lover or a hiking enthusiast we strongly recommend an excursion to **Piano del Vescovo**, **Monte Pomiciano** and **Monte Zoccolaro**.

ON HONEYMOON

In Zafferana they produce 15% of the nation's **honey**, which is sent all over Italy and the world. You can buy honey of all kinds, with orange-blossom, chestnut and eucalyptus, from all the mostly family owned and run producers. We mention, among others, **La Cantina del Miele** run by Caterina Arcidiacono, in via G. Verdi, where you can also see for yourselves how this incredible product is extracted from nature; **Apicoltura** run by Sebastiano Costa, in via San Giacomo; the Sicilian Beekeepers Consortium **Co.A.Si**, in via IV Novembre.

The cakes made in Zafferana are delicious and fragrant, particularly the biscuits, made according to traditional recipes, such as the "skiers", covered in chocolate.

You will find these and other specialities can be found at the confectioner's **Donna Peppina**, in via Roma, which also serves exquisite Sicilian pizzas (topped with anchovies and cheese); you should also try the specialities of the **Bar Torrisi**, comfortably seated, in summer, in Piazza Umberto.

In Zafferana they make excellent **wine**. If you are in town just after the grape harvest you must try the new wine. You can taste it and purchase it directly from the producers and from private wineries.

Mushrooms are the undisputed champions of Etna cuisine in general, and of Zafferana in particular, and can be picked in autumn if you are expert, or bought in town. They are used to make starters, first and second courses in all the restaurants of the area, cooked in a thousand different ways. The 'porcino' variety is particularly valued.

The calendar of annual events and festivals in Zafferana is rich and varied, including some very prestigious ones.

Left: Cathedral.

From July to September there is a review of cinema, drama and dance in the streets called **Etna in Scena**; in August, on the first Sunday of the month, the **patronal Feast of Our Lady of Providence** is celebrated; in the same month the **Silver Polyphemus Prize** is awarded.

The prize was instituted in 1965 with the intention of rewarding Sicilian personalities who have distinguished themselves in various fields and brought honour to Sicily.

Among those who have won the prize in the past are the writer Gesualdo Bufalino, the poet Salvatore Quasimodo and the scientist Antonino Zichichi.

In September the **Brancati Literary Prize** is awarded.

The prize has been running for 33 years and has the aim of spreading culture and love for knowledge. The past editions have been won by important personalities such as Eugenio Montale, Elsa Morante and Leonardo Sciascia; every Sunday in October Zafferana is enlivened by the **Ottobrata**, which includes the festival of grapes, must-cake, mushrooms, honey, wine and chestnuts.

The festival is a picturesque autumn festival and is an opportunity for trying delicious traditional recipes, such as fig or grape must-cake flavoured with cinnamon or topped with flakes of chocolate; in mid-November the **Wine and Chestnut Festival** is held.

RESTAURANTS

- AIRONE: via Cassone, 67 (tel. 095 7081819). Restaurant of the hotel of the same name. We recommend the traditional caserecci 'all'Airone'. Piano bar on request.
- AL PARCO PISANO: via Fossa Galatea.
- BELVEDERE DELL'ETNA: Piazza Belvedere.
- C'ERA UNA VOLTA: via IV Novembre, 7 (tel. 095 7083355). On a hilltop just outside Zafferana. Panoramic summer terrace. Typical Sicilian cuisine. Specialities include dishes made with Etna mushrooms. Also an excellent pizzeria.
- DEL BOSCO: via Zafferana Milo, 160 (tel. 095 7082003). We recommend the maccheroni with mushroom ragù and tri-coloured conchiglie.
- DEL BOSCO EMMAUS: via Cassone, 75 (tel. 095 7081888). Traditional cuisine.
- IL GIRASOLE: via Riggio, 14 (tel. 095 954161). Restaurant-pizzeria-reception room. Excellent mushroom based dishes.
- IL PORCINO: via Alcide De Gasperi, 2 (tel. 095 7082801).

We recommend all the mushroom based dishes. Also a pizzeria in the evening.
- LA FENICE: via Cassone (tel. 095 7081036). We suggest the ravioli with mushrooms and the roulades 'alla palermitana' with mushrooms.
- LA LOCANDA: via Garibaldi, 276 (tel. 339 2838561). Try the dishes typical of Mediterranean tradition and country cooking, including stock-fish, mixed meat and mushroom grill, pulses and tripe. In the evening the restaurant becomes a beer-hall and serves excellent crêpes and salad.
- MOULIN ROUGE: via Zafferana Milo, 21 (tel. 095 7082424). Restaurant-pizzeria. Traditional cuisine. Excellent maccheroni with mushrooms and maccheroni 'alla Boscaiola'.
- ORCHIDEA: via Libertà, 1 (tel. 095 7082575). Restaurant-pizzeria-bar. Specialised in mushroom based dishes. Special pizzas with Etna mushrooms, Sicilian pizza. Excellent must-cake.
- PARCO DEI PRINCIPI: via delle Ginestre, 1 (tel. 095 7082335). On the outskirts of Zafferana, in an old villa. Specialities include 'crostoni' with mushrooms, linguine with mushrooms and pistachios, meat roulades with aubergines, almond ice-cream cake.
- PASSOPOMO: via Passopomo, 47 (tel. 095 950297). Restaurant on the farm of the same name. In an old farmhouse, with a chapel and mill from the 1700s. Sicilian cuisine, with extensive use of produce from ecological crops grown on the farm, which is also equipped to offer accommodation for tourists. Specialities include fresh pasta, mushrooms.
- POGGIO DEL RE: via A. De Gasperi, 19.
- PRIMAVERA: via Cassone, 86 (tel. 095 7082348). Re-

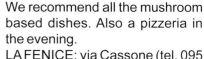

Top: votive altar built in front of the 1992 eruption.

HOTELS

- HOTEL AIRONE ♥♥♥: via Cassone, 67 (tel. 095 7081819 fax 095 7082142). In a panoramic position, on the road to Etna. All rooms with satellite TV and telephone.
- PRIMAVERA DELL'ETNA ♥♥♥: via Cassone, 86 (tel. 095 7082348 fax 095 7081695). In a panoramic position, halfway between the sea and Etna. With restaurant, bar, discotheque, meeting room, tennis court. Rooms with satellite TV, telephone, heating.
- DEL BOSCO EMMAUS ♥♥: via Cassone, 75 – contrada Airone (tel. 095 7081888 - fax 095 7083824). With restaurant, bar, car park and meeting rooms. Situated in a large chestnut wood, an ideal place for a relaxing stay. Beautiful views of Etna and the coast. Owned by the Salesians.
- VILLA PINA ♥: via dei Gerani, 19 (tel./fax 095 7081024).

ROOMS FOR RENT

- REDITUS ♥: via Passopomo, 47 (tel. 095 950297 fax 095 950298). With restaurant. Rooms with telephone and all the normal hotel services.

staurant-pizzeria in the hotel Primavera dell'Etna. Dishes made from Etna mushrooms and fresh fish from the Ionian sea, typical Sicilian and Italian cuisine. We recommend the tagliatelle 'alla Primavera' and the girelle with mushrooms.
- VILLA MIRADOR: SP Zafferana-Milo, 23 (tel. 095 7082890). Restaurant-pizzeria-cocktail parties-meetings. Air conditioned, car park, large park with ornamental fountain.

PIZZERIAS

- LA BUCA: Piazza Regione Siciliana, 6/8 (tel. 095 7081991).

FARM HOLIDAYS

- PASSOPOMO: via Passopomo, 47 (tel. 095 950297). Old farmhouse, 20 minutes from crater of Etna and 10 from the sea, surrounded by orchards and ecologically grown crops: wine, olive oil, peaches, apricots, pears and various vegetables sold on the premises. Rooms with private bathroom and TV. The restaurant is specialised in Sicilian cuisine.

Top: Town Hall. Right: Municipal Park.

FROM PIANO DELL'ACQUA
TO THE 1991/93 FLOW

From the Municipal Park in Zafferana you take via della Montagna, following the signposts to the scene of the eruption: after about 4 kilometres of tarmacked road you come to Piano dell'Acqua (800 metres), identifiable from a clearly visible water spring and a wide lay-by.

This is the place in which the long fast lava flow that started in December 1991 came to a stop, a flow that threatened part of the town of Zafferana.

ZAFFERANA: 10th ITINERARY ROUTE
Duration: 2 hours
Total distance: 4 km
Difference in height: 300 metres

As part of this continual struggle between life and death, danger and opportunity, that characterises the Etna district, today this area has become a tourist attraction, thanks also to the widespread live TV coverage at the time of the eruption, which made it famous all over Italy.

Here then you find yourself face to face with the 'monster': immobile, black and solid, no longer able to advance towards the rural houses and villas just a short distance away, now prey to the human 'ants', who, after having fought against it during the eruption (with bulldozers and explosives), are now ready to take back the land conquered by the volcano.

If you want to get a better idea of the force and violence of that eruption, climb up along the pretty paved track that initially runs alongside the course of the lava flow and then climbs up to a high viewpoint from where you can get a good view over the valley through which the violent river of fire ran.

After about twenty minutes of steep climbing you continue along a track made by the bulldozers on the lava flow itself in order to reach the narrow pass (at an altitude of about 1,000 metres) that once led to the forgotten paradise of the Calanna Valley (an ancient crater covered with fruit trees and little houses built of dry-stone). Today the sight that meets your eyes at the top of the climb is that of lunar landscape, ruled over the god Vulcan, who channelled all his anger here for months because of an embankment built to defend the town.

Considering the roughness of the recent lava flow, we recommend wearing strong walking boots.

FROM PIANO DELL'ACQUA
TO THE SCALAZZA

You have to leave the tarmacked road that climbs up from Zafferana towards Piano dell'Acqua when you are near the spring that gives this place its name. On the left there is a narrow rough track that goes downhill for about a hundred metres into the wide depression where the San Giacomo Valley and the inhospitable Cavasecca Gorge meet.
The Scalazza begins right at the base of the ridge (*'u cugnu di mezzu*) that separates the two valleys near an old house built of lava stone, now almost completely covered by the vegetation. It is an old mule track, completely surrounded by the chestnut wood, which is paved most of the way and thanks to a hundred hairpin bends allows you to easily climb up almost 500 metres, from the 700 metres of Piano dell'Acqua to the 1,200 metres of the Cassone area.
In order to reach the orchards of Cassone, where the Scalazza rejoins the tarmacked road from Zafferana to the view-

ZAFFERANA: 11th ITINERARY ROUTE
Duration: about 2 hours
Total distance: 4 km
Difference in height: 430 metres

point over the Calanna Valley, you need to walk for about an hour up a steep incline through the chestnut wood. It should be underlined that this mule track (unfortunately seriously damaged in the upper stretch) is of great anthropological importance, since for a long time it was the only access road to the fruit orchards kept by the people of Zafferana at the foot of Monte Pomiciaro.
Today you can follow it for the whole of its length thanks to the maintenance carried out by local volunteers, who have cleared away the weeds from some stretches so allowing walkers to enjoy one of the last remaining historical pathways in the Etna area. The return trip is along the same track.

THE SAN GIACOMO VALLEY

ZAFFERANA: 12th ITINERARY ROUTE
Duration: 2 hours
Total distance: 3.8 km
Difference in height: 260 metres

Access to the San Giacomo Valley is by the same route just described for the Scalazza: you have to turn left a hundred metres before reaching the spring of Piano dell'Acqua, you continue along a rough track slightly downhill and after about a hundred metres you leave the track leading to the Scalazza (see description) on the left and go straight on until you come to a chain blocking the way to cars.

From here the track begins to get narrower until it becomes a narrow footpath through the San Giacomo Valley.

The walk is made quite difficult in some parts by sharp climbs or descents that need a little agility.

This excursion is interesting above all from a botanical point of view, since there are numerous valuable and rare species that can be found in this narrow valley.

It is therefore important to pay the greatest attention and do not damage the vegetation growing alongside the pathway.

Your visit to the valley can be completed (including return) in a couple of hours.

Once you arrive at the head of the San Giacomo Valley, where the incline suddenly rises sharply and the vegetation gives way to vast piles of rocks, it is better to turn back.

FROM THE VIEWPOINT OVER THE CALANNA VALLEY (1,470 M) TO MONTE ZOCCOLARO (1,741 M)

ZAFFERANA: 13th ITINERARY ROUTE
Duration: 1 hour 30 mins.
Total distance: 2.2 km
Difference in height: 270 metres

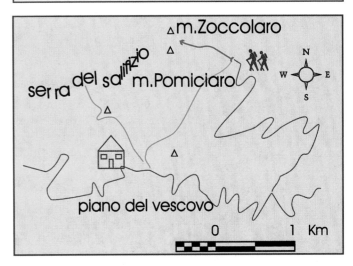

Going up the provincial road from Zafferana to the Sapienza mountain hut, about 6 kilometres from the town you come to a turn off sign-posted Monte Pomiciaro.

Turn into this secondary road and after a few minutes driving through a fruit growing district you will find yourself at a splendid viewpoint from where you can look down onto the Calanna Valley, and on clear days it is even possible to see the Aspromonte mountains and the coast of Calabria. Here, where the tarmacked road ends, is one of the base points for excursions in the Etna Park and a short but spectacular route to the Bove Valley starts here.

The path is sign-posted by the Park Authority and begins very near the end of the road, where you can park your car. A 50 minute walk will give you the chance to admire the breathtaking views in the ancient heartland of Etna.

This walk is interesting because it takes you to see the most important sites of the thousands of years of evolution of the volcano, which has moved its principal eruptive areas from the Calanna Valley, to the Bove Valley area (with the Trifolium complex) and then to the ancient and recent Mongibello, where the present summit craters are now situated.

Along the way, there are numbers indicating places of particular interest where you can stop off; for example, your attention is drawn to some beech trees and the presence of fruit orchards at an altitude well above a thousand metres.

There are no particular difficulties along this route since the pathway is well sign-posted, even though it is quite steep.

The only piece of advice we give you is not to wander off the pathway because there are dangerous precipices a short distance away that drop down into the Giumenta canyon. At the end of the climb (Monte Zoccolaro 1,740 metres) you are suddenly confronted with the horrid and peculiar landscape of the Bove Valley.

From Serra delle Concazze north-eastwards as far as the outline of the Montagnola there is an unbroken series of lava flows and high rocky outcrops above which you will often see birds of prey circling, sometimes even the golden eagle, which has been nesting on the volcano again since the mid-1980s.

FROM PIANO DEL VESCOVO
TO THE BOVE VALLEY

ZAFFERANA: 14th ITINERARY ROUTE
Duration: 3 hours
Total distance 4.6 km
Difference in height: 340 metres

This is one of the shortest and easiest walks to reach the Bove Valley: from Piano del Vescovo (1,370 metres) towards the Salfizio Ridge (1,720 metres) and finally a steep descent across an easily accessible gorge, partly covered with majestic beech trees.

If you drive along the road from Zafferana towards the Sapienza mountain hut, after about eleven kilometres you come to Piano del Vescovo, a place easily recognised because of the presence of some partially ruined buildings on the right hand side of the road and a wide rough track that heads off up the mountain.

Leave your car here and start along the Etna Park nature path that cuts across the plain towards a wide wooded canyon.

Once you have passed the sign indicating the edge of Zone 'A' of the Park (integral reserve), the path continues for a while in the shade of some large beech trees and then begins to climb up the steep incline (by means of a series of steps) that separates the plain from Acqua Rocca degli Zappini.

Once you arrive here, it is worth stopping for a few minutes to take a close look (but with great care) at a very smooth basalt rock face that drops straight down for about fifty metres.

A short distance away from this precipice there is a majestic secular beech tree and at the foot of this tree there is a spring that gives its name to this location.

This spring has been channelled to allow walkers to freshen up after the first steep climb of the route. You continue along this path, which gradually becomes sandier and winds among beech trees, broom and pulvini of milk-vetch as far as the Salfizio Ridge.

At this point the hardest part is over.

Look over the crest of the ridge and you will be irresistibly attracted by the scenario of the Bove Valley, with its lava flows, massive 'dykes' (ancient internal canals through which lava flows passed and which are now visible because of erosion) and the impressive surface of the 1991/93 flow.

Walk along the ridge following a clear pathway that starts on your left, looking at the valley, and after crossing a sandy canyon you enter a beech wood that will lead you down into the ancient valley.

Once you are in the valley you will find the imposing mass of recent lava in front of you (40-50 metres thick on the old bottom of the Bove Valley) and on this lava flow you will see the route of the "Carmelo and Riccardo" footpath, marked by piles of stones, and if you follow it you can extend your walk in the valley (see the description of the fifth stage of the GTE hike).

From a technical point of view the excursion is not particularly difficult in summer. In winter, on the other hand, you can easily find snow inside the canyon that leads up from Acqua Rocca and ice on the first part of the pathway down into the Bove Valley (which faces north).

If this is the case you will have to use crampons to attach to your boots.

Finally, we advise you to keep a waterproof in your rucksack at all times as the weather in the Bove Valley in summer is very unpredictable.

Left: Bove Valley.

MILO: SEARCHING FOR LOST TIME

Situated on the eastern side of Etna, **Milo** is the highest town on this part of the mountain, situated at an altitude of 700 metres.

It is popular with tourists, especially during summer, because of its pleasant climate and because it is an ideal base for numerous excursions.

Like Sant'Alfio, Milo was part of the county of Mascali and was a district of Giarre until 1955, when it became an autonomous municipality.

The origins of the town can be traced back to the 14th century, when the Duke of Randazzo, Giovanni d'Aragona, had a church dedicated to Saint Andrew built in the feud of Milo, along with a house where he spent a lot of time in summer.

Around this a town began to develop and flourish, above all thanks to the production and export of wines. The appearance of the town, surrounded by green woods and vineyards, is particularly pleasant, with typical lava stone houses and rural buildings scattered around the countryside, almost like a step back into the past.

Indeed, although the town has been threatened by serious eruptions, the centre of the town has remained unscathed and has not undergone extensive rebuilding work like other towns around Etna.

You should see the **Cathedral**, dedicated to Saint Andrew, preceded by a stairway in lava stone, characterised by a lin-

Bottom: Cathedral.

ear facade in white stone with flat pilaster strips. Above the broken line cornice stands the harmonious bell-tower, flanked on both sides by a balustrade decorated with sculptures.

The outlying districts of Milo are of considerable interest from the point of view of nature: **Fornazzo**, which earned the name of the ideal Italian village in a competition organised by the magazine Airone, **Praino** and **Caselle**, above all because of the presence of farmhouses and mansions, some of which date back to the 18th century, examples of the rural architecture of the past.

These small villages owe their existence to the activities that were carried on in the area (such as wood working and the cultivation of vines) and are real oases of tranquillity, places in which man's presence is in true harmony with nature.

If you really want to immerse yourself in nature, we advise excursions to **Monte Fontana** and **Monte Rinatu**.

Don't leave Milo without having stocked up on wines for your cellar at home.

The vineyards of the area produce **DOC wines**, particularly the Etna white, which has earned the denomination of superior Etna white because of its peculiar characteristics.

The first two weekends of September are dedicated to wine and culinary specialities with **ViniMilo**, a wine and gastronomic festival and exhibition and sales of local wines, in via Etnea.

There is tasting of many specialities of local cuisine, including the tasty sausages, mushrooms and home-made cakes.

On 11th November, in the village of Fornazzo, the **Feast of Saint Martin** is celebrated with gastronomy, tasting of wines and typical local produce, folklore and entertainment.

In July the **patronal Feast of Saint Andrew** takes place with religious traditions and folklore, and the **Autoslalom**.

Finally, in August **Milo's Venus** is a beauty contest held in Piazza Madonna delle Grazie.

RESTAURANTS

- AL BRACIERE: Corso Italia, 38/40 (tel. 095 955576).

We recommend the meat, barbecued, stewed or roasted, and mushroom dishes such as the caserecci with mushrooms.

- BELVEDERE DELL'ETNA: via Del Bosco, 20 (tel. 095 955253). In a panoramic position, with a garden. Rustic mountain cuisine. We recommend the pappardelle with mushrooms and the caserecci 'Belvedere'.
- IL TORCHIO: via Del Bosco, 30 (tel. 095 7082163). Restaurant-pizzeria of the Mareneve Campsite. Try the mushroom based dishes.
- LA VOLPE: via Mongibello, 41 - Fornazzo (tel. 095 955500). Restaurant-pizzeria-bar. We recommend the mushrooms, the wild-boar and the rabbit.
- NONNA VITA: via A. Meli - Fornazzo (tel. 095 955214). Restaurant-pizzeria. Try the Nonna Vita pizza.
- QUATTRO ARCHI: via F. Crispi, 9 (tel. 095 955566). Typical Etna cuisine and excellent Sicilian wines. Also a pizzeria in the evening. Try the fresh tagliatelle with mushrooms and the roast lamb.

FARM HOLIDAYS

- BARONE DI VILLAGRANDE: via Del Bosco, 25 (tel. 095 7894339). Tasting of the excellent wines produced from the vineyards of the estate. Overnight stays and visits to the estate available by booking.

CAMP SITES – RESIDENCES

- MARENEVE ♥ ♥ ♥: via Del Bosco, 30/b (tel. 095 7082163 fax 095 7083417). In the greenery of a thick chestnut wood, can accommodate tents and caravans. With restaurant, swimming-pool, stables, bar, bowls and tennis courts. Typical Sicilian cuisine. Excursions organised.

HOLIDAY CENTRES

- VILLAGGIO A. MUSCO: via Angelo Musco, 5 (tel. 095 955129 - 095 955112). Holiday chalets.

Top: excellent Milo grapes.
Left: village of Fornazzo.

SANT'ALFIO: THE TOWN WITH THREE PATRONS

On the eastern slopes of Etna, at a moderate altitude of about 500 metres, stands **Sant'Alfio**, an ancient feud of the county of Mascali, and district of Giarre until 1923.

The tourist potential of the town is fully revealed in summer when it is particularly pleasant to take a stroll through the town with its pure clean air.

Sant'Alfio is famous above all for the **"chestnut tree of a hundred horses"**, a thousand year old tree that holds the European record for age and size.

According to legend Queen Joan of Anjou was near the tree one day during a hunt, accompanied by a hundred horsemen. Caught in a storm, they were all able to shelter under the tree.

This monument to nature is situated about two kilometres from the town, behind a wide square at the start of the provincial road to Linguaglossa. The tree is striking because of the size of its foliage and trunk and is made all the more attractive by the splendid scenery behind it: Etna with its old black lava flows, the intense green colour of the Mediterranean scrub, the vineyards and the woods. A short distance away you can admire another example of chestnut tree which, because of its size, is called "the ship".

The town first grew up in the late 17th century. The same period saw the construction of the **Cathedral**, dedicated to the three martyred Saints Alfio, Cirino and Filadelfo. Originally, the building had a single nave, but in the 19th century it was enlarged and in the following century the rough lava stone facade was rebuilt.

This is notable for the harmony of its shape and the beautiful bell-tower that stands above it. Inside the three naves you should see the valuable marble altars and the altar piece depicting the three Saints, attributed to D'Anna. From the viewpoint near Piazza Duomo you can enjoy a breathtaking view.

Nearby you will find the **Municipal Park**.

Apart from the Cathedral you should also visit the **Magazzeni Church**, in the locality of the same name, and the 19th century **Church of Calvary**, preceded by a lava stone stairway that makes it stand out even more, in a charming panoramic position on a hilltop.

The **Nucifori** district is interesting because of its characteristic streets paved in lava stone and the church of the same name.

Don't forget to make some excursions into the surrounding

Bottom: Cathedral.

areas; we particularly recommend a walk to the **eruptive mouths** of 1928 and to the **Cerrita wood**, a particularly beautiful wood of Turkey Oaks, the only place on Etna that these trees can be found.

WINE AND THE LIKE

The **gastronomic specialities** of Sant'Alfio can be bought at the market selling typical produce on Sundays and holidays in the chestnut tree square (honey, wine, apples and fresh fruit, mushrooms).

Honey can also be purchased from signor Mauro Alfio, in via Crispi.

Wine can be purchased from signor Papandrea, in via Fossopoliti.

Sant'Alfio is a member of the National Association of **Wine Towns**. Indeed, the quality of its grapes is famous and is due to the fertile volcanic soil and continual exposure to intense sunlight, thanks to the favourable position of the town. The wines produced here are among the best in the whole Etna district. The most common vines are those with the black grape 'nerello mascalese', but there are also white grapes of the 'Carrici' variety.

Wine producing is the theme of the municipal Museum "Vines and Wines" in via Coviello, with two exhibition rooms in which you can see several hundred objects donated by local people, connected with wine producing and crafts.

The Museum highlights and explains an activity that has always been and still is important for the life of the whole community.

It is also interesting to pay a visit to the workshop in via L. Capuana, where signor Santo Maccarone weaves **baskets** with reeds and elm canes. This is an art that very few people now practise and is passed on from father to son.

The typical dishes of the town are home-made pasta, especially maccheroni with tomato, and grilled meat dishes (lamb, pork, beef and mutton). The pulse soups are also excellent.

The most original cakes include 'mustaccioli', filled with nuts and cooked wine.

You can find exquisite pastries with nuts, almonds and pistachios at the **bar-confectioner's Papotto**, in Piazza Duomo, and **La Spina**, in via V. Emanuele.

If you want to try real traditional Sant'Alfio cuisine we suggest: **Associazione Enogastronomica Sicilia Nostra**, in via Castagno dei Cento Cavalli, 2 (tel. 095 968007), a typical trattoria situated in a rural house made of characteristic local lava stone. You will be served the typical caserecci with aubergine pesto. Booking is advised. The association also organises nature walks, meetings and excursions; **Associazione Belvedere**, in via Costantini - contrada Nucifori (tel. 095 965544). Booking essential. Fixed menu. Speciality home-made maccheroni with tomato; **Associazione Il Castagno**, in via Castagno dei Cento Cavalli (tel. 347 4680103). With garden, situated in an old renovated wine cellar. The **Association Le Betulle** organises attività sporting and cultural activities for tourists (hiking, climbing competitions, guided excursions, nature days and study holidays) in via F. Crispi, 8/a (tel. 095 7824026).

EVENTS ALL YEAR ROUND

The rich and varied calendar of annual events in Sant'Alfio includes religious and secular celebrations that we advise you to attend in order to share the most important moments of community life with the local people, giving you the chance to get a glimpse of the true nature of life here.

In February the **Feast of Saint Biagio** is celebrated on the 3rd, with the distribution of *'cuddureddi sammrasi'*, characteristic blessed bread, in the Church of Calvary; in the same month the **Nordic Ski Meeting** is held, with excursions along the nature path of the Monti Sartorius.

Top: interior of a wine-cellar. Left: the Chestnut Tree of a Hundred Horses.

From the last Sunday in April to the second Sunday in May you can take part in the **Feast of Saints Alfio, Cirino and Filadelfo**. The celebrations begin on the last Sunday in May with fireworks and the recreation of episodes from the patron Saints' lives and martyrdom. On the following Thursday and Friday the traditional illumination called "dera" takes place: infront of every house bonfires are lit using resinous wood in order to commemorate the passing of the three martyrs on their way to Lentini, where they were martyred. The celebrations end on the first Sunday in May when the statues of the three Saints are placed on a monumental litter and carried in procession by thousands of devotees.

In the second half of May the **Festival of the Mountain** is held, a day for promoting Etna with a series of excursions to the most interesting places on the volcano. After a stop at the Citelli mountain hut (base for the Etna Park) for lunch, the event comes to an end in the town square with an exhibition and mountain songs.

From 10th July to 12th September there are various events as part of **Etna Music**, a review of music, drama, dance, culture, cabaret, food and wine. Among the many concerts and plays we can also mention the award of the silver plaque "Chestnut tree of a hundred horses" to Sicilian personalities who have distinguished themselves in sport, entertainment and culture in general and the event called "Chalices of Stars" with star-gazing on the night of Saint Lawrence, tasting of Etna wines and typical local gastronomy.

In October and November **Etna-Wines** takes place, a festival of local wine and food with the aim of showing off Etna wine production, spreading the culture of "healthy drinking" and arousing the interest of tourists for local food. The programme includes: exhibition of typical agricultural produce and crafts, tasting, wine competitions, conventions on food and wine, photographic and art exhibitions and musical entertainment.

On 3rd November there is a **procession** to commemorate the miraculous event of 1928 when the lava stopped in the presence of the patron Saints of the town. The procession ends at the church-sanctuary in the locality of Magazzeni, the site of this happening.

Sounds and Lights of Christmas from 20th December to 10th January includes exhibition of cribs, musical events, theatre shows and a living crib.

RESTAURANTS

- ASSOCIAZIONE CULTURALE SICILIA NOSTRA: Via Castagni dei Cento Cavalli, 5 (tel. 095 968007). Risotto with wild fennel, pennette cooked in paper and pork ribs 'alla Sicilia nostra'.
- CASE PERROTTA: via Andronico, 2 - locality Perrotta (tel. 095 968928). Gourmet restaurant belonging to the farm of the same name, in a 17th century Benedictine convent.

Bottom: panorama of Sant'Alfio.

Try the mushroom or broad bean soup, the maccheroni in Perrotta sauce and the penne with pistachio.
• CASTAGNO DEI CENTO CAVALLI: Piazza Castagno dei Cento Cavalli (tel. 095 968886 - 360 285330). Country-style restaurant with its own mill serving maccheroni 'alla montanara', pappardelle with mushrooms and Etna mixed grill.

• RIFUGIO CITELLI: Mareneve Road (tel. 095 930000). Base Point number 15 of the Etna Park. Just a few minutes away from the ski-lifts. Restaurant, bar and overnight accommodation. We recommend: the caserecci 'all'Etna', all the barbecued dishes and all the mushrooms you like.

FARM HOLIDAYS

• LA CIRASELLA: via Trisciala, 13 – contrada Magazzeni (tel./fax 095 968000). Farm holiday centre with overnight accommodation, just three kilometres outside town, situated in the woods of the Etna Park and not far from the sea (about 12 km). Guided excursions up Etna, cooking and yoga courses. Bowls, football and children's playground. Also a restaurant with garden. Guests of the farm can try the fruit, the jams and the wine produced here.
• L'ASTRAGALO: via Taverna, 42 - Pietra Fucile Estate Puntalazzo di Mascali (tel. 095 7824205 fax 095 606170). Just outside Sant'Alfio, in a panoramic position. Country style hospitality. Large camp site. Also a restaurant with country Mediterranean cuisine.

A CAVE FOR BRIGANDS

Duration: 5 minutes
Total distance: 200 metres from the Mareneve provincial road, Piano delle Donne
Sant'Alfio.

This cave certainly has an interesting name, bringing to mind the times when the woods on Etna were ruled over by bands of feared brigands. The Cave of Thieves is situated at an altitude of 1,540 metres in the locality of Piano delle Donne and has a surprising shape, in some ways quite disturbing, which may have inspired the name by which the cave has been known for several decades.
The main characteristics are three vertical shafts, partially lined with stone blocks placed there by man, which drop straight down into the cave from a height of 5-6 metres. The use of these shafts (probably originally vents for volcanic gases) has been the subject of popular speculation and legends. One of these tells that the brigands that once hid in this area as a refuge used to drop their booty down these shafts and then come back to collect it once they had shaken off their chasers.
Others simply connect these shafts and the work carried out to perfect them with the need to provide the cave with air and light, making life easier for the shepherds and hunters that used it. Certainly you can still see today the remains of what was probably once a 'pagghiaru 'n petra', that is a primitive circular stone construction, flanked by a wall, that must have been used as a pen for animals. So was it all just a simple 'mannira' to keep animals during the summer? We do not wish to simply ignore these charming legends, which, as researchers will tell you, often contain a good measure of historical truth. We would like to think, therefore, that the cave has been put to a whole series of different uses by a various people, including not only brigands (why not?), shepherds and hunters, but also very probably snow sellers. They were probably responsible for cutting out the steps in the living rock of one of the two entrances, making access easier, especially when leaving the cave with their heavy 'cufini' (baskets) used to carry their freezing load down to the valley.
The curious cave we have just described is situated deep in a beautiful wood of aetnensis birches, a very short distance from the Mareneve road: in order to reach it you go uphill from Fornazzo towards the Citelli mountain hut and park about a kilometre before the turn off for the hut. From a small lay-by at the side of the provincial road (which is well sign-posted in any case) a narrow pathway leads north-eastwards and brings you to the cave after just a hundred metres. The area where the cave is situated can be recognised by the presence of wooden fencing that the Forestry Service has wisely put around the shafts.

MONTI SARTORIUS
NATURE PATH (1,769 M)

SANT'ALFIO: 15th ITINERARY ROUTE
Duration: 1 hour 45 mins.
Total distance: 3.5 km
Difference in height: 100 metres

From Fornazzo, a small town on the eastern slopes of the volcano, follow the road that leads to the small but welcoming Citelli mountain hut.

About a kilometre from the latter you will notice, on the right,

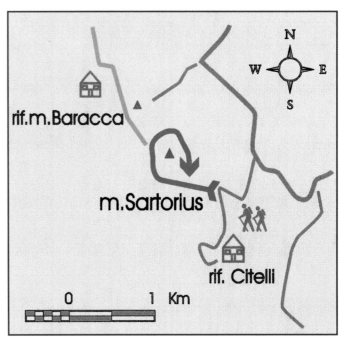

the signposts for the nature path. At first the itinerary runs through countryside characterised by broom and above all by Etna birches, before bringing you to the centre of an eruptive apparatus.

In the first part the path climbs gradually, with good views of the imposing mass of the Pizzi Deneri, which hide the crater summits from sight.

As you come closer to the Monti Sartorius, other features come into view: the large crater of Monte Frumento delle Concazze (2,151 metres), one of the most imposing temporary craters on Etna, and the smaller Monti Conconi and Monte Zappinazzo. The Monti Sartorius bear the name of one of the famous and enthusiastic expert on the volcano, Sartorius von Waltershausen, who stayed in Sicily for a long time; they were formed during the eruption that began on 30th January 1865 and lasted 150 days.

The nature path goes around the western side, crossing a wide stretch of land littered with volcanic bombs, as far as a sheep pen, after which it enters a charming birch wood, easily recognisable from the white colour of the bark on the trees.

A sharp rise brings you up to a small

ridge that runs along the eruptive apparatus and gives you a view over the whole grandiose lava flow (over 8 km^2 in area).

In order to get back to your departure point you go down among the ashes, colonised by typical pioneering plants (astragalus, rumex, soapwort) that should be seen during their very brief flowering period at the beginning of summer, when they form intense blotches of bright colour that stand out sharply against the dark background of the black volcanic sand.

Top: Monte Sartorius in spring. Right: winter view of Monte Sartorius.

ENTRANCE TO THE CERRITA WOOD
FLOW OF 1865 - SERRA BUFFA HOUSE

SANT'ALFIO: 16th ITINERARY ROUTE
Duration: 2 hours
Total length: 4.1km (excluding visit to the Cerrita Wood). Difference in height: 130 metres

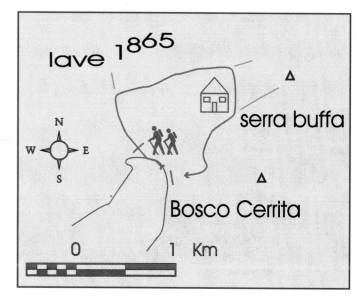

This is an itinerary for enthusiasts who appreciate the traces left by generations of mountain walkers that have used it.

If you want to try out a walk at a moderate altitude, through a mixture of landscapes and full of charm, then park your car in the lay-by on the Mareneve road from where you can enter the Cerrita Wood (1,360 metres), shown by a large sign indicating the beginning of the state-owned forest. In order to recognise the lay-by just remember it is the only one in the stretch between Fornazzo and the turn off for the Citelli mountain hut.

After parking your car, you have to walk about 100 metres further along the Mareneve road until, on the right, you come to a clear forest track that heads off into the woodland. Follow it for about 1.3 kilometres until you come to the lava flow of 1865, the flow that came out of the Monti Sartorius.

After reaching the flow there is a short descent and you enter the hollow of casa Bada: you then turn right onto a mule track, which is one of the most interesting parts of the itinerary.

With its rough surface and intelligent route it demonstrates the presence of intense grazing activity in the area, an activity which made a mule track necessary in order to link the towns lower down with the higher slopes of the volcano.

It is a pleasant surprise to notice that the mule track you are following still today makes the going easier among the twisted lava flows. Moreover, since it was made by experts, it allows you to touch the small 'daggers' set in the lava flows.

To follow our itinerary you have to follow the mule track north-eastwards for about a kilometre (up to an altitude of 1,358 metres), until you come to a clear pathway that heads to the south-east. Here the landscape is characterised by Corsican pines, which have courageously colonised the lava and stick up solitarily among mounds of dark stones.

After less than a kilometre you come to the end of the flow at the abandoned house and sheep pen at Serra Buffa (1,315 metres).

The buildings belong to the Forestry Service and are usually closed. The water tank in front of the house was once used to water the livestock.

You are now on the edge of the Cerrita Wood (which is so called because it is mostly composed of Turkey Oaks, a particular type of oak that can be found in woodland only in this zone of Etna).

Here you have two alternative routes: firstly you can head into the Cerrita Wood, going down the track alongside the house, in order to admire the beautiful woodland, or alternatively you can end your walk by going back up the track for a couple of kilometres until you arrive back at the lay-by on the Mareneve road, where you parked your car at the beginning of the itinerary (1,358 metres).

Both choices are a very pleasant way of ending the walk, you need only choose one or the other according to how fit you feel after your exertions.

FROM MAGAZZENI TO
THE CRATERS OF 1928

It is remembered as the eruption that destroyed the town of Mascali and overran the railway line. The newspapers of the day gave wide coverage of the bitter resignation of the population, who suddenly found themselves in a state of poverty.

The people of Sant'Alfio also suffered the destruction of fields and country houses, but they avoided the worst: the destruction of the town.

The crucial moment of the eruption was the night after the pilgrimage of 3rd November 1928, when the devotees, accompanied by three priests, carried the relics of the three martyred Saints in procession as far as the church of Magazzeni, which was then part of large rural building.

The river of lava coming down from the upper slopes of the volcano was heading straight for the town of Sant'Alfio and, at that time, was only a couple of kilometres away. As the procession was nearing the lava flow, accompanied by the cries of the devotees, something disturbing happened.

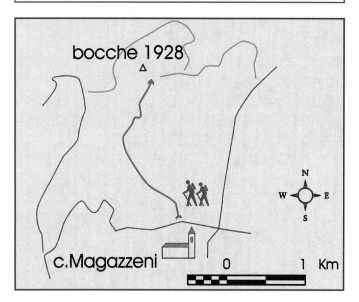

The devotees heard – as reports of the time say – a strange sound coming from the bowels of the earth and saw the lava flow slow down, while all around them the fog came down. The next day the inhabitants learnt that a new eruptive mouth had opened up a little further to the east, in the Cerrita area, and therefore the lava flow threatening the town was no longer supplied. The Saints had performed a miracle.

From that day the 3rd November is commemorated by the people of Sant'Alfio, who repeat the pilgrimage of that misty day.

For our excursion we have chosen as the point of departure the place where the lava stopped, the new church of Magazzeni, built to commemorate that historic event.

To get there you have to turn into the first tarmacked road on the left on the provincial road to Fornazzo (a district of Milo), heading towards Linguaglossa, at the point where you see a modern villa now in disuse. You climb up a steep incline until you come onto a wide tarmacked road that runs along the side of the mountain and is indicated by writing on the wall as "via Finaita".

In reality this is the old cart track that marked the boundary of the Cerrita feud and was the main thoroughfare of the district.

You follow it for several hundred metres and then turn left at the first junction you come to. 300 metres further on the road suddenly widens and gives you a view of the church of Magazzeni (1,000 metres) here you can park your car and head off along the track that starts on the other side of the church and heads in a north-easterly direction.

Your walk immediately takes you through a harmonious rural landscape, mostly made up of hazel groves with pretty country houses.

Gradually the cultivated areas give way to chestnut woods,

until – after a stretch of apparently flat ground – you catch sight of the 1928 lava flow, at an altitude of 1,200 metres, above the Naca Escarpments.

It is easy to identify the explosive and eruptive mouths, which are situated just a little higher up from the point where the cart track you just have followed comes out.

In order to explore the mouths go into the eruptive crack among the numerous hornitos.

One of these (you will discover it with a little patience) is easily accessible and therefore gives you the chance to descend to the point where the heart of the eruption was situated, the point of violent separation between the gases, which came out in whirling explosions, and the lava, which ran out and fed the river of fire.

If you want to extend your excursion to the eruptive mouths of 1928, head back down to the main square of the town and climb back up following the signposts for the "Castagno dei cento cavalli" (Chestnut tree of a hundred horses). Just after turning right at a votive shrine, leaving behind you the Sant'Alfio – Fornazzo provincial road, you take a wide road that starts off to the left very near the chestnut wood.

The road goes uphill for about 600 metres and then suddenly comes to an end. From here you can follow the prettiest part of the "3rd November way", part of the route followed on that dull morning in 1928 in pilgrimage, and every year since.

Leaving the disproportionately wide tarmacked road, the cart track, paved with roughly cut stones, climbs straight up a picturesque slope, passing high drystone walls, charming rural houses, the bed of a torrent with sharp ups and downs.

In all there is about a kilometre of beautiful unspoilt countryside, a little gem not to be missed.

INDEX

MAPS

Printed in March 2001
by Avvenire 2000 - Messina

Benvenuti

Fascicolo omaggio allegato al volume "Etna il Vulcano"

EDIZIONI AFFINITÀ ELETTIVE

CALENDARIO FESTE
SAGRE E MANIFESTAZIONI

Gennaio
- **Festa patronale di Sant'Antonio Abate**: Misterbianco, Aci Sant'Antonio, Camporotondo Etneo, Pedara. Il 17. In particolare a Pedara rituale benedizione degli animali e degli automezzi, vendita dei prodotti naturali offerti al Santo.
- **Festa di San Sebastiano**: Maniace, Piedimonte Etneo.
- **Festa e Fiera San Sebastiano**: Santa Venerina. Ultima domenica del mese.
- **Fiera Bestiame e degli Attrezzi Agricoli**: Viagrande.
- **Tre giorni dell'Etna**: Nicolosi. Da gennaio a marzo. Gara internazionale di sci.

Febbraio
- **Festa di San Biagio: Bronte, Sant'Alfio**. Il 3. In particolare a Sant'Alfio distribuzione dei cuddureddi sammrasi, tipici pani benedetti, nella chiesa del Calvario.
- **Sagra della Porchetta**: Calatabiano.
- **Raduno Escursionistico Sci di Fondo: Sant'Alfio**. Escursioni lungo il sentiero-natura dei Monti Sartorius.
- **Carnevale: Acicatena, Belpasso, Biancavilla, Calatabiano, Castiglione di Sicilia, Fiumefreddo, Giarre, Mirabella Imbaccari, Misterbianco, Motta Sant'Anastasia, Palagonia, Paternò, Piedimonte Etneo, Tremestieri Etneo**.

Marzo
- **Maccheronata: Calatabiano**. Il 4. A Pasteria.

Aprile
- **Festa di San Giuseppe: Adrano, Biancavilla, Fiumefreddo di Sicilia, Maletto, Mascalucia, Mirabella Imbaccari, Nicolosi, Raddusa, Ramacca, Randazzo**. Il 19 marzo. A Maletto tradizionali sfilateddi che ciciri e crespelle di riso al miele. A Raddusa e Ramacca allestimento di sontuose tavolate con ogni genere di pietanza e con i tipici pani votivi.
- **Festa di Maria Santissima Annunziata**: Bronte, Pedara. Il 25 marzo.
- **Mostra Mercato del Tombolo: Tremestieri Etneo**. In marzo.
- **Sagra degli Agrumi: Motta Sant'Anastasia**. Fine marzo-primi di aprile.
- **Venerdì Santo: Bronte, Giarre, Militello in Val di Catania, Randazzo, Sant'Alfio**. A Bronte e Randazzo processione. A Sant'Alfio corteo dalla chiesa Madre alla chiesa del Calvario da dove il simulacro del Cristo Morto è condotto alla Matrice.
- **La Diavolata: Adrano**. Domenica di Pasqua. Rappresentazione del dramma religioso risalente al 1752.
- **Sagra dei Formaggi: Aci Bonaccorsi**. 3ª domenica di aprile. Prodotti tipici siciliani.
- **Mostra Artigianato: Linguaglossa**. Dal 29 aprile all'1 maggio.
- **Aprile in Festa: Nicolosi**. In aprile. Folclore e degustazione di prodotti tipici.

Maggio
- **Sagra dei Formaggi, della Ricotta e dei prodotti tipici siciliani: Aci Bonaccorsi**. L'1 e il 2.
- **Festa patronale di Maria SS. della Catena: Castiglione di Sicilia**. 1ª domenica del mese.
- **Festa dei SS. Alfio, Cirino e Filadelfo: Trecastagni**. Dal 7 al 12. A Trecastagni processione dei devoti detti "nudi" e fiera in cui si distinguono le bancarelle di aglio fresco. Specialità a base di carni ovine.
- **Sagra del Carretto Siciliano: Trecastagni**. Il 10. In concomitanza alla festa dei santi patroni.
- **Sagra Regionale del Folkore: Trecastagni**. 1ª domenica dopo il 10.
- **Festa dei Fiori e dell'Artigianato: Aci Bonaccorsi**. 2ª domenica del mese. Con festival degli aquiloni.
- **Sagra della Nespola: Calatabiano**. 2ª domenica del mese.
- **Festa di Mompilieri: Mascalucia**. 3ª domenica del mese. In ricordo del ritrovamento della Madonna della Sciara.
- **Festa della Montagna: Sant'Alfio. 2ª metà del mese**. Escursioni nei luoghi più suggestivi dell'Etna, mostre e canti.
- **Festa di Sant'Alfio: Adrano**. Ultima domenica del mese. Carretti siciliani trainati da cavalli sontuosamente bardati, suonatori di antichi strumenti tipici.
- **Festa di Primavera: Bronte**. Fine mese. Artigianato e degustazione di prodotti tipici.
- **Maggio Ecologico: Mascalucia**. Per tutto il mese.
- **Trofeo degli Ulivi: Pedara**. Fine mese-primi di giugno. Arcieri in competizione allo stadio comunale.
- **Torneo Internazionale di Hockey su prato: Catania**. Maggio-giugno.
- **Maggio Mascalese: Mascali**. Giochi tradizionali.
- **Antich...età: Motta Sant'Anastasia**. Mostra dell'artigianato antico.
- **Madonna di Valverde: Valverde**. Con processione dal luogo di apparizione della Madonna al santuario.

Giugno
- **Festa patronale di S. Antonio da Padova: Gravina di Catania, Nicolosi**. Il 13.
- **Festa patronale di San Vito: Mascalucia**. Il 15 ed anche il 15 agosto.
- **Sagra della Fragola: Maletto**. 2ª metà del mese. Mostra-mercato delle fragole e dei prodotti tipici, degustazioni, folclore, teatro e musica.
- **Estate Piedimontese: Piedimonte Etneo**. Da giugno a settembre. Teatro, spettacoli e gastronomia in piazza.
- **Notturna di Fuoco: Misterbianco**. Rassegna italiana del ferro battuto.
- **Corpus Domini: Mascalucia, Riposto, Valverde**. A Riposto processione per il paese con soste dinanzi alle edicole votive e agli altarini allestiti per l'occasione.
- **Sagra delle Ciliegie: Ragalna**.

Luglio
- **Festa Medioevale: Randazzo**. Dall'11 al 18. Nel centro storico. Rievocazione della storia di Bianca di Navarra. Concerti, tavole rotonde, mostre e cene medievali.

- **Settimana dell'Etna: Linguaglossa**. Dal 18 al 25. In piazza. Tra le manifestazioni più interessanti "Pentathlon dell'Etna" e "Legni e pennelli".
- **Etna Jazz: Mascali**. Il 23. A Puntalazzo. Rassegna itinerante di musica jazz.
- **Etna Jazz: Bronte**. Il 25. In piazza. Rassegna itinerante di musica jazz.
- **Mostra Mercato dei Prodotti Artigianali Locali: Fiumefreddo**. Metà mese. In piazza Botteghelle.
- **Estate Sanconese: San Cono**. Dal 26 luglio al 31 agosto. In piazza. Giochi, gare e concerti.
- **Esposizione Antiquariato: San Giovanni La Punta**. Il 27.
- **Sere d'Estate in Musica: Mascali**. Dal 28 luglio al 12 settembre. Rassegna d'arte e spettacolo in piazza.
- **Festa patronale di Sant'Andrea: Milo**. Ultima domenica del mese. Tradizioni religiose e folclore.
- **Estate Adranita, Belpassese, Biancavillese, Malettese: Adrano, Belpasso, Biancavilla, Maletto**. Luglio-agosto. Rassegne di musica, teatro, danza, cabaret.
- **Brontestate: Bronte**. Luglio-agosto. Rassegna di musica, teatro, cabaret, moda in piazza.
- **Estate Fiumefreddese e Premio Asclepio: Fiumefreddo**. Luglio-agosto. Musica, cinema, teatro, danza.
- **Etneadi: Nicolosi**. Luglio-agosto. Rassegna di musica, danza e teatro, cinema e cabaret.
- **Rocca Normanna: Paternò**. Luglio-agosto. Musica, teatro, cinema e balletto in piazza.
- **Pedarestate: Pedara**. Luglio-agosto. Teatro, musica e sport presso il parco Belvedere.
- **Fiera d'Estate: Pedara**. Luglio-agosto. Al parco comunale ed in piazza Don Bosco.
- **Giarre Estate: Giarre**. Luglio-settembre. Rassegna di musica e teatro.
- **Estate Palagonese: Palagonia**. Luglio-settembre. Musica, teatro, film all'aperto.
- **Estate Mottese: Motta Sant'Anastasia**. Luglio-settembre. Rassegna di musica, danza e teatro in piazza.
- **Etna in Scena: Zafferana Etnea**. Luglio-settembre. Rassegna di cinema, musica, teatro e danza in piazza.
- **Autoslalom: Giarre-Milo**.
- **Etna Jazz: Trecastagni**. Rassegna itinerante di musica jazz.

Agosto
- **Festa patronale della Madonna della Provvidenza: Zafferana Etnea**. 1ª domenica del mese.
- **Premio Poseidone: Fiumefreddo**. 1ª settimana del mese. Premio conferito ad un personaggio che si sia distinto nella diffusione della cultura ambientalista.
- **Festival Nazionale dei Fuochi d'Artificio e Festa patronale di Santo Stefano: Aci Bonaccorsi**. Il 2.
- **La Volata dell'Angelo e Festa di San Nicolò Politi: Adrano**. Il 3 e il 4.
- **Sagra delle Pesche e delle Pere: Maniace**. Dal 6 all'8. Con degustazione in piazza.
- **Festival Cinema: San Gregorio**. Dall'8 al 18. Al campo sportivo di Piano Immacolata.
- **Notte di San Lorenzo: Nicolosi**. Il 10. Al rifugio Sapienza. Musica e picnic.
- **Festa patronale di San Lorenzo: Sant'Agata Li Battiati**. Il 10.
- **Feste Medievali: Motta Sant'Anastasia**. Dal 10 al 22. Folclore e cortei storici.
- **Estate Puntese: San Giovanni La Punta**. Dal 10 al 4 settembre.
- **Festa patronale di Sant'Antonio di Padova: Nicolosi**. Il 15. Mostra mercato dell'artigianato e del folclore.
- **'A Vara: Randazzo**. Il 15. Solenne processione del carro trionfale dell'Assunzione con personaggi viventi.
- **Rock Evolution: Bronte**. Dal 18 al 20. Rassegna di musica rock in piazza Cimbali.
- **Sagra del Pane Casereccio: Piedimonte Etneo**. Il 20. A Vena.
- **Show sotto le Stelle: Viagrande**. Il 20. In piazza S. Mauro.
- **Raduno Bandistico: Santa Maria di Licodia**. Il 21 e il 22. In piazza.
- **Festa patronale di Sant'Anastasia: Motta Sant'Anastasia**. Dal 22 al 25. Con Festival degli sbandieratori.
- **Festa patronale di Santa Venera: Santa Venerina**. Il 26.
- **Festa patronale di San Giuseppe: Santa Maria di Licodia**. Dal 28 al 30.
- **Festa di San Gerardo: Piedimonte Etneo**. Il 29.
- **Arte Mestieri e Gastronomia: San Gregorio**. Dal 31 agosto al 5 settembre. Degustazione di salsiccia, polenta e vino.
- **Festa del Villeggiante: Mascali**. Fine agosto-primi di settembre.
- **Motoraduno Internazionale dell'Etna: Belpasso**.
- **Agosto Calatabianese: Calatabiano**. Iniziative ricreative e culturali sul litorale San Marco.
- **Etnalquantara: Castiglione di Sicilia**. Rassegna di musica, teatro e danza in piazza.
- **Torneo Internazionale di Tennis Femminile: Catania, Mascali, Tremestieri, Nicolosi**.
- **Sagra del Pesce: Mascali**. Sulla spiaggia di Fondachello.
- **La Venere di Milo: Milo**. Concorso di bellezza. In piazza Madonna delle Grazie.
- **Manifestazione Nazionale di Pallacanestro: Nicolosi**.
- **Fiera Mostra Artigianato: Nicolosi**.
- **Ferragosto Randazzese: Randazzo**. Manifestazioni di varia natura durante tutto il mese.
- **Effetto Battiati: Sant'Agata Li Battiati**. Rassegna di musica, teatro e cabaret in piazza.
- **Fiera dell'Artigianato: Trecastagni**. Mostra dei prodotti tipici dell'artigianato locale.
- **Sagra dell'Acciuga: Valverde**. Nell'ambito dei festeggiamenti in onore del patrono. Degustazione di panini con acciughe e vino a volontà.

Settembre
- **Sagra delle Nocciole e delle Mele Delizie dell'Etna: Mascali**. Dall'1 al 10. A Puntalazzo.
- **Vini Milo: Milo**. Il 4, 5, 11 e 12 in via Etnea. Mostra mercato dei vini milesi e dell'Etna.
- **Fiera dell'Artigianato: Santa Maria di Licodia**. Dal 4 al 12. Mostra mercato e spettacoli.

- **Sagra dei Fiori: San Gregorio**. 1ª domenica del mese. Mostra mercato e spettacoli.
- **Fiera di Settembre: Paternò**. Dal 13 al 23. Artigianato e gastronomia. Presso la Villa comunale.
- **Enoetna: Santa Venerina**. Il 17, 18, 19, 24, 25. Mostra mercato di vini siciliani e dell'Etna. In piazza Roma.
- **Etna-Vini: Sant'Alfio**. 1ª metà del mese. Vini dell'Etna e prodotti tipici.
- **Sagra d'Ampanata: Misterbianco**. 3° sabato del mese.
- **Festa della Vendemmia: Piedimonte Etneo, Viagrande**. A Piedimonte dal 24 al 26. Musica, folclore, personaggi in costume tipico, pigiatura dell'uva con i tradizionali sistemi, gastronomia e artigianato. A Viagrande il 24.
- **Mostra Mercato del Cotto, della Pietra Lavica e del Legno: Gravina di Catania**. Dal 30 settembre al 4 ottobre.
- **Mercato dei Funghi: Nicolosi**. Settembre-ottobre-novembre.
- **Palio della Madonna delle Grazie: Belpasso**. Nel corso principale.
- **Settembre Gravinese: Gravina di Catania**. Teatro popolare presso il parco Borsellino.
- **Corsa dell'Etna: Nicolosi**. Cronoscalata.
- **Premio Letterario Brancati: Zafferana Etnea**.

Ottobre
- **Sagra dell'Uva e dei Vini: Sant'Agata Li Battiati**. Il 3 e il 4.
- **Sagra dell'Uva e della Salsiccia: Trecastagni**. 2ª domenica del mese. Degustazione, mostra, folclore.
- **Sagra del Pistacchio: Bronte**. 2ª settimana del mese. Esposizione e degustazione di prodotti tipici al pistacchio.
- **Sagra del Fico d'India: San Cono**. 2° fine settimana del mese.
- **Sagra del Miele e del Dolce: Trecastagni**. 3ª domenica del mese. Degustazione e folclore.
- **Sagra delle Castagne e del Vino: Trecastagni**. 4ª domenica del mese.
- **Meletna: Pedara**. Dal 23 al 31. Promozione delle gustose mele locali.
- **Festa dell'Ulivo: Biancavilla**. Fine mese.
- **Festa del Pane Condito e delle Caldarroste: Aci Sant'Antonio**. A Lavinaio. In piazza Maggiore.
- **Mostra della Pietra Lavica: Belpasso**. In piazza.
- **Mostra Mercato dell'Artigianato e dell'Agricoltura: Belpasso**. Al Giardino Martoglio.
- **Ottobrata: Calatabiano**. Fiera mercato e manifestazione gastronomica.
- **Open Internazionale Femminile di Golf: Castiglione di Sicilia**.
- **Mostra dell'Artigianato: Gravina di Catania**.
- **Sagra dell'Uva: Maletto**.
- **Autunno Mascalese: Mascali**. Teatro, musica e manifestazioni sportive.
- **Sagra della Mostarda: Mascali**. In piazza.
- **Mostra Micologica e Sagra dei Funghi: Nicolosi**. In piazza della Cisterna.
- **Sagra del Fungo: Pedara**. Nel parco comunale e in piazza Don Bosco.
- **Festa delle Mele: Ragalna**. Ogni sabato e domenica. Mercatino dei prodotti etnei.
- **Festa della Vendemmia: Randazzo**. Animazione e degustazioni.
- **Sagra del Castagno: Trecastagni**. Degustazione di funghi, pane casereccio, ricotta, miele, mostarda.
- **Ottobrata Zafferanese: Zafferana Etnea**. Tutte le domeniche del mese. Sagra dell'uva, della mostarda, dei funghi, del miele, del vino e delle castagne.

Novembre
- **Fiera dei Morti e del Giocattolo: Trecastagni**.
- **Sagra della Salsiccia, Caliceddi e Vino: Ragalna**. 1ª settimana del mese.
- **Festa di San Martino: Linguaglossa, Milo (contr. Fornazzo), Raddusa, Ramacca**. L'11. Gastronomia, degustazione vino e prodotti tipici etnei, folclore, spettacoli. A Raddusa concorso enologico e salsicciata.
- **Sagra delle Castagne Caliate: Piedimonte Etneo**. Il 13.
- **Sagra del Vino e delle Castagne: Zafferana Etnea**. Metà mese.
- **Festa di Santa Caterina: Pedara, San Pietro Clarenza**. Il 25.
- **Mostra Vini Locali: Linguaglossa**.
- **Secolare Fiera del Bestiame: Mascali**. Mostre, antiquariato e folclore.
- **Sagra del Buongusto: Misterbianco**. Prodotti tipici siciliani. In piazza Mazzini.
- **Sagra dell'Olio d'Oliva: Motta Sant'Anastasia, Santa Maria di Licodìa**.
- **Estate di San Martino: Nicolosi**. Preparazione e degustazione della ricotta, mostra mercato dei prodotti agricoli locali e spettacoli folcloristici.
- **Festa e Fiera della Madonna del Lume: Santa Venerina**.

Dicembre
- **Festa di Santa Barbara: Paternò**. Il 4.
- **Festa patronale di San Nicola di Bari: Trecastagni**. Il 6.
- **Festa del Patacò: Licodia Eubea**. 1ª o 2ª domenica del mese. Degustazione del patacò, legume tipico della zona, con broccoli e salsiccia.
- **Sagra dell'Olio d'Oliva e dei Prodotti Locali: Ragalna**. 2ª settimana del mese.
- **Festa patronale di Santa Lucia: Belpasso**. Il 12-13-14. Sfilata di carri allegorici e competizione canora tra i vari quartieri.
- **Suoni e Luci del Natale: Sant'Alfio**. Dal 20 dicembre al 10 gennaio. Mostra di presepi e manifestazioni musicali.
- **Natale in Strada: Randazzo**. Presepe vivente, novene in dialetto. Nella notte di Natale accensione degli zucchi.
- **Festa patronale di San Giovanni Evangelista: San Giovanni La Punta**. Il 27.
- **Natale a Nicolosi**: Nicolosi. Concerti e presepi.
- **Festa dei Parchi: Randazzo**. Escursioni a cavallo e in mount-bike. Animazione nel centro storico.